D1796956

Synthese Library

Studies in Epistemology, Logic, Methodology, and Philosophy of Science

Volume 413

Editor-in-Chief
Otávio Bueno, University of Miami, Coral Gables, USA

Editorial Board Members
Berit Brogaard, University of Miami, Coral Gables, USA
Anjan Chakravartty, University of Notre Dame, Notre Dame, USA
Steven French, University of Leeds, Leeds, UK
Catarina Dutilh Novaes, VU Amsterdam, Amsterdam, The Netherlands

The aim of *Synthese Library* is to provide a forum for the best current work in the methodology and philosophy of science and in epistemology. A wide variety of different approaches have traditionally been represented in the Library, and every effort is made to maintain this variety, not for its own sake, but because we believe that there are many fruitful and illuminating approaches to the philosophy of science and related disciplines.

Special attention is paid to methodological studies which illustrate the interplay of empirical and philosophical viewpoints and to contributions to the formal (logical, set-theoretical, mathematical, information-theoretical, decision-theoretical, etc.) methodology of empirical sciences. Likewise, the applications of logical methods to epistemology as well as philosophically and methodologically relevant studies in logic are strongly encouraged. The emphasis on logic will be tempered by interest in the psychological, historical, and sociological aspects of science.

Besides monographs *Synthese Library* publishes thematically unified anthologies and edited volumes with a well-defined topical focus inside the aim and scope of the book series. The contributions in the volumes are expected to be focused and structurally organized in accordance with the central theme(s), and should be tied together by an extensive editorial introduction or set of introductions if the volume is divided into parts. An extensive bibliography and index are mandatory.

More information about this series at http://www.springer.com/series/6607

Mark Addis • Peter C. R. Lane • Peter D. Sozou
Fernand Gobet
Editors

Scientific Discovery in the Social Sciences

 Springer

Editors
Mark Addis
Centre for Philosophy of Natural
and Social Science
London School of Economics
and Political Science
London, UK

Peter D. Sozou
Centre for Philosophy of Natural
and Social Science
London School of Economics
and Political Science
London, UK

Peter C. R. Lane
Department of Computer Science
University of Hertfordshire
Hatfield, UK

Fernand Gobet
Department of Psychological Sciences
University of Liverpool
Liverpool, UK

Synthese Library
ISBN 978-3-030-23768-4   ISBN 978-3-030-23769-1   (eBook)
https://doi.org/10.1007/978-3-030-23769-1

© Springer Nature Switzerland AG 2019
This work is subject to copyright. All rights are reserved by the Publisher, whether the whole or part of the material is concerned, specifically the rights of translation, reprinting, reuse of illustrations, recitation, broadcasting, reproduction on microfilms or in any other physical way, and transmission or information storage and retrieval, electronic adaptation, computer software, or by similar or dissimilar methodology now known or hereafter developed.
The use of general descriptive names, registered names, trademarks, service marks, etc. in this publication does not imply, even in the absence of a specific statement, that such names are exempt from the relevant protective laws and regulations and therefore free for general use.
The publisher, the authors, and the editors are safe to assume that the advice and information in this book are believed to be true and accurate at the date of publication. Neither the publisher nor the authors or the editors give a warranty, express or implied, with respect to the material contained herein or for any errors or omissions that may have been made. The publisher remains neutral with regard to jurisdictional claims in published maps and institutional affiliations.

This Springer imprint is published by the registered company Springer Nature Switzerland AG.
The registered company address is: Gewerbestrasse 11, 6330 Cham, Switzerland

Contents

Part III   Formalising Theories in Social Science

Contributors

Peter Abell Department of Management, London School of Economics and Political Science, London, UK

Mark Addis Centre for Philosophy of Natural and Social Science, London School of Economics and Political Science, London, UK

Adam Arvay Department of Computer Science, University of Auckland, Auckland, New Zealand

Maria Dimarogkona Department of Humanities, Social Sciences and Law, National Technical University of Athens, Athens, Greece

Fernand Gobet Department of Psychological Sciences, University of Liverpool, Liverpool, UK

Catherine Greene Centre for Philosophy of Natural and Social Science, London School of Economics and Political Science, London, UK

Tobias Henschen Faculty of Philosophy, University of Konstanz, Konstanz, Germany

Maria Koumenta Department of Business and Management, Queen Mary University of London, London, UK

Peter C. R. Lane Department of Computer Science, University of Hertfordshire, Hatfield, UK

Pat Langley Institute for the Study of Learning and Expertise, Palo Alto, CA, USA

Jakub Bazyli Motrenko Institute of Sociology, University of Warsaw, Warsaw, Poland

Clayton Peterson Munich Center for Mathematical Philosophy, Ludwig-Maximilians-Universität München, München, Germany

Peter D. Sozou Centre for Philosophy of Natural and Social Science, London School of Economics and Political Science, London, UK

Petros Stefaneas Department of Mathematics, National Technical University of Athens, Athens, Greece

Michael T. Stuart Centre for Philosophy of Natural and Social Science, London School of Economics and Political Science, London, UK

Ben Trubody School of Liberal and Performing Arts, University of Gloucestershire, Cheltenham, UK

Chapter 1
Introduction: Scientific Discovery in the Social Sciences

Fernand Gobet, Mark Addis, Peter C. R. Lane, and Peter D. Sozou

Abstract Is it reasonable to talk about scientific discoveries in the social sciences? This chapter briefly reviews the status of scientific research in the social sciences and some of the arguments for and against the notion of scientific discovery in those sciences. After providing definitions of "scientific discovery" and "social sciences", the chapter notes the large variety of epistemological views and methodologies drawn on by the social sciences. It discusses the extent to which the social sciences use precise formalisms for expressing theories. Critiques of the use and reliability of the scientific method in the social sciences are discussed. In spite of these critiques, it is argued that it is possible to speak of scientific discovery in the social sciences. The chapter ends with a preview of the book.

Keywords Deconstruction · Falsification · Formal theory · Grounded theory · Information theory · Postmodernism · Pseudoscience · Psychoanalysis

1.1 Introduction

When asked about scientific discoveries, people typically think of Pasteur's discovery of vaccination, Le Verrier's discovery of Neptune and Einstein's discovery of the theory of relativity. Discoveries from the social sciences are rarely mentioned, if at all. The social sciences are also conspicuously absent from lists of the most

F. Gobet (✉)
Department of Psychological Sciences, University of Liverpool, Liverpool, UK
e-mail: fernand.gobet@liverpool.ac.uk

M. Addis · P. D. Sozou
Centre for Philosophy of Natural and Social Science, London School of Economics and Political Science, London, UK
e-mail: m.addis@lse.ac.uk; p.sozou@lse.ac.uk

P. C. R. Lane
Department of Computer Science, University of Hertfordshire, Hatfield, UK
e-mail: p.c.lane@herts.ac.uk

© Springer Nature Switzerland AG 2019
M. Addis et al. (eds.), *Scientific Discovery in the Social Sciences*,
Synthese Library 413, https://doi.org/10.1007/978-3-030-23769-1_1

1

influential scientific discoveries in books and on the internet. However, there are many discoveries in the social sciences. Just to take the fields of linguistics and cultural studies, advances have ranged from the nineteenth century theory of laryngeals in Indo-European linguistics to the current controversy about the Luwian civilization, which offers a radical different view of the Mediterranean in the Bronze Age. Why are such discoveries missing?

Scientific discovery can be defined as the discovery of new objects, phenomena, mechanisms, cures, technologies and theories (including the unification of theories). It involves a range of activities and methods, including observations, formation of taxonomies, finding empirical rules and devising theoretical explanations (Sozou, Lane, Addis, & Gobet, 2017). Whilst philosophers of science have focused on how to best test and falsify theories, following Popper's (1959) influence, psychologists have studied the mechanisms leading to scientific discoveries. For example, Langley, Simon, Bradshaw, and Zytkow (1987) emphasise heuristic search whilst Simonton (1999) argues that search is essentially random but that successful scientists use efficient selection processes.

The social sciences can be defined as the application of scientific methods to the study of societies and the individuals within societies. They cover a wide range of fields of which a good summary is offered by the sciences represented in this book: anthropology, business, economics, law, liberal and performing arts, management, psychology and sociology. Other fields have important things to say about the social sciences – including computer science, mathematics and philosophy – as they do in this book. For example, Maymin (2011) argues that polynomial time computational complexity theory provides strong evidence for the efficient market hypothesis in financial economics being false. The social sciences use a dizzying variety of epistemological views and methodologies. In some cases, the boundaries between the natural sciences and the social sciences can be fuzzy. For instance, subfields of psychology such as the study of cognitive processes using brain imaging technologies clearly belong to the natural sciences, whereas other subfields of psychology such as psychoanalysis find a more suitable home in the social sciences.

1.2 Popper – An Incorrect Critique?

As is well known, philosopher of science Popper (1959) directed his attack against pseudo-science with a condemnation of two subfields belonging to the social sciences: Marxism and psychoanalysis. His key argument was that theories cannot be proven: they only can be refuted. However, for testing and possibly refuting scientific theories, it is necessary that these theories are formulated precisely. Popper's argument was that this was not the case with Marxism and psychoanalysis: these theories were formulated in such a way that it was always possible to generate post-hoc explanations to account for any recalcitrant empirical data. Some authors argued that Popper's criticism was incorrect and that, in fact, theories in psychoanalysis can be tested and refuted. Grünbaum (1984) showed that psychoanalysis did make testable predictions. For example, Freudian theory postulates that repressed homosexuality leads to paranoia. Thus, a falsifiable – and, as it turns out, incorrect – prediction is that a reduction in repression of homosexuality should lead to a reduction of paranoia. However, even Grünbaum agrees that some schools of psychoanalysis develop theories that are not refutable. In a similar way, some scholars have claimed that Popper's objections to Marxism are unjustified and that theories in Marxian economics are capable of testing and refutation. Roemer (1981) formulated Marxian economics using neoclassical economics as a theory of dynamic macroeconomics processes to explain class and exploitation. Despite this, there are a number of versions of Marxism which are expressed in fundamentally ideological terms where the theories produced cannot be refuted.

It is important to note that, within individual social sciences, there is a large variability in the extent to which precise formalisms are used for expressing theories. For example, in economics, theories of microeconomics tend to be expressed mathematically, while behavioural economics tends to have more descriptive formulations. Similarly, in psychology, whilst some theories are implemented as mathematical or computer models, most are expressed informally and lack precision. By the same token, there is considerable variety in the types of methodologies used in the social sciences. In particular, in many social sciences there is a tension between quantitative data and qualitative data. For example, psychological research based on brain imaging uses vast amounts of quantitative data whilst other subfields of psychology, such as existential psychotherapy, use exclusively qualitative data such as introspection and case descriptions.

1.3   Are the (Social) Sciences Reliable?

Our brief discussion has so far assumed that the natural sciences are a good model for the social sciences to emulate – emphasis on precise theories, tests with empirical data and sound methodologies. But there has also been strong scepticism in the social sciences about the reliability of the natural sciences themselves, and indeed science in general. In the field of science and technology studies, Latour and Woolgar (1979) argued that science is not objective but socially constructed; rather than consisting of principles and procedures, science is a culture. Thus, science is not about refuting or verifying theories but about making alliances. A similarly negative analysis is that offered by Derrida's (1967) deconstruction, where the natural, "obvious" meaning of a text is critiqued and deconstructed to show that language cannot carry truth unambiguously. While influential, these postmodernist critiques cannot at face value be correct. For example, progress in technology, such as in computer science and space exploration, has produced scientific theories that are not devoid of truth nor solely socially constructed: computers can beat the best human players at chess and Go, and space probes have been sent to Mars and beyond.

It remains the case that the terms "mechanism" and "law" are frowned upon in several social science circles, primarily in anthropology and sociology, where such terms are often uttered inaudibly and with trusted colleagues. Rather than focusing on solving problems, emphasis in these fields is put on identifying, understanding and possibly deconstructing them. Some popular methodologies explicitly negate the cumulative construction of scientific knowledge. The textbook example is "grounded theory", an inductive methodology according to which pre-existing theoretical views should be ignored and qualitative data should be analysed in such a way that new theories emerge. The theories are "grounded" in the data in the sense that they are specific to these data (Strauss & Juliet, 1994). Generalisation and incremental development of theories are thus excluded by definition.

A final critique of the possibility of objective science is the idea that scientific theories reflect biases and prejudices of the individuals enjoying power, a line for example adopted by feminism with respect to "male science". Whilst it is possible that the prevailing intellectual and political environment can influence the probability of different sorts of ideas being put forward in science, the effect is likely to be stronger with respect to the kind of scientific objects studied in the social sciences.

Overall, there is no doubt that these criticisms have had considerable influence on the social sciences. At the same time it is obvious that if scientific theories cannot be built or if there is no objective reality, then it is not possible to speak of scientific discoveries. There are other consequences as well, of which two will be briefly mentioned here. The first is that the self-corrective nature of science would disappear if the criticisms mentioned above are correct. The second relates to research funding. Funders in many countries emphasise the impact of research: curiosity and creation of new knowledge is not enough, and research must have measurable implications for society, such as better health, less crime, a booming economy and improved instructional methods. One might disagree with this notion of impact, and rather argue that science should be about exploration and understanding and should not be systematically pressured to produce measurable practical applications, but the point is that, without objective experiments or observations, and indeed testable theories, it is hard to see how any impact could happen. Of course, organising a conference on discovery in the social sciences and editing a book on this topic implies that we believe that there are indeed discoveries in the social sciences. It also implies that we believe that there exists an objective reality, which might be far from our current scientific understanding, but which is there nonetheless.

1.4   Preview of Chapters

The following chapters are based on papers presented at the *Scientific Discovery in the Social Sciences* international conference, an interdisciplinary event which was organised by the editors of this book and held at the London School of Economics and Political Science on 30–31 January 2015. The conference brought together some of the leading authorities in the field of scientific discovery in the social sciences from computer science, economics, management, philosophy and psychology.

The first part of the book deals with the type of methods – broadly construed – used in scientific discovery. In Chap. 2, Peter Abell and Maria Koumenta discuss the opposition between quantitative and qualitative methods. While causal inference has traditionally been the province of quantitative methods, Abell and Koumenta argue that qualitative causal inference has an important role to play as well. It is possible to develop causal models using qualitative data. As a specific method, they describe Bayesian Narratives based on ethnographic data. The chapter also discusses the limits of quantitative and qualitative methods.

Just like the natural sciences, the social sciences use latent constructs (or theoretical terms) to develop theories. Not directly observable, these variables are essential in making predictions. In Chap. 3, Clayton Peterson provides a philosophical analysis of one of the main methods for identifying latent variables: factor analysis. He provides a discussion of both exploratory and confirmatory factor analysis, and identifies some of the statistical and philosophical issues associated with these techniques. In the end, pragmatic considerations are emphasized in using these techniques.

In Chap. 4, Michael Stuart broadens the scope of what counts as a method of discovery and investigates what is needed for letting machines make scientific discoveries in the social sciences. Compared to the natural sciences and mathematics, the social sciences impose new constraints for scientific discoveries. As noted above, in several subfields the data are not quantitative but rather qualitative, and the difficulty is in reaching a correct interpretation. Whilst standard quantitative algorithms are ill-suited for such data, there is nothing in principle to prevent the development of new algorithms for dealing with them. Considering the kind of abilities that computers would need to successfully interpret qualitative data, Stuart concludes that there is one common prerequisite: imagination.

Chapter 5 deals with an extreme "method" for scientific discovery: fraud. Ben Trubody uses Kuhn's (1970) concept of a scientific paradigm to argue that, depending on the strength of a given scientific paradigm, it is easy or difficult to "successfully" commit scientific fraud. Whilst examples of scientific misconduct exist in all sciences, including the "hard" sciences such as physics, it is easier to commit fraud (such as omitting anomalous data points or even faking data) in the softer sciences. One reason is that the difference between contributing expertise and interactional expertise (Collins & Evans, 2007) blurs in those sciences. Several examples are provided from social psychology. To remain undetected but still have some influence on a field, fraudsters need to reach a fine balance between making reasonable claims and claims that are significant.

The second part of the book presents examples of scientific discovery in specific fields. In Chap. 6, Catherine Greene sheds new light on the role of information in financial markets. The concept of information plays a central role in the Efficient Market Hypothesis – that share prices incorporate all available information. However, Greene notes two important ambiguities in the way the concept of information is used: there is disagreement not only about the nature of information but also about what information means for different individuals. Using Skyrms's (2013) definition that information is whatever changes probabilities, she discusses examples showing that these two ambiguities raise serious doubts about previous analyses of the Efficient Market Hypothesis.

Chapter 7 addresses the issue of scientific discovery in macroeconomics. Tobias Henschen notes that, in this field, scientific discoveries aim to explain causal relations. However, the data available are not strong enough for testing the presence of causal relations. Henschen argues that, as a consequence, it is incorrect to describe scientific research in macroeconomics as following Lakatos's (1970) notion of a research program. Rather, research in macroeconomics fits Kuhn's (1970) description of scientific research. Specifically, it is motivated by ideology and not empirical data. As Kuhnian logic has motivated many policies that turn out to be failures, Henschen argues that macroeconomics should use a different type of logic – a variant of Popper's (1963) situational logic.

In Chap. 8, Jakub Motrenko first discusses why sociologists rarely talk about scientific discoveries in their field. He then argues that scientific discoveries do indeed happen in sociology, and typically take the form of "That-What discoveries" (Kuhn, 1962). With such discoveries, a new object is found first, and a theory is developed to explain it. Adapting Kuhn's notion to sociology, Motrenko applies it to the study of Solidarność (Solidarity), the Polish trade union which successfully challenged Poland's communist government in the 1980s. He shows how research carried out by Polish sociologists can be described as That-What discovery.

The third and final part of the book deals with formalising theories in the social sciences. In Chap. 9, Maria Dimarogkona, Mark Addis and Petros Stefaneas argue that the theory of institutions offers a powerful means for formalising theories in the social sciences. This theory, originally developed in computer science for addressing the problem of the vast number of logics developed in this field, has the advantage that it can be used independently of the specific nature of the underlying formal language. It thus presents an elegant solution to the philosophical debates about the relative merits of the syntactic and semantic views of scientific theories. The authors discuss several advantages of using this approach for formalising scientific theories in the social sciences, including formalising systems that use a different theoretical vocabulary and facilitating analysis at different levels of abstraction.

Building computational models is an important way of developing theories in psychology and cognitive science. Such models offer important advantages, such as precise predictions and the ability to simulate the behaviour under study, whatever its complexity. However, this endeavour is notably difficult and time consuming. In Chap. 10, Mark Addis, Fernand Gobet, Peter Lane and Peter Sozou describe a novel way to develop computational models, whereby computational models are semi-automatically generated by genetic programming algorithms, which use analogues of Darwinian selection processes. The chapter also addresses several philosophical issues raised by this approach, including the nature of the explanations proposed by this approach and how they relate to the notion of fictional modelling.

While Chap. 10 focuses on data obtained under experimental control, Chap. 11 considers the use of correlational data, which are omnipresent in the social sciences.

Specifically, Pat Langley and Adam Arvay focus on modelling research aimed as inducing numeric laws. Whilst early research focused on finding mathematical relationships between variables independently of domain knowledge, more recent efforts have aimed at using such knowledge for explaining data, in particular with the use of multivariate time series. Applications have been mostly carried out in biology and ecology, and Langley and Arvay discuss ways similar methods could be used in the social sciences. These methods offer the prospect of discovering new explanations for data that characterize dynamic systems evolving as a function of time.

Acknowledgments The *Scientific Discovery in the Social Sciences* international conference and the preparation of this book was supported by Economic and Social Research Council grant ES/L003090/1.

References

Collins, H. M., & Evans, R. (2007). *Rethinking expertise*. Chicago: University of Chicago Press.

Derrida, J. (1967). *De la grammatologie*. Paris: Les Éditions de Minuit.

Grünbaum, A. (1984). *The foundations of psychoanalysis. A philosophical critique*. Berkeley, CA: University of California Press.

Kuhn, T. S. (1962). The historical structure of scientific discovery. *Science, 136*, 760–764.

Kuhn, T. S. (1970). *The structure of scientific revolutions*. Chicago: University of Chicago Press.

Lakatos, I. (1970). Falsification and the methodology of scientific research programs. In I. Lakatos & A. Musgrave (Eds.), *Criticism and the growth of knowledge* (pp. 91–196). Cambridge, UK: Cambridge University Press.

Langley, P., Simon, H. A., Bradshaw, G. L., & Zytkow, J. M. (1987). *Scientific discovery*. Cambridge, MA: MIT press.

Latour, B., & Woolgar, S. (1979). *Laboratory life: The social construction of scientific facts*. Los Angeles: Sage.

Maymin, P. (2011). Markets are efficient if and only if P=NP. *Algorithmic Finance, 1*, 1–11.

Popper, K. (1959). *The logic of scientific discovery*. New York: Basic Books.

Popper, K. (1963). *The poverty of historicism*. London: Routledge.

Roemer, J. (1981). *Analytical foundations of marxian economic theory*. Cambridge, UK: Cambridge University Press.

Simonton, D. K. (1999). *Origins of genius*. Oxford, UK: Oxford University Press.

Skyrms, B. (2013). *Signals: Evolution, learning and information*. Oxford, UK: Oxford University Press.

Sozou, P. D., Lane, P. C., Addis, M., & Gobet, F. (2017). Computational scientific discovery. In L. Magnani & T. Bertolotti (Eds.), *Springer handbook of model-based science* (pp. 719–734). New York: Springer.

Strauss, A., & Juliet, C. (1994). Grounded theory methodology: An overview. In N. Denzin & Y. Lincoln (Eds.), *Handbook of qualitative research* (1st ed., pp. 273–284). Thousands Oaks, CA: Sage.

Part I
Methods of Scientific Discovery

Chapter 2
Case Studies and Statistics in Causal Analysis: The Role of Bayesian Narratives

Peter Abell and Maria Koumenta

Abstract Case study method suffers from limited generalisation and lack of extensive comparative method both of which are prerequisites for the standard co-variation approach to causality. Indeed, in the standard model co-variation and comparative method are logical prerequisites for any causal explanation. Nevertheless, those that advocate case studies characteristically aspire to make causal inferences whilst promoting the virtues of detailed study and eliminating artificial comparison enforced by statistical samples. It is this latter aspect that recommends case methodology to many qualitatively orientated social scientists. It is proposed that the social sciences should find a "small N" (qualitative) conception of causal inference which is logically prior to any inter-unit comparison and generalisation and which complements "large N" (quantitative) statistical studies where this is not the case. The method advocated is called Bayesian Narratives which can depend upon subjective causal and counterfactual statements. Bayesian Narratives, in turn, require ethnographic data collection, in contrast to statistical sampling, in the pursuit of causal connections.

Keywords Bayesian narrative · Causal analysis · Causal inference · Constructivism · Directed acyclic graph · Ethnographic enquiry · Large N · Qualitative comparative analysis · Small N

2.1 Introduction

The social sciences, perhaps with the exception of economics (but see North, 2005), are beset by perpetual conflict between the advocates of "quantitative" (i.e. broadly

P. Abell (✉)
Department of Management, London School of Economics and Political Science, London, UK
e-mail: p.abell@lse.ac.uk

M. Koumenta
Department of Business and Management, Queen Mary University of London, London, UK
e-mail: m.koumenta@qmul.ac.uk

© Springer Nature Switzerland AG 2019   11
M. Addis et al. (eds.), *Scientific Discovery in the Social Sciences*,
Synthese Library 413, https://doi.org/10.1007/978-3-030-23769-1_2

speaking statistical) and "qualitative" (often in the form of case-based studies) approaches. However, the juxtaposition of these two terms is not entirely fortunate as statistical models utilising non metric (ordinal and nominal) variables is routine and case-based studies can embrace metric variables. They, nevertheless, have come to identify styles of research grounded in very different philosophical precepts and research methods occasioning much mutual disparagement. Whereas quantitative (i.e. statistical) methods in many respects tend to ape the aspirations of the natural sciences, qualitative methods often, though not universally, invite us to draw a line with "natural science"; rather favouring various forms of in-depth ethnographic inquiry taking account of the social construction of the meaning of concepts and the truth (or perhaps more accurately the justified belief) of propositions. The starting point of such enquiries is almost invariably the observation that actors/agents can themselves characteristically provide descriptions and sometimes explanations of what they are doing (and forbearing to do) formulated in their own, culturally derived, vocabulary (discourse). This provision then carries the assumption that agents have a contextual self-understanding of their activity which should engage (for some exclusively) social scientists. The question then arises, if exclusivity is rejected, as to what the relationship, if any, this discourse should bear to any alternative one which the social scientist might wish to impose.

The social construction of the actor's vocabulary implies a perspective whereby evidence always under-determines the "definition" of concepts and the "truth" of propositions connecting them, by making space for partially determining contingent social factors. Indeed, for some Constructionists the very concept of what constitutes evidence is itself socially constructed. There is, thus, no available concept of truth falling beyond the reach of socially constructed belief.

Some Constructionists even fail to detect a dividing line between the social and natural sciences, enjoining that both are equally socially constructed endeavours. Social construction is, thus, a beguiling portmanteau term that one has to be particularly careful in interpreting.[1] Nor is there, for many Constructionists, a pragmatic instrumental route to truth by virtue of prediction which is occasioned by their insistence that systematic comparison and generalisation are invariably unfeasible without undue surrender of case detail.

Inter-case comparison and generalisation (regularity) are, to a significant degree, surrendered by case analysts in favour of unique or, at best, only similar in-depth

---

[1] The phrase "social construction" is open to a myriad of interpretations as the voluminous literature testifies. Reviews of this literature are available (such as Searle, 1995) and the details fall beyond the competence of these authors. We shall, however, interpret the phrase to imply the rejection of a simple concept of truth which is determined by the structure of an objective world. Other related terms could also be used here like "Verstehen", "Hermeneutics" and "Interpretation" and a number of others. Although the details of these differing conceptions vary, most agree that there is both an epistemological and an ontological discontinuity between the social and natural sciences. However, as the "science wars" testify, there are those for whom both the social and natural sciences are equally socially constructed endeavours. In this essay we try to explore how any discontinuity, which may exist within social science is, at least in part, derivative of different conceptions of causal inference.

descriptions. This creates little intellectual frisson if the objective is only to describe phenomena, and this does appear to be the intellectual horizon for many case based study advocates. But causal explanation is another matter. Many qualitative analysts, however, disavow the whole vocabulary of causality in social inquiry, believing that it necessarily implies unwarranted forced comparison and generalisation across otherwise descriptively unique cases. In this respect case-based studies tend to find common ground with some historical scholarship (Carr, 1987) though judicious comparisons are sometimes entertained by historians.

Peter Winch's book, *The Idea of a Social Science* (1990), strongly influenced by late Wittgenstein (1953), leads the charge against the idea of a generalising social science but did open up the idea of family resemblance. Indeed, much may not be lost, from a Constructionist standpoint, by interpreting social construction as the social construction of family resemblance or similarity and indeed dissimilarity (Abell, Engel, & Wynn, 2016)[2]? Both identity and similarity/dissimilarity licence comparison which is of course necessary if one is to escape the assumption that everything is unique.

We shall assume that the ultimate purpose of social science is to furnish causal explanations which are at least in part generated by voluntary human actions – individual and collective – and, as such, may be conceived as socially constructed by actors when "making sense" of the appropriateness of their actions (and forbearances) in given contexts. This implies that events are to be conceived as causally connected by generative mechanisms involving human activity intervening between the events. The phrase generative mechanism has recently become popular in social science (Hedstrom & Bearman, 2009). In this context it is probably important to recognise that the adjective generative implies that the mechanism involves human actions and forbearances which construct and connect the context of action and its outcomes. Thus, in a sense, two causal links are involved the first connecting the context to the action and the second the action to the outcomes.[3]

There have of course been many attempts to bridge the gap between "qualitative" and "quantitative" analysis in the social sciences. Qualitative Comparative Analysis (QCA) (Ragin, 1989) is perhaps the most successful applying a Boolean Analysis to a handful of cases each exhibiting a binary outcome, in an attempt to extract a causal model comprising a number of alternative case types each exhibiting the conjunctive presence and absence of a number of binary variables. Reducing such

---

[2]Family resemblance concepts engender a network of similarity relations amongst the resembling units. A similarity relation, like an identity, is reflexive and symmetric but is not necessarily transitive. Thus, units of analysis cannot be conceptualised into exclusive classes with unequivocal boundaries which is normally deemed a necessity for units exhibiting a causal connection between concepts.

[3]For those who controversially respect the logical connection argument, the connection from intentional action to outcomes is not correctly conceived as causal but rather definitional. Taking sides on this controversial debate is not necessary for the purposes of this paper. We shall treat the connection between context and outcomes, generated by the action(s), as a single causal hypothesis.

a Boolean model to its prime implicants can then surrender a parsimonious, but deterministic, causal structure. Consistency of such models can then be assessed by applying de Morgan's Law[4] to cases that do not exhibit the outcome. Although this is all far from a Constructionist's picture of things it does enable a limited form of generalisation and the binary variables can be carefully extracted from ethnographically rich descriptions.

A ready criticism of QCA is its apparent deterministic nature, but which is, nevertheless, sometimes justified by asserting that detailed (ethnographic/ "thick description") case studies are observed without error. QCA has, however, been extended into fuzzy set analysis (Ragin, 2000) where this controversial assumption is dropped.

The purpose of this paper is to try and fashion some common understanding about the limits of both "quantitative" and "qualitative" analysis, such that the current mutual disparagement might be, to some extent, mitigated leading to the recognition of their complementary roles in causal analysis.

The paper will proceed as follows. First, we shall briefly outline the orthodox observational (as opposed to experimental) statistical approach to causality. Here many observations are required either longitudinally or in cross-section; N is "large". Indeed, N is large enough to render tests of significance operative when only a sample is observed. This leaves little room for one or just a few (N is "low") historically based case studies net of their possible exploratory role as a preface to statistical modelling. Any repeated observation internal to a case does not characteristically generate a time –series of identical events, but rather a chronology of diverse events and actions which is not amenable to time series analysis.[5] The insertion of causal links into a chronology produces a Narrative.

Second, we shall examine the apparent achievements and limitations of the orthodox approach, which we shall, in order to avoid the awkward terms quantitative and qualitative, re-label as large N as opposed to small N. These terms seem better to capture the essential differences between the two approaches when causal analysis is at stake.

Third, we shall pose the question as to whether the large N method needs complementing (not substituting as some low N analysts might aver) by causal inference when N is intrinsically low. We shall answer in the affirmative which confers a role upon case studies beyond merely providing an exploratory method.

Fourth, we shall outline a small N method of causal inference, which we term Bayesian Narratives (Abell, 2004, 2009, 2010), and which, we argue, can complement statistical large N modelling.

---

[4]De Morgan's law takes the Boolean formula for the presence of a binary outcome and derives the formula for its absence by inverting all the logical connectives in the former.

[5]Interrupted time series (Shadish, Cook, & Campbell, 2001) analysis can allow causal inference as can Grainger causality between time series.

2.2   The Large N (Orthodox) Approach to Causal Inference

Here we are not concerned with the details of statistical technique but rather with the underlying logic of whatever technique is appropriate given the available data. We shall assume that the focus is upon observational studies not randomised experiments. The number of observational studies far outreaches the number of experimental studies in the social sciences. Experimental studies do allow careful causal inference with only a few observations (N is low) through the device of randomized controls where the investigator is able to select the experimental treatment. But it would obviously be difficult to advocate a marked reliance upon experiments in the social sciences. In observational studies the investigator is not in a position to select treatments though the sharp line between experimental and observational studies has been significantly eroded by recent developments of the do-calculus (Paul & Hall, 2013; Pearl, 2009) which allows the investigator to intervene in the context of an observationally based study expressed as directed acyclic graph (DAG).

A necessary, though far from sufficient, component of any causal inference in the large N tradition is a significant co-variation of the cause and effect variables (at any level of measurement). As Pearl (2009) has observed some additional causal assumptions are always required. The elementary treatment of both observed and unobserved confounding variables is a case in point. Neither the joint nor the conditional probability distributions of cause and effect and a potential confounder will alone distinguish between (i.e. identify) confounding and mediation causal models. Whilst the appropriate statistical assumptions for causal inference depend upon sample size, causal assumptions are not so dependent; they rather contribute to the possibility or otherwise identification of a causal link prior to any estimation procedure.

Despite accusations mounted against its supposed metaphysical foundations (Dawid, 2000), the most persuasive conception of causality in the statistical tradition is the potential outcomes model due to Rubin (2005) and his colleagues. These authors note that in order to establish a causal link connecting C (cause) and E (effect) for a particular case (unit of analysis), evidence for that particular unit is required of the value of E both in the presence and absence of C. That is to say counterfactual ideas are inevitably invoked. In neither a cross-sectional nor an experimental context are both immediately accessible and in longitudinal studies (including test retest experiments) inevitable dependence of values at different points in time rapidly creates analytical complications. That is, we can rarely assume that exposures of the same unit on different occasions are independent. Taking sample expectations across an assumed homogeneous sample of units in the presence and absence of C is the standard inter-unit comparative and generalising way around this problem under the Stable Unit Treatment Value Assumption (SUTVA) (Heckman, 2005). SUTVA is however, especially with human subjects, rather fragile; it requires that the potential outcomes of each unit are not influenced by the treatment status of all the other units.

SUTVA is violated when units of analysis do not derive their value on the effect (E) independently, but rather influence one another. That is to say, when network effects are operative and are not explicitly incorporated into the picture. In an experimental context individual units subject to a treatment variable (C) and the network effect variable must be compared with units exposed to neither. In observational studies this requires conditioning out of the network effect. Needless to say, this imposes immense constraints upon statistical models.

In the face of this complexity it is appropriate to pose the question as to whether individual case studies can offer some help. Indeed, recently there has been some misgivings aired in statistical circles as to the sometimes careless assumption that causal states (which usually comprise of a nominally designated conjunction of constituent states[6]) are the most apposite starting point from which to infer stable causal connections without a detailed understanding of the causal mechanisms connection each of the constituents to the effect (Reed, 2011). Cartwright (2007) is particularly critical of social science in this respect, she writes of "imposter counterfactuals" derivative of aggregated causal variables. No doubt many case based enthusiasts would concur. They urge that detailed case based studies can more effectively address complexity, though they are rather silent as to how causality is to be embraced. Moreover, in so far as they commence ethnographic studies using the vocabulary of the actors themselves they argue that aggregated concepts are unlikely to capture "what is really going on". But, the nagging question is still insistent – can causal connections be identified and estimated in case studies? Let it be clear we are searching for a more elaborate role for case studies than one whereby the case is suggestive of a causal link in the elaboration of a causal model which is to be subsequently identified and estimated using appropriate large N methods.

The practical consequences of unpacking all the constituent elements in a theoretically aggregated causal concept are, of course, manifest. To use the social scientists' terminology, each of the operational concepts defining a descriptively theoretical causal variable would have to be disaggregated and stand alone in a complex causal structure (Pearl, 2009). It is, however, the use of aggregate concepts that often generates a sufficiently large N to enable statistical analysis to be applied.[7] Multiplying the number of variables in a model can quickly run up against degrees of freedom issues.

Whatever the sophistication of the statistical model chosen the underlying logic of any explanatory causal inference is manifestly clear: Both inter-unit comparison and generalisation (some might, in the spirit of the hypothetico-deductive and inductive models of explanation, even say law) are necessary prerequisites for any causal inference; no explanation without comparison and generalisation. A particular ordering of a trinity is established whereby the determination of a causal

---

[6]The social sciences are replete with statistical techniques for aggregating "operational" indicator variables into "theoretical" variables (e.g. factor analysis, latent structure analysis and so on).

[7]When aggregation is used then the imperfect correlation between operational indicators allows similar but not identical units to be classified together.

explanation is always posterior to comparison and generalisation (co-variance). Thus, large N becomes a sine qua non.

We all know that such inferences are always precariously provisional in the light of unexplored confounding effects but Pearl's (2000, 2009) back and front door analysis in Structural Causal Models (SCM) has significantly advanced our understanding of causal inference (Morgan & Winship, 2015). It does so by explicitly tying causal analysis and its assumptions, in the large N context, to Directed Acyclic Graphs (DAGs) and matching non parametric structural equations. Structural Causal Models based upon DAGs are a development of earlier linear Structural Equation Models (SEMs) and path analysis.

2.3   What Has the Orthodox Model Achieved?

In our view the answer to this question is, most of what we have learned about the social world. Notwithstanding, Fig. 2.1 depicts the average variance explained (when reported), in empirical papers published from 1960 onwards, in the American Sociological Review; one of the world's leading social science journals. For good reasons, maximising variance explained is not the usual objective of empirical researchers, nor are many studies explicitly directed at a complete causal explanation. It is worthy of note, nevertheless, that despite the unprecedented advances in statistical analysis and the availability of data since 1960, the average variance explained has not significantly improved and remains rather modest. One might have

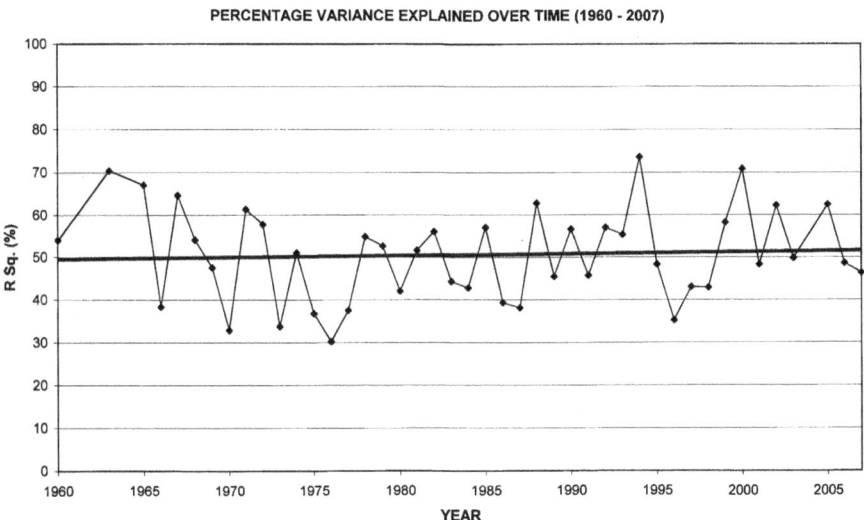

Fig. 2.1 Trend in variance explained (R^2) in the American Sociological Review (1960–2007). (Source: Authors' calculations)

expected with the accumulation of published studies and subsequent incorporation of control variables into models that we would have witnessed a significant upward trend? Alternatively it could be conjectured that statistical modelling of social phenomena is about as good as it is going to get, reflecting the fundamentally stochastic nature of social phenomena; or maybe early low hanging fruit is partially responsible for the flat profile. But whatever interpretation we care to put upon the analysis, it invites the question as to what we might reasonably expect in the future. Will the recent development of big data and perhaps improved statistical modelling likely improve the situation? This query is difficult, even for those much more versed in statistics than we, to give a definitive answer to. But these observations do, we believe, give us grounds for thought.

The advocates of case studies would also demur at the frequent resort to devices like dummy variable in statistical modelling, feeling that apples and oranges are often forced into the same category, generating superficial homogeneity across units which is entirely unwarranted. Indeed, they are deeply sceptical about the existence of large populations of causally homogeneous cases open to statistical sampling and treatment. They prefer carefully selected cases studies, using detailed ethnographic techniques, which make no claim to be representative of a population. As we have noted above it is, however, difficult to comprehend how causality (if it is embraced at all) is inferred in such situations, beyond the instantiation of already established generalisations (from large N studies).

How should we react to the apparent limitation of current statistical practice and the sceptical claims of ethnographic case study researchers? Firstly, we should always be open to the incorporation of improved statistical modelling and developments in causal analysis. Nevertheless, we shall argue below that we need to search for an alternative and complementary approach to causal analysis which is appropriate in low-N situations. Let it be clear we are, unlike many Constructionists, not seeking to substitute low-N approaches for statistical modelling but rather pondering whether each could play a significant role under their respective appropriate conditions.

2.4   A Small N Approach to Causality

Can case-based studies, often historically (i.e. longitudinally) formulated, play a role in causal analysis which is more than merely exploratory? There is little disagreement that exploratory studies can prove to be highly suggestive, providing causal insights which can subsequently be studied using large N statistical methods. Such insights are usually delivered in a manner whereby a causal event characteristically comprises a complex conjunction of sub-events. Furthermore, cases are usually reported as a jumble of events and actions /decisions. The logical prerequisites for a single or just a few cases to directly surrender causal information are, however, clear; the large N "trinity", whereby inter-unit comparison and generalisation (co-variance) are prerequisites for any causal explanation, needs to be inverted. Thus, causal explanation then stands as prior to any possible inter-case comparison and thence tentative generalisation. So, we could then cogently ask how general a case based causal explanation is, as revealed by inter-unit comparison across, a likely severely limited set of similar case studies. Note, that even if N were to be large enough, this is not a procedure equivalent to statistical induction because the question being asked is not whether there are sufficient grounds for inferring a causal connection but rather how general the already established the causal connection is. It is, thus, important to draw a line between this procedure and the standard inductive and deductive nomological models of scientific explanation. Any limited induction is rather across a small N number of established singular causal explanations.

What is required is a case-based technique which:

1. In the spirit of QCA, allows for complex interactive causality in the recognition that causes usually comprises a conjunction of events.
2. Is, contrary to the assertions of many low N advocates, stochastic in nature. The oft claimed notion that ethnographic observation is, by virtue of its attention to detail, entirely deterministic must be rejected (Goldthorpe, 2001).
3. Shows how "the world" is transformed from state E_1 to state E_2 by virtue of human activity which generates singular causal connections.

We shall argue below that Bayesian Narratives (Abell, 2009) have such properties, but first we define a narrative.

2.5   A Brief Introduction to Narratives

A Narrative is a time ordered acyclic directed graph (DAG) where:

1. The nodes represent a chronology of defined states/events.
2. The edges are action driven causal connections running between pairs of states.
3. The structure is an "and" graph in the sense that edges incident into a given node are conjointly sufficient for the occurrence of the node at a particular time. If more than one edge is incident out of a node then the node contributes to the causes of each of the nodes reached.

Figure 2.2 depicts a very simple Narrative transforming E_0 into E_1 and thence to E_2 and E_3. The major puzzle is how the causal edges can be inserted into the chronology of events, consequently generating the Narrative? Namely, what is the evidence permitting the insertion of the various causal links in the absence of sufficient comparators to enable systematic treatment?

It is noteworthy that historians, when proffering narratives as an explanatory mechanism, do not usually fall out over the ordering of a chronology of states but often do struggle to agree on their relative importance which, in turn, is often implicitly linked to what causes what. Compiling evidence for events/states of the world

Fig. 2.2 A narrative directed
graph

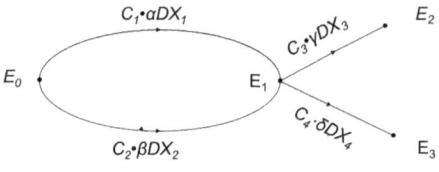

α, β, γ, δ– Actors
C_1, C_2, C_3, C_4 – Conditions
DX_1, DX_2, DX_3, DX_4 – Actions Performed
E_0, E_1, E_2, E_3 – States

appears to be much easier than doing so for causal connections.[8] Interestingly, the classic paper by Hempel (1965) introducing (the now much disputed) hypothetico-deductive model of causal explanation was partially motivated in terms of whether or not history could deemed to be a science. We have no idea of what the current thinking amongst historians is on these matters but what does seem clear is that historical generalisations are hard to come by and exclusively linking causal analysis to generalisation does not appear to pay dividends.

2.6   Bayesian Causal Analysis of Narratives

The basic idea behind Bayesian Narratives is to mount a search for items of evidence – some maybe supporting and others undermining the action driven causal connections – between states (nodes), without recourse to inter-case comparison and co-variance across cases. In case based ethnographic research evidence will usually be forthcoming from participants, both active and passive and from observers in interaction with the investigator.

We shall argue below that subjective past tense causal statements by participants like: "I did Y because of X" and counterfactuals, "I would not have done Y if X had not happened" provide probabilistic evidence for the causal statement that "X caused the actor to do (bring about) Y". Collective actors would use the first person plural (we). Observers would use the third person singular or plural. Although subjective statements of this sort are clearly open to all sorts of possible distortions, certainly ruling out a deterministic interpretation of their possible impact upon the truth of the actual causal relation, they should not be summarily dismissed as many

---

[8]Historians frequently debate the granularity of their explanations. Should individuals, groups or social movements be construed as the causal agents connecting events? A similar debate has occupied sociologists since at least Durkheim. The statistical and causal issues involved are usually handled in terms of ecological inference (King, Rosen, & Tanner, 2004) and the Coleman diagram (Coleman, 1990). Case study analysts appear not to have given this issue as much attention often mixing a variety of units of analysis in the same case (but see Ragin, 2000).

large N researchers tend to do. Recall that case based studies usually assemble evidence in the context of deep ethnographic interviews which, to use the much promoted phrase, enable an understanding of "what is really going on"! The X and Y will characteristically be defined in terms of the culturally derived vocabulary (discourse) of the participants themselves.

So, consider a particular causal link in a narrative whereby it is hypothesised that X causes α to do Y which, in turn causes Y. Call the causal link between X and Y, hypothesis H and the absence of such a link $\sim$H. Now, assume there are n items of evidence $b_1, b_2 \ldots , b_n$ pertaining to H and $\sim$H, like subjective causal and counterfactual statements. Assume initially that the items of evidence are conditionally independent given H; then, making use of Bayes Theorem:

$$P(H|b_1, b_2, \ldots , b_n) \cdot P(b_1) \cdot P(b_2) \cdot \ldots \cdot P(b_n) =$$
$$P(H) \cdot P(b_1|H) \cdot P(b_2|H) \cdot \ldots \cdot P(b_n|H). \tag{2.1}$$

$$P(\sim H) | b_1, b_2 \ldots , b_n \big) \cdot P(b_1) \cdot P(b_2) \ldots P(b_n) =$$
$$P(\sim H) \cdot P(b_1| \ \sim H) \cdot P(b_2| \ \sim H) \cdot \ldots \cdot P(b_n| \ \sim H). \tag{2.2}$$

Thus,

$$\text{Log Odds}(H: \sim H|b_1, b_2 \ldots b_n) - \text{Log Odds}(H: \sim H)$$
$$= \text{LogL}_{b1} + \text{LogL}_{b2} \cdots + \text{LogL}_{bn} \tag{2.3}$$

where, $L_{bi}(i = 1, 2 \ldots , n)$ are likelihood ratios for each item of evidence. This analysis is easily extended to evidential items which are not conditionally independent of each other (Abell, 2009).

The global log likelihood ratio, $\text{Log L}_B = \sum_i^n \log L_{bi}$ now provides a summative measure of the probative force of the evidential items in changing the prior to the posterior odds of H compared to $\sim$H. Concentrating upon odds ratios is superior to what might appear to be a more natural comparison in terms of probabilities (e.g. $P(H| b_1, b_2, \ldots , b_n) - P(H)$ or $P(H| b_1, b_2, \ldots , b_n)/P(H)$) because an item of evidence will have the same incremental impact upon the posterior odds whatever the prior odds. This is in contrast to differences or ratios of posterior and prior probabilities.

It is clear from Eq. (2.3) that log L_B would provide a direct measure of the impact of all of the evidential items upon the log odds ratio of H to $\sim$H if the log of prior odds could stand at unity. In the absence of any evidence prior to the accumulation of B, assuming this to be the case seems reasonable. One has no reason to believe in H rather than $\sim$H. This is rather like assuming the null hypothesis in statistical modelling. Accumulating evidence across a limited number (small N) of studies would however require an appropriate updating of the prior which departs from unity.

The next step is to determine how the global and individual likelihood ratios in Eq. (2.3) should be estimated. The items of evidence assessed will often comprise subjective statements reflecting upon the probity of H and $\sim$H. Those statements may be derived from the commissioning actor or close observers of the causal connection of the form:

$$X \rightarrow \text{do}Y \rightarrow Y$$

where X in general is a conjunction of states and Y is the realised state.[9] The advocates of small-N, ethnographic case based studies enjoin us to explicitly take account of the social interaction of the actors and observers with the investigator in the "social construction" of the above scheme.

Let us concentrate upon subjective causal statements proffered by the commissioning actor. Thus, the investigator may pose, to such an actor, the question: "Why did you do Y?", having negotiated with the actor that categorising the action as doing Y is "consistent" with the way the actor would categorise matters. Consistency here is tricky. In order to head off the possibility of uniqueness the investigator will seek a categorisation which is potentially comparative with other similar actions, with a view, however limited in scope, to the location of generalisation. Ethnographic Constructionists, on the other hand, will verge in the direction of uniqueness. The negotiation in essence involves effective inter-conceptual translation where the target is perhaps best described as a matter of family resemblance (Wittgenstein, 1953) rather than identity. Resemblance or similarity, unlike identity, is not necessarily a transitive relationship and, thus, does not break the world into neat equivalence classes; in a sense the world retains its qualitative character. Thus, "doing Y" across a limited set of comparators takes the form of a network of similar relations rather than a clean equivalence (Abell et al., 2016).

The commissioning actor, in reply to the above question may proffer: "I did Y, because of X to realise Y" and, on prompting, "If X had not happened I would not have done Y". So, if these are credible statements, we are in possession of a causal statement and its counterfactual for the same actor. This is in sharp contrast to the potential outcomes approach, for large N, outlined above. Although the credibility of personal testimony may be less secure than many other forms of evidence, it has an intra-unit aspect that may begin to offset its questionable credibility, especially if we can take the claim of ethnographers seriously that they get closer to what is really going on. Subjective causal and counterfactual statements may then stand as evidential items standing in favour or against the odds ratio that a causal link

---

[9]To keep the presentation straightforward we shall gloss over the complexity of action descriptions in terms of beliefs and intentions (but see Abell, 2009). Further, the relation between do Y and event Y will be construed as causal despite the urging of those who maintain the logical connection argument. Nothing is gained for the analysis presented here in taking a position one way or another on this vexed issue.

connects X and Y. The investigator then needs to compute the odds likelihood for each item of such evidence. The investigator could make use of a "jury "of experts or observers to make the estimates and take their mean value as a measure of the odds. There is a long tradition in the social sciences of making use of expert and "key" observers to make estimates of difficult to observe phenomena. Using the word jury is perhaps particularly apposite. Jury members are charged with the responsibility of making a decision which is beyond all reasonable doubt or on the balance of probabilities (Schum, 1994). The parallel with assessing evidence in case based causal analysis is evident. The internal consistency of estimates is at hand if the estimations are also made of L_B which should equal the product of all the item specific likelihood odds ratios.

2.7 Bayesian Narratives

Bayesian causal analysis offers a method whereby estimates of the probability of each causal link are inserted into an evolving chronology of states. The derived Narrative can then stand alone as a singular explanation of how the starting state(s) get translated into the final state(s). However, given a small number of case based Narratives the question arises as to whether they can be generalised (small N induction). Abell (1987) proposed an algebraic method of achieving this through the agency of homomorphic mappings, and Abell (2009) suggested a Boolean approach to causal paths which we shall now briefly outline.

If all the causal paths in a narrative connecting the starting and final state(s) are labelled (they may intersect at nodes) then a case can be described as the conjunction of those paths and the absence of any other paths that may appear in any comparator cases (cf. Ragin, 1989). Thus, across the comparator cases (low N), the alternative conjunctions of the presence and absence of paths describe the causal structures of the comparators. The set of cases generating alternant sets of conjunctions can then be reduced to prime implicants giving the generalised causal picture in terms of causal paths.

Given the intellectual pre-eminence of large N statistical models alongside the recent developments of DAG causality, it is finally pertinent to ask how Bayesian narratives may complement SCM.[10] Assume a causal DAG is postulated, but in practice it proves too complex, given the limited number of comparators, to enable a large N statistical investigation. Then each link in the DAG can be interpreted as an action driven narrative, depicting a generative mechanism. Typically, a DAG

---

[10]One of the major contributions of Pearl (2009) to causal analysis is his claim that the do-calculus (i.e. "experimental" intervention by setting the value of certain variables in a DAG) enables one to observe the impact of counterfactuals. Pearl also notes that the assumptions underlying any DAG amount to the absence of a direct causal link. Subjective causality, does allow a direct test of such assumptions as actors can be asked if such causal connections exist garnering a reply along the lines of - "I would not do-Y because of X".

will comprise of alternative front and back door paths of causal connections running between pairs of states which would, if statistical treatment were possible, imply a pattern of statistical co-variances. Statistical treatment absent, however, each link in each path may be associated with independent case studies cast within a narrative framework. These narratives may comprise of single actions connecting two states (nodes) or networks of paths of interactions directly connecting pairs of states in the parent DAG.[11]

2.8 Conclusion

We have argued that social scientists, rather than defending the exclusive virtues of small N (qualitative) or large N (quantitative) studies, should all recognise the virtues of both types of study and their respective methods of causal inference. They complement each other, small N occupying a space where large N studies are not feasible because of a poverty of comparators or the likelihood of over-forced comparisons. Small N case based studies invert the relationship between causal explanation and comparison and generalisation by giving explanation priority. This calls for a distinctive form of causal evidence where subjective causal and counter-factual statements feature which convert chronologies of events into Narratives by the insertion of evidence based causal links.

References

Abell, P. (1987). *Comparative narratives: The syntax of social life*. Oxford, UK: Oxford University Press.

Abell, P. (2004). Narrative explanation: An alternative to variable centred explanation. *Annual Review of Sociology, 30*, 287–310.

Abell, P. (2009). A case for cases: Comparative narratives in sociological explanation. *Sociological Methods & Research, 38*, 38–70.

Abell, P. (2010). Singulare Mechanismen und Bayesch narrative. In T. Kron & T. Grund (Eds.), *Die Analytische Soziologie in der Diskussion*. Weisbaden, Germany: V.S. Verlag.

Abell, P., Engel, O., & Wynn, H. (2016). *Ethnographic causality. Mimeo*. London: LSE.

Carr, E. H. (1987). *What is history?* (2nd ed.). Harmondsworth, UK: Penguin.

Cartwright, N. S. (2007). *Hunting causes and using them: Approaches in philosophy and economics*. Cambridge, MA: Cambridge University Press.

Coleman, J. S. (1990). *Foundations of social theory*. Cambridge, MA: Cambridge University Press.

---

[11] Since SCM is based upon non parametric models, Bayesian techniques administered amongst observers/experts could be used to directly estimate causal links in a DAG. Case study analysts would find this lacking where the connecting inter-actions are complex. Recently, the do calculus has been extended to what is termed meta-synthesis whereby causal results can be synthesised from heterogeneous populations and multiple studies. Although it falls beyond the scope of this paper, this sort of analysis may provide a bridge into case study results.

Dawid, A. P. (2000). Causal inference without counterfactuals. *Journal of the American Statistical Association, 95*, 407–424.

Goldthorpe, J. H. (2001). Causation, statistics and sociology. *European Sociological Review, 17*, 1–20.

Heckman, J. J. (2005). The scientific model of causality. *Sociological Methodology, 35*, 1–97.

Hedstrom, P., & Bearman, P. (Eds.). (2009). *The Oxford handbook of analytical sociology.* Oxford, UK: Oxford University Press.

Hempel, C. (1965). *Aspects of scientific explanation and other essays in the philosophy of science.* New York: Free Press.

King, G., Rosen, O., & Tanner, M. A. (2004). *Ecological inference: New methodological strategies.* Cambridge, MA: Cambridge University Press.

Morgan, S. L., & Winship, C. (2015). *Counterfactuals and causal inference. Methods and principles for social research.* Cambridge, MA: Cambridge University Press.

North, D. C. (2005). *Understanding the process of economic change.* Princeton, NJ: Princeton University Press.

Paul, L. A., & Hall, N. (2013). *Causation: A user's guide.* Oxford, UK: Oxford University Press.

Pearl, J. (2000). *Causality: Models, reasoning and inference.* Cambridge, MA: Cambridge University Press.

Pearl, J. (2009). Causal inference in statistics: An overview. *Statistics Surveys, 3*, 96–146.

Ragin, C. C. (1989). *The comparative method: Moving beyond qualitative and quantitative strategies.* Berkley, CA/Los Angeles, CA: University of California Press.

Ragin, C. C. (2000). *Fuzzy-set social science.* Chicago: University of Chicago Press.

Reed, I. (2011). *Interpretation and social knowledge: On the use of theory in the human sciences.* Chicago: University of Chicago Press.

Rubin, D. B. (2005). Causal inference using potential outcomes: Design, modeling, decisions. *Journal of the American Statistical Association, 100*, 322–331.

Schum, D. A. (1994). *The evidential foundations of probabilistic reasoning.* Evanston, IL: Northwestern University Press.

Searle, J. R. (1995). *The construction of social reality.* New York: Free Press.

Shadish, W. R., Cook, T. D., & Campbell, D. T. (2001). *Experimental and quasi-experimental design for generalized causal inference.* Boston: Houghton Mifflin.

Winch, P. (1990). *The idea of a social science.* London: Routledge.

Wittgenstein, L. (1953). *Philosophical investigations.* New York: Macmillan.

Chapter 3
Scale Development in Human and Social Sciences: A Philosophical Perspective

Clayton Peterson

Abstract Explanation of human and social phenomena is often formulated using unobservable constructs, otherwise known as latent constructs. In this context, latent constructs are broadly understood as latent characteristics. Formally, latent constructs are interpreted as latent variables that influence the behavior of observed variables (items). Latent constructs are identified through measurement instruments, which are tested in specific samples using measurement models, representing the relationship between the latent variable and the items. Depending on the methodological guidelines that are followed during the development of measurement instruments, these measurement models will be tested using factor analytic techniques such as exploratory and confirmatory factor analysis. Historically, these techniques have been surrounded by various controversies and have generated their share of confusion. This chapter explores the conceptual and philosophical issues related to scale development in human and social science research and discusses the main problems associated with these techniques.

3.1 Introduction

Explanation of human and social phenomena is often formulated using unobservable constructs, otherwise known as latent constructs (e.g., personality traits or degrees of life satisfaction). Formally, latent constructs are interpreted as latent variables, influencing the behavior of observed variables. These observed variables can take the form of items (i.e., individual statements) that are scored on specific scales (e.g., a Likert-type scale, ranging from 5 = never to 1 = always). Scales meant to identify latent constructs are developed on the grounds of these items, which are taken as plausible empirical consequences of the constructs.

C. Peterson (✉)
Munich Center for Mathematical Philosophy, Ludwig-Maximilians-Universität München, München, Germany
e-mail: clayton.peterson@outlook.com

© Springer Nature Switzerland AG 2019   27
M. Addis et al. (eds.), *Scientific Discovery in the Social Sciences*,
Synthese Library 413, https://doi.org/10.1007/978-3-030-23769-1_3

Scale development in human and social sciences is accomplished using factor analytic techniques. Historically, these techniques have been surrounded by various controversies and have generated their share of confusion. This chapter explores the conceptual and philosophical issues related to scale development in human and social science research. It provides a bird's eye view of the points that should be known and taken into consideration. We begin by discussing the role statistics can play within this context, and which kind of statistics are required to develop scales meant to identify latent constructs. Then, we present the statistical techniques as well as the issues pertaining to model selection, causal explanation, realism and theory-ladenness.

3.2   Statistics in Social Sciences

Human and social science research can be applied and conceived in different ways. One aim is to describe human and social phenomena. Mathematically speaking, this is accomplished using *descriptive* statistics. Descriptive statistics are tools that are used to describe samples. As such, descriptive statistics yield information regarding what is happening in the data. Examples of descriptive statistics are means, modes, medians, quartiles, frequencies, etc. Descriptive statistics are used to summarise the information that is contained within a data set. To some extent, descriptive statistics can be understood as a form of statistical journalism, relating what is going on in the data (cf. Kiers & Mechelen 2001).

Research in social sciences, however, is not limited to the description of human and social phenomena. Indeed, researchers often want to draw conclusions that go beyond the samples and that apply to populations (cf. Aron, Coups, & Aron 2013; Tabachnick & Fidell 2013). From a quantitative perspective, this can be accomplished using *inferential* statistics. Examples of inferential statistics are hypothesis testing (with significance levels), t-tests, factor analysis, etc. One interest of inferential statistics is that they include techniques that can be used to argue in favor of causal explanations of human and social phenomena.

3.3   Measurement Models for Latent Constructs

Scales meant to identify latent constructs are developed using methods of inferential statistics. The rationale behind that conception is quite simple: Latent constructs are, by definition, not directly observable. Hence, one must employ statistical methods that go beyond the data at hand. Formally, these latent constructs are interpreted as latent variables (cf. Mulaik 1987). Latent variables can be understood in contradistinction to observed variables (cf. Borsboom 2008). Examples of observed variables are age, sex or the score of a participant on a Likert-type scale. Although observed variables are not directly observed by researchers per se (e.g., researchers do not directly observe that participants are male or female; they only see their answer on the questionnaire), they are empirically accessible to researchers. In comparison, latent variables are mathematical constructions that are either conceived as causes or as effects of the observed variables.

Measurement in human and social sciences is obtained via subjects' responses to items. Examples of items are dichotomous items (e.g., male or female), Likert-type scales (e.g., 1 = never, 2 = rarely, 3 = sometimes, 4 = often and 5 = always), indication of points on continuous lines, time taken to answer items, or psychophysical measurements (see Mellenbergh 1994). These items can be classified as either categorical or continuous data (cf. Stevens 1946). Categorical (i.e., discrete) data include nominal and ordinal data. In nominal data, numbers are assigned to individuals, concepts or classes. For instance, one might assign 0 to an incorrect answer and 1 to a correct one, 0 to male and 1 to females, or 0 to a negative answer and 1 to a positive one. Ordinal data is order preserving (e.g., a Likert-type scale). Continuous data include interval and ratio scales. The main different between these two is that in the former, 0 is a convention (e.g., $0°$ C or $0°$ F), although in the latter it might never be achieved (e.g., a 'mass' of 0 kg).

There are two types of measurement models that can be obtained on the grounds of items (cf. Edwards & Bagozzi 2000). In a *formative* measurement model, latent variables are defined in function of the items (see Fig. 3.1). An example of such a latent variable would be the socioeconomic status (e.g., White 1982). This variable is defined using observed variables such as the level of education of the parents, their occupation, the income of the family, etc. Thus represented, the latent variable, otherwise known as a principal component, is an effect of the observed variables. That is, a between-subjects variation on the items (observed variables) explains a variation on the latent variable (principal component). It is because some have, say, a better salary than others that they will have a different socioeconomic status. As such, the socioeconomic status is conceived as an effect of the observed variables (i.e., it can be described by the observed variables).

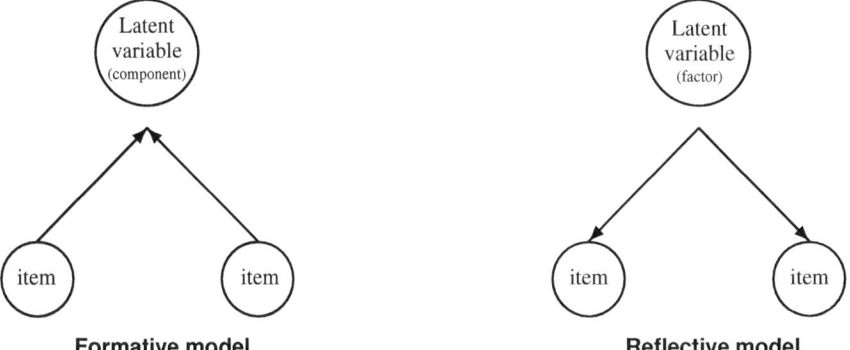

Formative model   **Reflective model**

Fig. 3.1 Measurement models

Reflective measurement models rather conceive items as effects of the latent variable. The rationale behind that conception is that the latent variable causally explains the between-subjects variation on the items (cf. Spirtes et al. 1991, 2000; Glymour 2001; Borsboom et al. 2003). The observed variables are considered as indicators of the latent variable. As such, the items are understood as testable empirical consequences of the latent construct, which is modeled by a latent variable. In this case, we rather speak of a latent factor.[1] The construct of *depression* would be a good example of this phenomenon (e.g., Zung 1965). Items considered as indicators of depression are, among others, "I have trouble sleeping at night", "I get tired for no reason" and "I feel hopeful about the future". They are rated on a Likert-type scale ranging from 1 to 4, 1 representing "A little of the time" and 4 "Most of the time". The rationale behind the measurement model is that the latent construct *depression*, modeled by a factor (latent variable), causally explains why some people score high while others score low on the items. For example, if a person is depressed, then researchers conceive that it is likely that this person will score high (i.e., 3 or 4) on an item such as "I get tired for no reason". Similarly, if a person is not depressed, then it is expected that this person will score low on the item (i.e., 1 or 2). Note that some items are reversed score items. For instance, a depressed person is expected to score low (not high) on the item "I feel hopeful about the future". Thus conceived, *depression* explains why there is a between-subjects variation on the items when participants answer questionnaires.

3.4 Statistical Techniques

Different statistical techniques can be used during the scale development process, and using one instead of the other depends on what one intends to achieve.

3.4.1 *Principal Component Analysis*

If researchers intend to provide an empirical summary of the data, then principal component analysis (PCA) may be used. PCA is tool of descriptive statistics that reduces the dimensionality of a data set (cf. ten Berge et al. 1992; Kiers & ten Berge 1994; ten Berge & Kiers 1997; Kiers & Mechelen 2001; Jolliffe 2002; Abdi & Williams 2010). One interest of this method is that it reduces a large number

---

[1] Anticipating on what follows, a factor is a latent variable within a reflective model, whereas a principal component is a latent variable within a formative model. Formally, items are defined as linear combinations of factors (plus error) within reflective models, while principal components are defined as linear combinations of items in formative models. The difference is that factors explain the between-subjects variation on items, whereas the between-subjects variation on items describes the variation on principal components.

of variables to a small number of principal components (i.e., latent variables) that can represent *most* of the variance in a data set. For instance, PCA can be used to determine the first x components that describe, say, 85% of the variance in the data. In this respect, PCA can be used to simplify the complexity of a data set and identify the most important components that can describe the variance. The socioeconomic status mentioned above is an example of such components.

Assume a data set with i variables (i.e., i items). This set can be represented using i-dimensions. For instance, the score of a participant on all items can be represented by a point in a i-dimensional space. In this set, some of the variables will be correlated. PCA can be used to reduce these i dimensions to $c \leq i$ dimensions, describing the variance in the data set. In other words, PCA reduces the i variables to (a usually much smaller number of) c components, which contain the most important information and can be used to simplify the description of the data set.

Principal components are defined as linear combinations of the observed variables. As such, components are effects of the observed variables. They possess two important properties. First, principal components are *orthogonal* (cf. Jolliffe 2002), meaning that they can be represented by perpendicular vectors. Mathematically speaking, one consequence of this property is that principal components are uncorrelated. Hence, PCA reduces the i variables to c independent components that can describe statistically the behavior of the observed variables. Second, principal components are *ordered*. This order is relative to the components' eigenvalues. Knowing precisely what an eigenvalue is not necessary to understand this order. Roughly, an eigenvalue represents the proportion of the variance described by the component (cf. Tabachnick & Fidell 2013). Each component describes part of the variance of a data set and, when taken altogether, principal components describe all the variance (the sum of the eigenvalues of the components equals the number of variables). An eigenvalue will be large insofar as it accounts for more variance in the data set (see also Huck 2012). A component that has an eigenvalue of 1 describes the same proportion of variance as would a variable. Consequently, a component that has an eigenvalue greater than 1 describes more variance than would a variable and, similarly, it describes less if it has an eigenvalue less than 1.

Although there are situations where one can find nonlinear relationships in the data (thus, where standard (linear) PCA does not work), it remains that there are available alternative techniques that can be used instead (e.g., nonlinear PCA, see Kramer 1991).

In the case of PCA, an important point that should be kept in mind is that, as a descriptive procedure, it accommodates the data and provides a unique solution. Given that principal components are defined as linear combinations of observed variables, PCA provides a formative model, where the latent variables are effects of the items.

3.4.2   Exploratory Factor Analysis

If researchers aim to *explain* the variance in the items (rather than provide an empirical summary of the data), then factor analysis should be used. The latent variables provided by a factor analytic model, known as factors, are interpreted as latent constructs. Given that latent constructs are taken as explanations of human and social phenomena, it follows that their formal representation should not be considered as idiosyncratic characteristics of samples. The aim is not only to explain the variance in the data set, but is also to explain the variance in the population. Exploratory factor analysis (EFA) is a tool of inferential statistics that can reach that goal. It goes beyond the data at hand and tries to explain why there is variance in the sample on the grounds of a model that is formulated with respect to the population.

During scale development, EFA is performed on data acquired via measured items (e.g., by a Likert-type scale). These measured items, however, are not likely to be error free. Indeed, it is likely that there will be noise in the data set. Statistics are used in human and social science research precisely to account for uncertainty and error (cf. Suppes 2007). Accordingly, EFA includes an error term for each variable, accounting for variance that might not be explained by the latent variables (factors) (cf. Borgatta & Stull 1986; Jolliffe & Morgan 1992; Finch & West 1997; Park, Dailey, & Lemus 2002; Abdi & Williams 2010; Tabachnick & Fidell 2013; Johnson 2016).

Although it is often said that the inclusion of the error term is the main distinction between EFA and PCA (cf. Borgatta & Stull 1986; Park et al. 2002; Henson & Roberts 2006), another important difference concerns the model provided by the analysis. While PCA models the latent variables (principal components) as linear combinations of the observed variables, EFA rather provides a reflective measurement model, where the observed variables are modeled as linear combinations of latent variables (factors) as well as error terms (cf. Jolliffe & Morgan 1992). Hence, in the measurement model provided by an EFA, the latent variables are taken as causal explanations of the (between-subjects) variance on the items.

EFA is a statistical procedure that can be summarised in two steps. The first step is factor extraction. There are various ways to carry out this process (see Tabachnick & Fidell 2013, section 13.5.1), each having its advantages and its inconveniences. The main difference between factor extraction techniques regards how they estimate the error term. A well-known and widely used extraction technique is *maximum likelihood factor extraction*, which is available in the usual statistical packages such as SPSS (i.e., the statistical package for social sciences). One benefit of this method is that it provides goodness-of-fit criteria and, further, it can be used in confirmatory factor analysis.

The second step of an EFA is rotation. It is applied after extraction. There are various ways to accomplish this (cf. Field 2009; Tabachnick & Fidell 2013).[2] We

---

[2]Formally, a rotation is accomplished by multiplying the matrix of factor loadings by an orthogonal or an oblique matrix. This amounts to a rotation of the axes of the f-dimensional space. Orthogonal

mentioned earlier that the score of a participant on all items can be represented by a point in a i-dimensional space, where the i-dimensions are the initial items (observed variables). EFA enables the representation of the *items* as points in a f-dimensional space, where the f dimensions (axes) are the factors (latent variables). The aim of rotation is to achieve a simple structure (cf. Thurstone 1947, 1954). This facilitates the interpretation of the factors by amplifying high loadings and reducing low ones (cf. Tabachnick & Fidell 2013). Roughly, a model is qualified as a simple structure when a variable loads only on one factor, each factor is determined by a specific subset of variables with high loadings, and the number of factors is as low as possible. Put differently, a simple structure is characterised by well-defined factors and a low complexity. Rotation to a simple structure makes the loadings tend to either 0 or their maximum value, which clearly shows which variables are important to which factor(s) (see also Jolliffe 2002).

3.4.3 Confirmatory Factor Analysis

Confirmatory factor analysis (CFA) is part of a broader framework known as structural equation modeling (cf. Schreiber, Nora, Stage, Barlow, & King 2006; Byrne 2012; Ullman 2013). It is a mixture of factor analysis and multiple regression analysis. While EFA accommodates the data under specific constraints (e.g., the number of factors to extract, the extraction technique, the rotation method, etc.), CFA allows models to be tested (see also Hurley et al. 1997). An important aspect of CFA and, more generally, of structural equation modeling, is that it allows a complete and simultaneous examination of all postulated relationships between the variables. By comparison to EFA, which can be performed without presupposition regarding the factorial structure that will result from the analysis, CFA specifies beforehand the relationships between the variables (latent or not) and then determines whether the model specified fits the data. CFA models are composed of two parts: Measurement models consider the relationships between the latent constructs and their empirical consequences (the items), whereas structural models posit relationships between these latent constructs (which are interpreted as latent variables).

Formally, CFA uses the model specified prior to the analysis to estimate a population covariation matrix.[3] This estimated covariation matrix is used to predict the variance in the data set (cf. Brown 2015) and is compared to the actual covariation matrix of the data using various goodness-of-fit criteria (cf. Browne & Cudeck 1992; Hu & Bentler 1998; Kline 2005; Bentler 2007; Byrne 2012; Ullman 2013). While the fit indexes allow judgement about whether or not a model

---

rotation implies that the axes will remain perpendicular, while an oblique rotation allows the axes to be non-perpendicular. Oblique rotation allows for correlations among factors.

[3] The factorial structure provided by an EFA is represented by a covariation matrix.

appropriately fits the data, chi-square difference tests are used to evaluate models and determine whether a gain in complexity is accompanied by a satisfactory gain in goodness-of-fit. Put differently, it is used to avoid overfitting and determine whether the gain in goodness-of-fit is really worth the more complex model.

3.5 Model Selection

3.5.1 Factor Retention

EFA is an accommodative technique that, given specific constraints, produces a unique solution. This method can be applied when the researcher does not have any preconceived idea regarding the number of factors that should be used to model the data (cf. Finch & West 1997; Huck 2012; Tabachnick & Fidell 2013). In this context, however, there is an issue of model selection: Researchers need to determine how many factors should be retained. There are a number of available criteria that can be used to accomplished this, including the Kaiser-Guttman rule and the scree test (cf. Velicer & Jackson 1990a; Finch & West 1997).

The Kaiser-Guttman rule specifies that factors with an eigenvalue greater than one should be retained. Although this rule is widely used (for instance, it is the default setting in SPSS), it is the least accurate of all factor selection criteria (cf. Velicer & Jackson 1990b). The scree test consists in looking at the graph of the eigenvalues in function of the number of factors in order to find a point at which the eigenvalues stabilise. As with the Kaiser-Guttman rule, however, there are problems associated with the scree test (e.g., graphs may be ambiguous; there can be more than one point followed by a stabilisation), which is considered as a subjective and arbitrary criterion for model selection.

Fortunately, however, there are other criteria that can be used for model selection with EFA. Parallel analysis, for instance, consists in simulating a normal distribution in order to determine the cut-off point at which a factor is statistically significant (cf. O'Connor 2000). It was initially developed for PCA by Horn (1965) but it has then been adapted for EFA. Horn's idea was to randomly generate data sets, extract components, note their eigenvalue and then do the average of these eigenvalues for each component (cf. Tabachnick & Fidell 2013). If the eigenvalue of the ith component for the actual data is greater than the average of the ith components randomly generated, then it should be retained. Horn's idea has been modified to fit the requirements of inferential statistics and, incidentally, has been adapted for EFA. Basically, the idea is still to use randomly generated data sets, but instead of comparing the eigenvalue e of the ith factor in the actual data with the average of the ith factor in the randomly generated data, one determines a level of statistical significance (e.g., $p < 0.05$) and then determines the eigenvalue e' over which e would be unlikely if the ith factor came from a population of randomly generated factors. The factors will only be retained when they are statistically significant, that is, when $e' \leq e$, which would be unlikely if the factors came from a randomly generated data set (i.e., which would be unlikely under the null hypothesis).

Furthermore, when factors are extracted using maximum likelihood extraction, there are goodness-of-fit criteria that can be used for model selection. Some of these criteria are relevant when we consider the curve fitting problem, which amounts to the usual incompatibility of two criteria generally used to evaluate models: Simplicity and goodness-of-fit (cf. Forster & Sober 1994). Simple explanations are preferable to complex ones. However, more complex models tend to have a better fit to the data. That being said, too complex models tend to overfit the data (i.e., they fit to the noise in the data set). This is undesirable given that models that overfit the data, although they have a good fit, are not predictively accurate (cf. Hitchcock & Sober 2004). Hence the curve fitting problem: During model selection, one needs to balance simplicity and goodness-of-fit. The Aikaike Information Criterion (AIC, Akaike 1987) can be used to accomplish this. AIC is computed by $(-2)max\,log\,likelihood + 2k$, where k is the number of parameters (i.e., the number of factors). AIC can be used to balance simplicity and goodness-of-fit and help determine whether it is worth selecting a more complex model (cf. Forster 2002; Preacher, Zhang, Kim, & Mels 2013).

3.5.2 Combining Fit Indexes

A sensitive issue that is not always taken into account by researchers is that combination of different fit indexes may result in an augmentation of Type I or Type II error (cf. Hu & Bentler 1999). A Type I error consists in rejecting the null hypothesis when it should be kept. In the context of model selection, it amounts to considering a model as an adequate explanation of the phenomenon under study although it is not. In contrast, a Type II error happens when one keeps the null hypothesis when it should be rejected. From the perspective of model selection, this means to reject a model as an adequate explanation of the phenomenon, although it is.

3.5.3 Methodological Guidelines

The role factor analysis should play during the scale development process is not as well understood as it should be (cf. Hurley et al. 1997). Looking at the literature in human and social science research, there are many dissimilar guidelines suggested for the scale development process. To some extent, there is a consensus on the role EFA can and should play during the scale development process: It is used to find an appropriate factorial structure. While researchers start with a large pool of items, it is used iteratively as a procedure to eliminate the items that are not good indicators of the latent constructs (cf. Mulaik 1991). Disagreement happens when one considers *how* to perform that role.

Some authors recommend use of EFA on the entire data set (e.g., Costello & Osborne 2005). Others suggest performing an internal cross-validation and randomly dividing the data set in two parts. On these grounds, researchers can either use EFA iteratively on the first part of the data set and then test the factorial structure using CFA on the second part (e.g., Comrey 1988; Hinkin 1998; Fabrigar, Wegener, MacCallum, & Strahan 1999), or they can use EFA iteratively on the first part of the data set but try to replicate the model using EFA on the second part (e.g. Thompson 1994, 2004).

The sensitive issue underlying these recommendations is about model selection. Depending on the criteria that are used, one strategy can be preferable to another. For example, if one uses a criterion that balances simplicity and goodness-of-fit to select the model (e.g., AIC), then one might argue that EFA should be used on the entire data set (e.g., Hitchcock & Sober 2004) given that accommodation should be accomplished on the grounds of all the available evidence (cf. Carnap 1947). Similarly, if one rather tries to maximise goodness-of-fit, then one might argue that an internal cross-validation should be performed using CFA on the second part of the data set, seeing that it would help determine whether the model is predictively accurate, and this can be used to safeguard against overfitting (cf. Hitchcock & Sober 2004). Finally, one could also argue that EFA should be performed on the second part of the data set during the cross-validation (e.g., Francis 2012; Asendorpf et al. 2013) insofar as a successful replication of the factorial structure would be a good indicator of its empirical adequacy (see also Norton 2015).

3.6 Default Parameters

The aforementioned considerations bring to light an important issue regarding EFA: One must be aware of the default settings in the computer programs meant to perform factor analysis. For instance, a researcher who would use SPSS with its default settings during scale development would use PCA as a factor extraction technique and would use the Kaiser-Guttman rule as a criterion for model selection. However, PCA is not a method that can (or should) be used to extract factors (recall that it provides a formative measurement model), and the Kaiser-Guttman rule is one of the worst criteria for model selection. Accordingly, one must be careful when performing an EFA.

Although it seems to be presented as such within classrooms, EFA is not something that can be performed without a thorough understanding of the steps that are required and, more importantly, of the rationale behind them. Flags were raised within the literature to warn researchers about this issue (cf. Ford, MacCallum, & Tait 1986; Fabrigar et al. 1999; Park et al. 2002; Russell 2002; Conway & Huffcutt 2003; Henson & Roberts 2006; Wetzel 2012). One important problem that was identified regarding the use of EFA during scale development was that PCA was often used as a factor extraction technique (see Sect. 3.7 below). However, another important problem thwarting the epistemic value of EFA is that researchers tend to not specify which settings are used during the analysis, including how the factors were extracted, how they were rotated, and which criteria for model selection were used. Consequently, it is often difficult to judge the overall quality of scales in human and social science research given the lack of information regarding how they actually were developed.

3.7 Using Principal Component Analysis

PCA does have a place in human and social science research (cf. ten Berge et al. 1992; Kiers & ten Berge 1994; ten Berge & Kiers 1997; Kiers & Mechelen 2001). This place, however, should not be misunderstood. In the human and social science literature, it has been reported that PCA is often confused with EFA and is used as a factor analytic technique (cf. Ford et al. 1986; Fabrigar et al. 1999; Jolliffe 2002; Park et al. 2002; Russell 2002; Conway & Huffcutt 2003; Henson & Roberts 2006; Wetzel 2012).

The problem amounts to the fact that *principal component* is used as a factor extraction technique during an EFA. Jolliffe (1995, 2002) pointed out that this confusion between PCA and EFA comes from the fact that PCA is usually presented as a part of an EFA in textbooks (cf. Huck 2012; Tabachnick & Fidell 2013), but also in computer programs. To emphasise this point, PCA is the default option for extracting factors in SPSS (cf. Field 2009). Although it is explicit in the literature that PCA should not be used as a substitute for EFA (see also Borgatta & Stull 1986; Hubbard & Allen 1987; Bandalos & Boehm-Kaufman 2009), some authors that are aware of this problem but still continue to use PCA as a factor extraction technique do so because it often leads to similar (comparable) results (cf. Velicer & Jackson 1990a,b; Jung & Lee 2011).

Besides technical problems related to using PCA as a factor extraction technique[4] there is a significant epistemic issue regarding the interpretation of the procedure. Borsboom (2006) provided a clear explanation of the reason why PCA should not be used during the development of scales meant to identify latent constructs: PCA, as a tool of descriptive statistics, provides a formative measurement model, where the components are effects (defined as linear combinations of) the items. Components do not explain the variation on the items. As such, they cannot (thus, should not) be used to provide a formal representation of latent constructs. If the aim of the research team is to identify latent constructs that can explain the

---

[4]For instance, the choice of the number of factors to extract changes the factorial structure in an EFA (i.e., it has an impact on the definition of the factors), whereas the choice of the number of components to retain does not have an impact on their definition. There are also issues regarding rotation of principal components (see Jolliffe & Morgan 1992; Jolliffe 1989, 2002).

between-subjects variation on the items, then PCA should not be used because it simply cannot reach that goal.

In addition to the fact that PCA models are not reflective, there is another reason why it would be inappropriate to use this procedure during the scale development process. Indeed, the factorial structure, which is statistically inferred from the sample, is meant to represent the factorial structure of the population. This sample, however, is not error-free. The between-subjects variation on the items is likely to be caused by other factors, not considered by the model. As such, researchers need to include error terms in their models, accounting for potential error in measurement. That is, researchers need to consider error factors that can account for the variance due to other aspects not considered during the statistical analysis. PCA should not be used during scale development insofar as it does not take error into consideration when describing the variance on the items.

3.8 Causal Explanation and Measurement

Two important assumptions underlying extraction techniques such as maximum likelihood extraction are that variables are continuous and normally distributed (cf. Byrne 2012). These assumptions can be criticised either from a technical or a foundational standpoint.

3.8.1 Continuity and Normality

From a technical standpoint, the data acquired in human and social sciences is often obtained on the grounds of nominal or ordinal scales. Likert-type scales, which produce ordinal data, are a good example of this phenomenon. These types of scale yield discrete data and, accordingly, they violate the assumption that variables are continuous. Hence, one might object to the use of categorical data in factor analysis. That being said, different estimators have been developed to deal with categorical data. In addition, when the data approximates a normal distribution, not addressing the fact that the data is categorical is likely negligible (see Byrne 2012, and the references therein).

Besides violation of the assumption of continuity, it might happen that the data acquired is not normally distributed. This poses a problem for maximum likelihood extraction and other techniques that rely on this assumption. Nonetheless, it remains that other extraction techniques can be used to address the violation of the assumption of normality (see Flora, LaBrish, & Chalmers 2012, and the references therein). Consequently, although these are technical points that need to be addressed, they should not be seen as arguments against the use of factor analysis during the scale development process.

3.8.2 *Continuous Attributes*

From a foundational standpoint, there are issues with the conception of latent constructs as continuous attributes. These issues appear when we consider how researchers try to capture these latent constructs: Researchers in human and social sciences often use Likert-type scales. This can be viewed as problematic for two reasons.

First, the measurement obtained through a Likert-type scale has a discrete structure (the value attributed is an integer). However, one might expect the structure of the measurement to be isomorphic to the structure of the attribute (e.g., Michell 1997). As such, it might be argued that a Likert-type scale, which provides a discrete measurement, is not adequate to measure a continuous attribute: Assuming that an adequate measurement should have a structure isomorphic to the structure of the attribute, and given that latent constructs are understood as continuous attributes, it follows that measurement should have a structure isomorphic to the real numbers.

This, however, is only an apparent issue. Indeed, any measurement is a discrete approximation, though this approximation can be (and usually is) interpreted as a real number.[5] For example, consider the case of a continuous quantity such as *length*. Any actual measurement of an object's length is discrete and is interpreted as the approximation of a real number. Even though an attribute is considered continuous, it is not a problem to provide a discrete measurement (e.g., in the rational numbers) that approximates its value in the real numbers. This is what is accomplished in exact sciences such as chemistry or physics. If it is not a problem for these disciplines, then it should certainly not be one for human and social science research. One can legitimately use a discrete quantity, such as one provided by a Likert-type scale, to approximate a continuous attribute. Besides, despite the assumption of continuity underlying factor extraction techniques such as maximum likelihood extraction, and given the internal structure of our computers, it remains that calculations are actually performed in the rational numbers, and rational numbers have a discrete structure.

Second, given that factor analytic techniques often rely on the assumption that data are continuous, Likert-type scales (providing discrete data) are often interpreted as approximations of interval scales (providing continuous data). It is unclear, however, whether one is justified to interpret a Likert-type scale as an approximation of an interval scale. An interval scale is characterised by equal intervals. In this respect, the difference between an interval and its predecessor is equal to the difference between another interval and its predecessor. This poses problems with a Likert-type scale. For example, consider a scale ranging from 1 to 5, where 5 = always, 4 = often, 3 = sometimes, 2 = rarely and 1 = never. Even though the difference between 5 and 4 equals the difference between 3 and 2, it is unclear whether or not the difference between 'always' and 'often' equals the difference

---

[5]There is also complex measurement, interpreted in the complex numbers.

between 'sometimes' and 'rarely'. Similarly, it is unclear whether the difference between 'always' and 'sometimes' (5 and 3) equals the difference between 'often' and 'rarely' (4 and 2). Hence, interpreting a Likert-type scale as an approximation of an interval scale is arguable.

3.8.3 Measurement

Some authors argue that *measurement* is simply not possible in human and social sciences. Such a position has been defended by Michell (1997, 2000, 2001, 2003) and can be summarised as follows: (i) the structure of an attribute can only be determined empirically, (ii) continuous quantity is an inherent property of reality and (iii) attributes can be measured if and only if they are quantitative. As a consequence, the only way to determine whether an attribute can be measured is by empirical verification.

Michell's point is that when one realises an **EFA**, one puts the cart before the horse: Researchers postulate that there are latent constructs that are measurable (hence quantitative) and these constructs are measured indirectly via items through factor analytic techniques. However, to legitimately apply factor analytic techniques, which assume continuity, Michell argues that researchers should first determine empirically that latent constructs have indeed the proper quantitative structure, otherwise the notion of *measurement* of attributes is unjustified. That is, before *measuring* an attribute, one must insure that the attribute is indeed measurable (i.e., that the attribute is quantitative; see also Hood 2008).

Michell's position relies on heavy realist assumptions that will be discussed below (see Sect. 3.9). Notwithstanding these assumptions, Michell's criticism is not as damaging as it may seem. First, researchers do test their factor models empirically. As Borsboom and Mellenbergh (2004) argued, even though the hypothesis that psychological attributes are quantitative is not tested in isolation, it remains that it is tested together with further hypotheses using factor analytic techniques. In this respect, Michell's objection against measurement in human and social sciences amounts to a failure to recognise the scope of the Duhem-Quine problem: Hypotheses cannot be tested in isolation.

But more importantly, Michell's criticism misses its target given that factor analytic techniques are not used during scale development to *measure* latent constructs. It might make sense to interpret the score of participant on the items as the position on a latent variable in a formative model, where the items are *not* interpreted as plausible empirical consequences of the latent variables but are rather used to define the components (which are understood as effects upon the items), but not in a reflective way. Although researchers speak of *measurement* models, this expression is a misnomer in the context of factor analysis. The measurement model provided by an **EFA** (or the one tested through **CFA**) is reflective. The latent variables, representing the latent constructs, are taken as causal explanations of the *between-subjects* variation on the items. This is important insofar as they are not meant to determine where one stands on a latent variable (cf. Borsboom 2008). That is, they are not meant to examine the *intra-subject* variation on a latent construct.[6]

For example, the aforementioned depression scale (cf. Zung 1965) does not *measure* to what extent one is depressed (or not). The interpretation of the measurement model provided by this scale regards the explanation of the between-subjects variation on the items: Some score high on items while others score low, and this can be explained using a latent construct known (conceptualised) as *depression*, which influences the between-subjects variation on the items. Though researchers infer that some are depressed while others are not, they do not infer to which extent they are. As such, reflective measurement models can *capture* or *identify* latent variables rather than *measure* them per se. They are used to explain the between-subjects variation on the items using latent variables as well as error, not to *measure* the latent variables.

3.9 Are Latent Constructs Real?

3.9.1 The Self-Evidence of Realism

Some researchers in human and social sciences tend to assume realism as a default and self-evident position. After all, they are studying human and social phenomena, so assuming that they do not have epistemic access to reality or that they cannot assert true statements with regard to said reality might appear counterproductive, and perhaps even inconsistent with what they are doing. Hence, realism is often seen as a self-understanding position that do not require further justifications (e.g., Michell 2004, 2005).

Nonetheless, arguments are sometimes put forward in favour of the self-evidence of realism in the context of human and social science research. Realism, understood as a necessary but self-evident epistemic standpoint, has been defended with respect to scale development and reflective models by Borsboom et al. (2003) and Borsboom (2005). Their argument in favour of a realist understanding of factorial structures and measurement models is threefold.

First, they appeal to the self-evidence of realism by considering the notion of *measurement*. If researchers are measuring latent constructs, then latent constructs must exist given that it would be impossible to measure something that does not exist. Taking error into consideration in factor analysis reinforces this idea. If researchers consider possible error in measurement, then they must assume that there is a 'truth' with respect to which this error is evaluated. Accordingly, reality must be accessible to researchers, and knowing it must be in their grasp.

---

[6]This would require a longitudinal research design, whereas EFA is performed in the context of a cross-sectional study.

The second argument runs along the same lines. In factor analysis, some parameters are estimated (e.g., error). When estimating values of parameters in a measurement model, one estimates the real (true) value of that parameter. Hence, in addition to the assumption that there are real parameters to be estimated, researchers also assume that it is possible to assert true or false statements with regard to these real parameters.[7] Further, researchers assume that it is possible to know whether one is right or wrong when asserting such statements, and this can be accomplished using factor analytic techniques.

The third argument appeals to the rationale behind hypothesis testing. When testing a measurement model through CFA, researchers need to assume that this measurement model is an adequate factorial structure explaining the between-subjects variation on the items. That is, researchers need to assume that the factorial structure corresponds to an actual state of affairs.[8] As such, researchers assume that (i) there are latent constructs explaining the between-subjects variation on the items, (ii) that the model that is tested corresponds to this reality and (iii) that it is possible to know, via statistical analyses, whether this statement is true or false.

3.9.2   Not Self-Evidence of Realism

Hood (2013) argued that Boorsboom's et al. position lacks nuances. In his view, researchers should distinguish between their semantic, epistemic and ontological realist commitments. Researchers that see realism as self-evident tend to treat realism as a unique and unambiguous position, and this is misleading. There are various formulations of realism (cf. Chakravartty 2007, 2015), and many ways to combine epistemic, semantic and ontological realism, notwithstanding that these aspects of realism are, to some extent (and arguably), independent from one another (cf. Shalkowski 1995; Horwich 1996).

Semantic realism, as endorsed by Borsboom et al., is a combination of the assumptions that scientific statements are declarative (i.e., capable of being true or false), and that their truth-conditions depend on the (objective) structure of reality (cf. Shalkowski 1995; Psillos 2009). Ontological realism postulates the existence of an objective and independent reality, which amounts to the belief that latent constructs exists. Whether these constructs are knowable, however, is an independent matter. Epistemic realism states that knowledge postulates this reality, which is epistemically accessible.

In the context of scale development, researchers that see realism as self-evident see the combination of semantic, ontological and epistemic realism as necessarily implying that latent constructs are real (i.e., they are part of an objective and independent reality), that we can study them using factor analysis (i.e., we have

---

[7]This amounts to understand truth as correspondence.

[8]This reasoning is incorrect if we consider that some researchers might rather try to refute models.

epistemic access), and that we can know whether the factorial structures are true or false using said techniques.

Against the self-evidence of realism, Hood (2013) objected that the semantic thesis does not necessarily implies ontological commitments. That is, one can postulate a hypothesis regarding the existence of latent constructs without being committed to the belief that these constructs are actually real entities. Rather, Hood argued that researchers need to assume that such claims regarding the existence of latent constructs can be justified and, further, that certain methodological choices require endorsement of this assumption.

Hood's position extends Leplin's (1986, 1997), who argued that some methodological choices in science require *minimal epistemic realism*, that is, they require that researchers be committed to the idea that their hypotheses regarding the existence of unobservable entities (here, latent constructs) can, in principle, be justified. Hood's and Leplin's position is named *methodological realism*, which amounts to the endorsement of the following thesis: Without an appeal to minimal epistemic realism, some methodological decisions appear to be arbitrary. In Hood's case, one argument regards the choice of the measurement model. In his view, choosing to model reflectively requires that researchers are committed to the idea that it is possible to justify the hypothesised factorial structure. Such a position is put forward against antirealist and empiricist positions, although it aims especially at a version of instrumentalism typically endorsed by researchers in human and social sciences, advocating that methodological choices can be explained using the pragmatic qualities of the instruments (e.g., predictive success; cf. Baird 1987; Sober 2002).

3.10 Theory-Ladenness

Another sensitive issue to consider during scale development is the extent of EFA's theory-ladenness (see Peterson 2016). Depending on the textbook one is using, different characteristics can be attributed to EFA. In the community, EFA is generally understood as a procedure that can generate theories and hypotheses (cf. Huck 2012; Tabachnick & Fidell 2013). The rationale behind that conception is that EFA accommodates the data. In comparison to CFA, EFA does not require the specification of a hypothesis prior to the analysis (cf. Hurley et al. 1997). As such, it can be performed without prior hypotheses regarding the factorial structure that will result from the analysis. EFA is therefore sometimes seen as a method that can uncover the factorial structure of human and social phenomena (cf. Haig 2005).

There are limits, however, to the extent to which EFA can be seen as a discovery tool allowing hypotheses and theories to be generated. When researchers say that EFA can be performed without prior hypotheses regarding the factorial structure that will obtain, they are considering EFA as an iterative procedure rather than a onetime analysis (cf. Mulaik 1991). Otherwise, researchers need to specify the number of factors to be retained to model the data.

Furthermore, to assert that EFA can be used to discover the factorial structure of human and social phenomena would be a bit hasty. Indeed, assuming that latent constructs can be used to explain human and social phenomena, this explanation will need to consider the relationships between said constructs. That is, it does not suffice to consider how the between-subjects variance on specific items can be explained using latent variables: One also needs to study how the latent constructs that are identified relate to each other. This can be accomplished through CFA.

3.11 Closing Remarks

All in all, the statistical tools that are used during scale development and further research in human and social sciences are worth philosophical consideration. Although we only provided a general review of the issues that are related to the statistical techniques used during the scale development process, we hope to have provided the reader with enough material and insight to pursue the investigation.

The important thing to remember from this chapter is not that some statistical techniques are good while others are bad. Rather, each tool has its idiosyncratic characteristics, and it can be used to reach precise predetermined goals. Researchers need to be aware of how the techniques work, how they should be used, what they can accomplish, and what their limits are. Otherwise, this will reduce the epistemic quality and the epistemic value of their research.

Acknowledgements I would like to thank Stephan Hartmann, Gregory Gandenberger, as well as Peter Sozou for valuable comments and suggestions. This research was financially supported by the Social Sciences and Humanities Research Council of Canada.

References

Abdi, H., & Williams, L. J. (2010). Principal component analysis. *Wiley Interdisciplinary Reviews: Computational Statistics, 2*(4), 433–459.

Akaike, H. (1987). Factor analysis and AIC. *Psychometrika, 52*(3), 317–332.

Aron, A., Coups, E. J., & Aron, E. N. (2013). *Statistics for psychology* (6th ed.). Upper Saddle River, NJ: Pearson.

Asendorpf, J. B., Conner, M., De Fruyt, F., De Houwer, J., Denissen, J. J. A., Fiedler, K., ... Wicherts, J. M. (2013). Recommendations for increasing replicability in psychology. *European Journal of Personality, 27*(2), 108–119.

Baird, D. (1987). Exploratory factor analysis, instruments and the logic of discovery. *The British Journal for the Philosophy of Science, 38*(3), 319–337.

Bandalos, D. L., & Boehm-Kaufman, M. R. (2009). Four common misconceptions in exploratory factor analysis. In C. E. Lance & R. J. Vandenberg (Eds.), *Statistical and methodological myths and urban legends: Doctrine, verity and fable in the organizational and social sciences* (pp. 61–87). New York: Routledge.

Bentler, P. M. (2007). On tests and indices for evaluating structural models. *Personality and Individual Differences, 42*(5), 825–829.

Borgatta, E. F., & Stull, D. E. (1986). A cautionary note on the use of principal component analysis. *Sociological Methods & Research, 15*(1–2), 160–168.

Borsboom, D. (2005). *Measuring the mind: Conceptual issues in contemporary psychometrics.* Cambridge, UK: Cambridge University Press.

Borsboom, D. (2006). The attack of the psychometricians. *Psychometrika, 71*(3), 425–440.

Borsboom, D. (2008). Latent variable theory. *Measurement, 6*(1–2), 25–53.

Borsboom, D., & Mellenbergh, G. J. (2004). Why psychometrics is not pathological: A comment on Michell. *Theory & Psychology, 14*(1), 105–120.

Borsboom, D., Mellenbergh, G. J., & van Heerden, J. (2003). The theoretical status of latent variables. *Psychological Review, 110*(2), 203–219.

Brown, T. A. (2015). *Confirmatory factor analysis for applied research* (2nd ed.). New York: Guilford Publications.

Browne, M. W., & Cudeck, R. (1992). Alternative ways of assessing model fit. *Sociological Methods & Research, 21*(2), 230–258.

Byrne, B. M. (2012). *Structural equation modeling with mplus.* New York: Routledge.

Carnap, R. (1947). On the application of inductive logic. *Philosophy and Phenomenological Research, 8*(1), 133–148.

Chakravartty, A. (2007). *A metaphysics for scientific realism: Knowing the unobservable.* Cambridge, UK: Cambridge University Press.

Chakravartty, A. (2015). Scientific realism. In E. N. Zalta (Ed.), *The Stanford encyclopedia of philosophy* (Fall 2015 ed.). http://plato.stanford.edu/archives/fall2015/entries/scientific-realism/.

Comrey, A. L. (1988). Factor-analytic methods of scale development in personality and clinical psychology. *Journal of Consulting and Clinical Psychology, 56*(5), 754–761.

Conway, J. M., & Huffcutt, A. I. (2003). A review and evaluation of exploratory factor analysis practices in organizational research. *Organizational Research Methods, 6*(2), 147–168.

Costello, A. B., & Osborne, J. W. (2005). Best practices in exploratory factor analysis: Four recommendations for getting the most from your analysis. *Practical Assessment, Research & Evaluation, 10*(7), 1–9.

Edwards, J. R., & Bagozzi, R. P. (2000). On the nature and direction of relationships between constructs and measures. *Psychological Methods, 5*(2), 155–174.

Fabrigar, L. R., Wegener, D. T., MacCallum, R. C., & Strahan, E. J. (1999). Evaluating the use of exploratory factor analysis in psychological research. *Psychological Methods, 4*(3), 272–299.

Field, A. (2009). *Discovering statistics using SPSS* (3rd ed.). London: Sage.

Finch, J. F., & West, S. G. (1997). The investigation of personality structure: Statistical models. *Journal of Research in Personality, 31*(4), 439–485.

Flora, D. B., LaBrish, C., & Chalmers, R. P. (2012). Old and new ideas for data screening and assumption testing for exploratory and confirmatory factor analysis. *Frontiers in Psychology, 3*(55), 1–21.

Ford, J. K., MacCallum, R. C., & Tait, M. (1986). The application of exploratory factor analysis in applied psychology: A critical review and analysis. *Personnel Psychology, 39*(2), 291–314.

Forster, M. R., & Sober, E. (1994). How to tell when simpler, more unified, or less ad hoc theories will provide more accurate predictions. *British Journal for the Philosophy of Science, 45*(1), 1–35.

Forster, M. R. (2002). Predictive accuracy as an achievable goal of science. *Philosophy of Science, 69*(3), S124–S134.

Francis, G. (2012). Publication bias and the failure of replication in experimental psychology. *Psychonomic Bulletin & Review, 19*(6), 975–991.

Glymour, C. (2001). *The mind's arrows: Bayes nets and graphical causal models in psychology.* Cambridge, MA: MIT.

Haig, B. D. (2005). Exploratory factor analysis, theory generation, and scientific method. *Multivariate Behavioral Research, 40*(3), 303–329.

Henson, R. K., & Roberts, J. K. (2006). Use of exploratory factor analysis in published research. *Educational and Psychological Measurement, 66*(3), 393–416.

Hinkin, T. R. (1998). A brief tutorial on the development of measures for use in survey questionnaires. *Organizational Research Methods, 1*(1), 104–121.

Hitchcock, C., & Sober, E. (2004). Preduction versus accommodation and the risk of overfitting. *British Journal for the Philosophy of Science, 55*(1), 1–34.

Hood, S. B. (2008). Comments on Borsboom's typology of measurement theoretic variables and Michell's assessment of psychometrics as "pathological science". *Measurement, 6*(1–2), 93–97.

Hood, S. B. (2013). Psychological measurement and methodological realism. *Erkenntnis, 78*(4), 739–761.

Horn, J. L. (1965). A rationale and test for the number of factors in factor analysis. *Psychometrika, 30*(2), 179–185.

Horwich, P. (1996). Realism and truth. *Noûs, 30*(10), 187–197.

Hu, L.-t., & Bentler, P. M. (1998). Fit indices in covariance structure modeling: Sensitivity to underparameterized model misspecification. *Psychological Methods, 3*(4), 424–453.

Hu, L.-t., & Bentler, P. M. (1999). Cutoff criteria for fit indexes in covariance structure analysis: Conventional criteria versus new alternatives. *Structural Equation Modeling: A Multidisciplinary Journal, 6*(1), 1–55.

Hubbard, R., & Allen, S. J. (1987). A cautionary note on the use of principal component analysis: Supportive empirical evidence. *Sociological Methods & Research, 16*(2), 301–308.

Huck, S. W. (2012). *Reading statistics and research* (6th ed.). Boston: Pearson.

Hurley, A. E., Scandura, T. A., Schriesheim, C. A., Brannick, M. T., Seers, A., Vandenberg, R. J., et al. (1997). Exploratory and confirmatory factor analysis: Guidelines, issues, and alternatives. *Journal of Organizational Behavior, 18*(6), 667–683.

Johnson, K. (2016). Realism and uncertainty of unobservable common causes in factor analysis. *Noûs, 50*(2), 329–355.

Jolliffe, I. T. (1989). Rotation of ill-defined principal components. *Applied Statistics, 38*(1), 139–147.

Jolliffe, I. T. (1995). Rotation principal components: Choice of normalization constraints. *Journal of Applied Statistics, 22*(1), 29–35.

Jolliffe, I. T. (2002). *Principal component analysis* (2nd ed.). New York: Springer.

Jolliffe, I. T., & Morgan, B. J. T. (1992). Principal component analysis and exploratory factor analysis. *Statistical Methods in Medical Research, 1*(1), 69–95.

Jung, S., & Lee, S. (2011). Exploratory factor analysis for small samples. *Behavior Research Methods, 43*(3), 701–709.

Kiers, H. A., & Mechelen, I. V. (2001). Three-way component analysis: Principles and illustrative application. *Psychological Methods, 6*(1), 84–110.

Kiers, H. A., & ten Berge, J. M. F. (1994). Hierarchical relations between methods for simultaneous component analysis and a technique for rotation to a simple simultaneous structure. *British Journal of Mathematical and Statistical Psychology, 47*(1), 109–126.

Kline, R. B. (2005). *Structural equation modeling*. New York: The Guilford Press.

Kramer, M. A. (1991). Nonlinear principal component analysis using autoassociative neural networks. *AIChE Journal, 37* (2), 233–243.

Leplin, J. (1986). Methodological realism and scientific rationality. *Philosophy of Science, 53* (1), 31–51.

Leplin, J. (1997). *A novel defense of scientific realism*. New York: Oxford University Press.

Mellenbergh, G. J. (1994). Generalized linear item response theory. *Psychological Bulletin, 115*(2), 300–307.

Michell, J. (1997). Quantitative science and the definition of measurement in psychology. *British Journal of Psychology, 88*(3), 355–383.

Michell, J. (2000). Normal science, pathological science and psychometrics. *Theory & Psychology, 10*(5), 639–667.

Michell, J. (2001). Teaching and misteaching measurement in psychology. *Australian Psychologist, 36*(3), 211–217.

Michell, J. (2003). The quantitative imperative positivism, naive realism and the place of qualitative methods in psychology. *Theory & Psychology, 13*(1), 5–31.

Michell, J. (2004). The place of qualitative research in psychology. *Qualitative Research in Psychology, 1*(4), 307–319.

Michell, J. (2005). The logic of measurement: A realist overview. *Measurement, 38*(4), 285–294.

Mulaik, S. A. (1987). A brief history of the philosophical foundations of exploratory factor analysis. *Multivariate Behavioral Research, 22*(3), 267–305.

Mulaik, S. A. (1991). Factor analysis, information-transforming instruments, and objectivity: A reply and discussion. *The British Journal for the Philosophy of Science, 42*(1), 87–100.

Norton, J. D. (2015). Replicability of experiment. *Theoria, 30*(2), 229–248.

O'Connor, B. (2000). SPSS and SAS programs for determining the number of components using parallel analysis and Velicer's MAP test. *Behavioral Research Methods, Intruments and Computers, 32*(3), 396–402.

Park, H. S., Dailey, R., & Lemus, D. (2002). The use of exploratory factor analysis and principal component analysis in communication research. *Human Communication Research, 28*(4), 562–577.

Peterson, C. (2016). Exploratory factor analysis and theory generation in psychology. *Review of Philosophy and Psychology, 8*(3), 519–540.

Preacher, K. J., Zhang, G., Kim, C., & Mels, G. (2013). Choosing the optimal number of factors in exploratory factor analysis: A model selection perspective. *Multivariate Behavioral Research, 48*(1), 28–56.

Psillos, S. (2009). *Knowing the structure of nature: Essays on realism and explanation*. Houndmills: Palgrave Macmillan.

Russell, D. W. (2002). In search of underlying dimensions: The use (and abuse) of factor analysis in *Personality and Social Psychology Bulletin*. *Personality and Social Psychology Bulletin, 28*(12), 1629–1646.

Schreiber, J. B., Nora, A., Stage, F. K., Barlow, E. A., & King, J. (2006). Reporting structural equation modeling and confirmatory factor analysis results: A review. *The Journal of Educational Research, 99*(6), 323–338.

Shalkowski, S. A. (1995). Semantic realism. *The Review of Metaphysics, 48*(3), 511–538.

Sober, E. (2002). Instrumentalism, parsimony, and the Akaike framework. *Philosophy of Science, 69*(S3), S112–S123.

Spirtes, P., Glymour, C., & Scheines, R. (1991). From probability to causality. *Philosophical Studies, 64*(1), 1–36.

Spirtes, P., Glymour, C., & Scheines, R. (2000). *Causation, prediction, and search*. Cambridge, MA: MIT.

Stevens, S. S. (1946). On the theory of scales of measurement. *Science, 103*(2684), 677–680.

Suppes, P. (2007). Statistical concepts in philosophy of science. *Synthese, 154*(3), 485–496.

Tabachnick, B. G., & Fidell, L. S. (2013). *Using multivariate statistics* (6th ed.). Harlow: Pearson.

ten Berge, J. M. F., & Kiers, H. A. L. (1997). Are all varieties of PCA the same? A reply to Cadima & Jolliffe. *British Journal of Mathematical and Statistical Psychology, 50*(2), 367–368.

ten Berge, J. M. F., Kiers, H. A. L., & Van der Stel, V. (1992). Simultaneous components analysis. *Statistica Applicata, 4*(4), 277–392.

Thompson, B. (1994). The pivotal role of replication in psychological research: Empirically evaluating the replicability of sample results. *Journal of Personality, 62*(2), 157–176.

Thompson, B. (2004). *Exploratory and confirmatory factor analysis: Understanding concepts and applications*. Washington, DC: American Psychological Association.

Thurstone, L. L. (1947). *Multiple factor analysis*. Chicago: University of Chicago Press.

Thurstone, L. L. (1954). An analytical method for simple structure. *Psychometrika, 19*(3), 173–182.

Ullman, J. B. (2013). Structural equation modeling. In B. G. Tabachnick & L. S. Fidell (Eds.), *Using multivariate statistics* (6th ed.). Harlow: Pearson.

Velicer, W. F., & Jackson, D. N. (1990a). Component analysis versus common factor analysis: Some further observations. *Multivariate Behavioral Research, 25*(1), 97–114.

Velicer, W. F., & Jackson, D. N. (1990b). Component analysis versus common factor analysis: Some issues in selecting an appropriate procedure. *Multivariate Behavioral Research, 25*(1), 1–28.

Wetzel, A. P. (2012). Factor analysis methods and validity evidence: A review of instrument development across the medical education continuum. *Academic Medicine, 87*(8), 1060–1069.

White, K. R. (1982). The relation between socioeconomic status and academic achievement. *Psychological Bulletin, 91*(3), 461–481.

Zung, W. W. K. (1965). A self-rating depression scale. *Archives of General Psychiatry, 12*(1), 63–70.

Chapter 4
The Role of Imagination in Social Scientific Discovery: Why Machine Discoverers Will Need Imagination Algorithms

Michael T. Stuart

Abstract When philosophers discuss the possibility of machines making scientific discoveries, they typically focus on discoveries in physics, biology, chemistry and mathematics. Observing the rapid increase of computer use in science, however, it becomes natural to ask whether there are any scientific domains out of reach for machine discovery. For example, could machines also make discoveries in qualitative social science? Is there something about humans that makes us uniquely suited to studying humans? Is there something about machines that would bar them from such activity? A close look at the methodology of interpretive social science reveals several abilities necessary to make a social scientific discovery (such as cognitive empathy and the ability to assign meaning) and one capacity necessary to possess any of them is imagination. Novel and significant interpretations required by social scientific discovery require imagination. For machines to make discoveries in social science, therefore, they must possess imagination algorithms.

Keywords Discovery · Ethnographic interpretation · Ethnographic method · Ethnographic novelty · Ethnographic significance · Imagination algorithm · Interpretive science · Machine discovery · Machine interpretation · Philosophy of social science

The question of whether machines could discover arose early in the history of artificial intelligence.[1] Since then, machine learning algorithms have been developed,

---

[1]Especially in the work of Herbert Simon and his students. See e.g. Newell, Shaw, and Simon (1958), Simon (1977, 1979), Bradshaw, Langley, and Simon (1980), Bradshaw, Langley, and Simon (1983), Langley, Simon, Bradshaw, and Żytkow (1987), Langley and Jones (1988), Shrager

---

M. T. Stuart (✉)
Centre for Philosophy of Natural and Social Science, London School of Economics and Political Science, London, UK
e-mail: m.stuart@lse.ac.uk

© Springer Nature Switzerland AG 2019
M. Addis et al. (eds.), *Scientific Discovery in the Social Sciences*, Synthese Library 413, https://doi.org/10.1007/978-3-030-23769-1_4

and there are now many putative examples of machine discoveries, for example: the BACON program that discovered Kepler's third law, Coulomb's law and Ohm's law (Langley, 1981); the KnIT program discovering features of a molecule important for cancer-prevention (Spangler et al., 2014) and the Automated Mathematician discovering Goldbach's conjecture (Lenat, 1982) (see also e.g. Giza, 2002; Lane, Sozou, Addis, & Gobet, 2014).

A common way to frame the possibility of machine discovery has been functionalist: if a machine can carry out some crucial set of processes, such as generating hypotheses, performing experiments, writing papers that pass peer-review, etc., it can discover. The thought is that scientists make discoveries with certain methods, so if machines can use those same methods, they can discover. This might be an effective framing if we want to suggest that machines can make some discoveries as opposed to none at all, but it will not tell us much about the limits of machine discovery. By analogy, teaching a computer to buy a canvass, paint with certain brushstrokes and sell the painting to a gallery might justify the claim that machines can do some art, but this would not tell us what kinds of art machines are capable of making.

A different kind of approach (call it "transcendental") would seek a set of necessary conditions for scientific discovery instead of sufficient ones. This approach presupposes that we do discover, and asks what makes this achievement possible. Applied to the case of machine discovery, we ask what capacities machines must possess as agents in order to discover in science. This begins in a piecemeal way since the features necessary for discovery in one domain might not be necessary in another, but the full account should provide the (perhaps disjunctive) combined set of features necessary for discovery in all domains of science. Since I am interested here in the *limits* of machine discovery, I propose we look at the social sciences, where no documented cases of machine discovery yet exist.

I argue in Sect. 4.1 that we should characterise discovery as an action (part of a discovery event). In Sect. 4.2, I develop this characterisation of discovery. In Sect. 4.3, I extract what is necessary for agents to discover in social science by an analysis of social science textbooks and methodology papers. In Sect. 4.4, I show that the ability to imagine is necessary for social scientific discovery, and I conclude that machine discoverers must possess imagination algorithms if they are to discover in the full sense of scientific discovery (which must include social science).

---

and Langley (1990), Langley, Shrager, and Saito (2002), Langley (2000), Dzeroski, Langley, and Todorovski (2007).

4.1 Reasons to Pursue an Action-Centered Account of Discovery

There are many ways of characterising scientific discovery,[2] but each of them portrays discoveries either as *events* or *objects*. According to the first, the *process* or *act* of discovery is emphasized. Think of Newton's discovery of universal gravitation: we typically emphasize what Newton did, and how he did it, rather than focusing on gravity itself. According to the second, a particular *object* is emphasized. Think of penicillin; we talk about what it is and why it is important. We should not claim that only one of these is the "true" sense of discovery, that would be to introduce a false dichotomy. Inquiry into both processes and products can illuminate the phenomenon of scientific discovery. Nevertheless, I will focus on discovery as an event for three reasons.

First, objects of discovery are not counted as discoveries until there is some recognition of those objects *being* discoveries, and this recognition takes place at a certain time. It makes little sense to say that penicillin was a discovery in 30,000 BCE, or that it was always a discovery. The number 0, democracy and Snell's law do not exist in time, although they seem to have been discovered at certain times. The temporal element of objectual discoveries suggests that we might take discovery events as conceptually primary to discovery objects, since events can be indexed to times and this is not true of all objects of discovery.

Second, the temptation to think of discovery as objectual is at least partially a result of scientific rhetoric. Since the foundation of the Royal Society, science has been portrayed as objective by removing the traces of particular agents (see, e.g., Schaffer & Shapin, 1985). Discoveries are made by science itself, that is, by no one in particular, in order to distance those discoveries from the doubts that might otherwise attend them if they were portrayed as products of a practice carried out by biased and imperfect humans. This rhetorical move masks important agential aspects of science, and we need not take the mask for the face.

Finally, the products of discovery can be anything from bacteria to equations to methods, and it seems far more difficult to look for commonalities in the set of all things that have been (or could be) discovered and ask if machines could produce them, than to ask what sort of action a discovery is and whether machines could be the sort of agent to perform it.

So, what kind of action is discovery?

---

[2] See e.g. Kuhn (1962), Achinstein (2001), Hudson (2001), McArthur (2011), Schindler (2015) and the entries in Schickore and Steinle (2006). See Schickore (2014) for an overview.

4.2   Elements of the Discovery Event

I propose we distinguish the following elements of a discovery event: (a) an agent (who discovers), (b) an object of discovery (that which is discovered), (c) a trigger event (that which prompts the discovery) and (d) an act of discovery (the agent's interpretation of the object, prompted by the trigger event).

The agent can be an individual or a community, whose mind can be extended or distributed. *The object of discovery* can be an idea, a fact, a value, an entity (concrete or abstract), a process, a problem, a kind, an ability or a method. Anything, really. *The trigger event* often takes the form of an observation, inference, experiment, simulation, model manipulation, statistical analysis, or combination of these. It need not be intentional and can even be accidental. Generally speaking, any event can be a trigger event. Finally, *the act of discovery* is the agent's interpretation of the object of discovery, prompted by the trigger event. In the simplest cases, this interpretation is a mere categorisation of the object of discovery. We must not confuse the act of discovery with the trigger event, however. The discovery of penicillin was not the Petri dishes left uncovered, or the mould growing on the dishes, or Flemming's walking into the lab and seeing the area surrounding the mould in which there was no Staphylococcus. All of these objects and events jointly constitute the trigger event, and the discovery of penicillin must be different from this event because we want to be able to praise a discoverer for their discovery, and we cannot do this if the discovery simply *is* the trigger event, which need not include the intentional action of any agent.

Interpretation is therefore the key *action* of discovery. I propose four specifications of interpretation that when satisfied (and combined with the other elements) yield what I think is a plausible explication of scientific discovery.

First, the interpretation of the object of discovery has to be *novel* – whether to the agent ("personal discovery") or to the agent's epistemic community ("historical discovery") (see Boden, 2004. Novelty is also a requirement for Kuhn, 1962; Schindler, 2015; and Hudson, 2001). An agent or community who discovers the same thing again still discovers it, but after the first instance we say that they *re*discover it. Something may be a personal discovery for an agent though only a rediscovery for her epistemic community. And one epistemic community can rediscover what another has discovered already. The same discovery can therefore be a discovery or a rediscovery depending on how broadly we understand the agent's epistemic community. Lastly, we should note that an interpretation can be more or less novel.

Second, for an interpretation to count as a scientific discovery, it must interpret the object of discovery as the solution to a scientific problem. This is too loose, however, because a scientist who learns that her assistant has been stealing lab equipment interprets an object of discovery (the lab assistant's actions) as the solution to a problem (the equipment going missing) in a scientific domain. So let us focus on acts of *theoretical* scientific discovery, which are those that solve theoretical scientific problems. Theoretical problems concern the phenomena studied in a scientific domain, while practical problems obfuscate our solving such problems. The distinction is contextual, but it will do for our purposes.

Third, a scientific discovery must not merely *appear* to solve a theoretical problem, it must actually solve it. (Or partially solve it for a partial discovery). Thus Poincaré wrote that a mathematical discovery has three steps, an unconscious combination of ideas, a flash of insight that suggests that one of these combinations solves the problem, and then the most important step: verification that the solution is correct.[3] Since we do not want to discuss the mere *feeling* of discovery (what William Whewell called "happy thoughts"), we must include some criterion of success (Achinstein, 2001; Hudson, 2001). The kinds of solution that count as successful for a given problem will vary according to context.

Fourth, in addition to producing a novel and successful solution to a theoretical scientific problem, we require that the problem solved be significant. This is to preserve the intuition that discoveries are in some sense special: not all novel solutions to theoretical problems are discoveries. A problem is significant when its solution possesses some minimum value in whatever the relevant set of weighted scientific values are. Examples of such values include descriptive and predictive adequacy, coherence with previous knowledge, fruitfulness, beauty and simplicity.

To summarise, scientific discovery events consist of an agent's novel interpretation of an object which successfully solves a significant theoretical scientific problem. A discovery is more or less momentous depending on how novel and complete the solution is, and how significant the problem solved is.

Can machines discover in this sense? Trigger events and objects of discovery can be almost anything, and tests for a solution's satisfactoriness can be programmed into computers in advance, so I will leave these to one side and focus on the question of whether machines can produce novel interpretations that provide solutions to significant theoretical problems. According to some characterisations of novelty, interpretation and significance, the answer will be, yes. As regards novelty, machines can do things that are novel (in the sense that they have not been done before) given the use of random number generators. Second, machines can interpret if by interpretation we mean categorisation. In this minimal sense of interpretation, computers already categorise certain states as solutions by checking them against programmed desiderata. Finally, machines can have significance encoded into them, insofar as they are designed by scientists to address problems that are antecedently deemed significant. In sum, there are senses of novelty, interpretation and significance that justify the use of the concept DISCOVERY as applied to machine behaviour.

But there are senses of novelty, interpretation and significance that will be more difficult for machines to satisfy. These can be found in many corners of science. We want to know what is required if machines are to satisfy even the most difficult.

---

[3]He writes, "Discovery consists precisely in not constructing useless combinations, but in constructing those that are useful, which are an infinitely small minority. Discovery is discernment, selection" (Poincaré, 1914, p. 51).

Good candidates can be found by considering qualitative discoveries like those made in the social sciences.

4.3 Social Scientific Discovery

A broad range of methods are used by social scientists, from surveys and statistics to interviews and observations. Naively, we can draw a continuum from positivist to interpretivist social science methods. Positivists focus on observables such as physical movements and questionnaire responses, and explicitly endorse the more "objective" methods of science, including standardised surveys and statistical analyses. They aim to draw generalisable lessons concerning human behaviour. Interpretivists argue that positivist methods cannot capture the rich complexity of human social life. To understand this complexity, researchers must be deeply immersed in the target system and recognise that they can only uncover a limited amount from a limited perspective. In light of this, interpretivists claim that their discoveries will not be widely generalisable.

Insofar as positivist social science employs quantitative methods of science, machines can make positivist social scientific discoveries if they can make quantitative discoveries in other fields of science, and I assume they can. A harder question is whether machines can discover in interpretivist social science. That is, can machines produce new interpretations of the shared experiences and meanings of agents as solutions to significant theoretical problems concerning how communities form, function and fall apart? The answer depends on the relevant senses of novelty, interpretation and significance, which can be extracted from what sociologists do and teach.

It would be impossible to review the notion of discovery across all interpretivist social sciences, so in what follows I focus on ethnography, which I take to be a paradigm interpretivist social science method shared across many subdisciplines of social science including sociology, anthropology, international relations, economics and history.

The ethnographic method discovers by means of field studies, which include participant observations and interviews. The main goal of this kind of research method is to tell us why people think and behave in the ways they do in terms of the meanings they ascribe to the objects and events that surround them. For example, Rosabeth Kanter's famous study, *Men and Women of the Corporation* (1977) found that secretaries in the 1970s had little or no upward mobility because of "trained incapacity," that is, "training that makes people fit for one position [but] progressively less fit for any other" (Kanter, 1977, p. 98). The skills developed by the secretaries studied by Kanter were highly specific to the needs of their particular bosses. While such specialisation might have provided job security, it also ensured that bosses typically would not let their secretaries move into other (higher) positions.

Another example is Annette Lareau's *Unequal Childhoods* (2003), which focused on how differences in social class affected parenting styles among American families. Middle class parents seemed to favour a style Lareau called "concerted cultivation," according to which children are allowed negotiation power concerning their life trajectories, are put into organised activities, and are taught to question authority. Lareau dubbed the other style "accomplishment of natural growth," which she found to be favoured by working class families. This style gives far less negotiation power to the child, but also imposes less organised structure on daily life. As a result, children are encouraged to respect authority figures while developing a sense of personal independence; both thought to be beneficial character traits in the context of working class life.

The above examples are typical of interpretivist social scientific discoveries: an agent or team performs observations and interviews motivated by a few general questions, and interprets the data to find patterns that explain why certain social phenomena take the forms they do. Now, in what sense are such discoveries *novel* interpretations that solve *significant* problems?

4.3.1 Ethnographic Novelty

According to two widely used ethnography textbooks, "A report may be perceived as new and noteworthy . . . in at least three ways: through theoretical discovery, extension, or refinement" (Lofland, Snow, Anderson, & Lofland, 2006, p. 173; see also Snow, Morrill, & Anderson, 2003, p. 186). The second, theoretical extension, "involves extending pre-existing theoretical or conceptual formulations to groups or settings other than those in which they were first developed or intended to be used" (Lofland et al., 2006, p. 173). There are difficult cases where it is not clear how to extend a conceptual formulation or how to determine what counts as a new domain of application, but in general this is something machines have been doing more and more effectively, especially in mathematics (Lenat, 1977), physics (Langley, 1981), chemistry (Żytkow & Simon, 1986) and biology (Kulkarni & Simon, 1990). We can expect this progress to continue, and it is only a matter of time before machines can apply existing models of human behaviour to new sociological data.

Theoretical refinement is "the modification of existing theoretical perspectives through the close inspection of a particular theoretical proposition or concept with new field data" (Lofland et al., 2006, p. 173). Again, there is no reason to deny this sense of novelty to machines. If something like the dominant view in philosophy of science is correct—that theories are collections of models—then we already have programs that can analyse data to create or refine models, which in this sense of theory, satisfy the requirement (for examples of programs that are capable of such novelty, see Valdés-Pérez, 1995, and Kocabas & Langley, 1998).

These are not the most interesting sorts of novelty. Indeed, it has been argued that if computers are limited to these sorts of novelty, they cannot really discover (Gillies, 1996). So let us turn to theoretical discovery.

Theoretical discovery requires categories to be devised and used in a way that interprets and explains data. This could be novel because the data is novel, the interpretation is novel, or both. For instance, we could use an old system of interpretation (e.g. looking at power imbalances) to analyse a new social phenomenon (e.g. Twitter behaviour). Or we could look at old data through a new interpretive scheme. Or we could produce a new interpretation of new data.

The first of these options can be achieved by computation as theoretical extension. What is interesting about the second and third is the production of a new interpretation. To give an account of the novelty relevant for social scientific discovery, therefore, we need to look at the nature of ethnographic interpretation. But first, a quick look at ethnographic significance.

4.3.2 Ethnographic Significance

According to Lofland et al. (2006, pp. 177–181), a significant ethnographic solution should do at least some of the following: (a) go against "common sense" or the "modern mind-set," (b) develop ideas that "establish broader implications," (c) be well-developed, that is, use or generate concepts that are elaborated in detail, with a good balance of conceptual elaboration and data presentation, and a high degree of interpenetration between the two, or (d) refine or extend existing social science ideas. Let us address these in turn with machine discovery in mind.

First, because computers are not typically programmed to reason as humans do, they generally go against common sense and the modern mind-set. We might nevertheless worry that they have their own computer common sense: patterns of reasoning and expression that they cannot deviate from. Machine novelty could then be thought of as the power to break free from such reasoning styles. This is something machines can currently do, as programmers regularly soften the criteria that define problem solutions and appropriate methods, as well as adding stochastic elements and evolutionary algorithms that encourage flexibility in problem solving.

The second way of achieving significance, namely, establishing broader implications, is an instance of theory extension, which we granted was within the purview of machines.

The third, which Lofland et al. (2006) call "developed treatment," merely requires that work be done "well": a significant study will be well-researched, have conclusions that are empirically or theoretically well-supported and were arrived at using scientific interventions that were carefully thought-out and cleverly brought-about. However, there is no (unique, finite, exhaustive) list of methods that are the "good" or "scientific" ones. The only list we have is open-ended. So, how could a computer go about choosing the *best* evidence and the *best* methods, when we cannot say in advance what those are? The computer will have to answer these questions by interpretation. Given the theoretical context, methods available and data collected, it must interpret one or some of the methods as the most appropriate. And it must interpret one of the many possible explanations as the best or most plausible. In other words, for a machine to satisfy this requirement it must interpret well.

The fourth sense of significance, namely, to refine an existing theory, is equivalent to theoretical refinement, which we granted above is achievable for machines.

In sum, to recognise and achieve significant solutions to theoretical social scientific problems, the only crucial element that machines do not yet obviously possess is the capacity to interpret. Just as an ethnographer is able to interpret the significance of the actions, questions, explanations and so on, that she observes, the social scientific community is able to interpret the significance of the ethnographer's results.

The cognitive requirements for producing a novel, significant interpretation must therefore be a superset of the cognitive requirements for interpretation alone. Novelty and significance are features of interpretations and problems respectively, and they are attributed *by interpretation*. If we want to uncover the cognitive requirements of producing a novel, significant interpretation, therefore, we will be off to a good start if we can identify the requirements for interpretation in general.

4.3.3   Ethnographic Interpretation

We can identify three main interpretive methodologies: analytic induction, grounded theory and the extended case method.[4]

To pursue analytic induction, we produce claims of universal generality that we aim to refute using particular cases, over and over, until only one irrefutable universal explanation remains. To reach this final end point (if it was also a novel solution to a significant theoretical problem) would be to discover. However, since we could never establish that any universal statement was forever immune to future disconfirmation (Katz, 2001), more recent versions of analytic induction have relaxed this requirement, and focus more generally on the method of hypothesis and counterexample. The role of interpretation in analytic induction is to turn data into counterexamples and to determine how to refine theory to avoid those counterexamples.

Grounded theory, in its strongest (and original) form, claims that theory must come from data and never the other way around. An often-quoted phrase is: "An effective strategy is, at first, literally to ignore the literature of theory and fact on the area under study, in order to assure that the emergence of categories will not be contaminated by concepts more suited to different areas" (Glaser & Strauss, 1967,

---

[4]For a statement of analytic induction, see Znaniecki (1934) and Lindesmith (1947). For statements of grounded theory, see Glaser and Strauss (1967), Corbin and Strauss (1990), Glaser (1978), Strauss (1987), and Strauss and Corbin (1990). For statements of the extended case method, see Burawoy (1991, 1998, 2000). In what follows, I try to distil the methods of ethnographic interpretation, but I cannot do them complete justice. Interested readers are encouraged to look at the sources listed for more details.

p. 37). As with analytic induction, criticism has softened grounded theory over time. For example, Strauss (one of the theory's originators) came to admit that it is not realistic to think we could generate theory *purely* from data and data alone (Strauss & Corbin, 1994, p. 277). The main idea is now something like the following. As much as possible, we must try to let themes and patterns present themselves to us instead of imposing existing categorisations and theoretical assumptions on our data. Then, we test the emerging notions against future observations and interviews, until we feel sure we have understood them correctly. The relevant notion of interpretation here is complicated, and we will return to it in a moment.

In the extended case method, the emphasis is on extending and developing theory through qualitative methods. Given some background theory, a researcher enters the field with a host of specific hypotheses inspired by theory. Fieldwork is then "a sequence of experiments that continue until one's theory is in sync with the world one studies" (Burawoy, 1998, pp. 17–18). Things not relevant to the background theory and initial set of questions can and should be ignored.

On a loose reading, these methodologies are not mutually exclusive. One can begin with a theory in mind to inform an investigation (as in the extended case method), but look for empirical counterexamples (as in analytic induction) and be ready to create new conceptual resources as necessary (as in grounded theory). However, the extended case method and analytic induction produce new interpretations in the senses of theory extension and refinement respectively. What we really want are cases where new theoretical understanding is born from the data. This is the promise of grounded theory.

A great deal has been written on the process of interpretation in grounded theory. In general terms,

> You get *from* data, topics, and questions, on the one side, *to* answers or propositions, on the other, through intensive immersion in the data, allowing your data to interact with your disciplinary and substantive intuition and sensibilities as these latter are informed by your knowledge of topics and questions (Lofland et al., 2006, pp. 198–199).

This kind of interpretation "occurs continuously throughout the life of any qualitatively oriented project" (Miles & Huberman, 1994, p. 10). It begins with coding the data, which is "the process of defining what the data are all about" (Charmaz, 2001, p. 340) or "relating (those) data to our ideas about them" (Coffey & Atkinson, 1996, pp. 45–47) by "sorting your data into various categories that organise it and render it meaningful from the vantage point of one or more frameworks or sets of ideas" (Lofland et al., 2006, p. 200). The codes themselves are "names or symbols used to stand for a group of similar terms, ideas, or phenomena" (LeCompte & Schensul, 1999, p. 55), "tags of labels for assigning units of meaning to information complied" (Miles & Huberman, 1994, p. 56) or just "the labels we use to classify items of information as pertinent to a topic, question, answer, or whatever" (Lofland et al., 2006, p. 200).

Once some codes are established, we move to "focused" coding. One way to do this is to sort the codes into *units* and *aspects*, which combine into *topics*. The unit is the scope of the sample (Lofland et al., 2006, pp. 122–132), for example, a practice (like getting ready for work), an episode (like divorce), an encounter (like a cocktail party), an organisation (like a school), or a larger community (like a refugee camp). An aspect of a unit might be the beliefs, norms, ideologies, emotions, relations, etc., of the people in the unit. These combine to form a topic (e.g. the faith of people in a sports team or the norms governing drug dealers). Topics should emerge and change naturally as the ethnography progresses.

These reflections ready us for writing "memos," which are "the intermediate step between coding and the first draft of your completed analysis" (Charmaz, 2001, p. 347). This is where we generate and develop possible explanatory relationships between data (organised in codes) and the topic. Again, coding and memoing must be done simultaneously with the data collection process, so that ideas can be brought back to the field, tested and updated.

But how do we select units and aspects and generate meaningful codes and memos? "Field researchers too rarely elaborate how they get from their data, topics and questions to their findings and conclusions. The result is a kind of 'black box' or ... 'analytic interruptus' ... between the data-gathering and writing phases of the fieldwork enterprise that contributes to the sense that qualitative analysis is often the result of a mystical process or romantic inspiration" (Lofland et al., 2006, p. 211). While we can identify the parts or milestones of this process (coding, memoing, etc.), there still appears to be some extra cognitive leap that is left undescribed. And this is why, admitting that some parts of this process can be performed by machines, Lofland et al. claim that data interpretation "is not a process that can be farmed out to independent analysts nor ... to computers and various software programs" (2006, p. 196).

Why not? I think it has to do with interpreting *well*, as opposed to merely interpreting. Perhaps a machine can select units, aspects and topics, generate codes from data and organise the codes into answers about a topic. But the thought might be that a machine cannot do this well. Interpretation can be a simple act of rule-governed categorisation, but it can also be one of the most difficult cognitive acts that an agent can perform, requiring creativity, patience, imagination and insight. Perhaps it is some of these underlying cognitive powers that ethnographers suspect are missing from machines. In the next section, I will try to identify some of the cognitive powers that make the most difficult acts of interpretation possible.

4.4 Machine Interpretation

Building on the work of Peter Winch (1958) and Charles Taylor (1971) I will argue that there are at least five abilities any agent must possess in order to interpret well. I leave out abilities like collecting data and performing calculations, which I take machines already to possess.

To begin with, explaining human social behaviour requires that we discern the meanings of utterances and actions. And this requires that we recognise the possibility of certain behaviours having meanings at all. A statement is not just the production of a sound wave, it is also the expression of a thought. Following from this, a machine must have at least the following two abilities:

1. It must be able to distinguish between the *presentation* of a datum and the *meaning* of that datum when such a difference obtains.

When someone says, "I'm fine", they *present* themselves as being fine. They might also *mean* that they are fine. But they might not. If we always assumed that speakers meant exactly what they said, no additional sense could ever be made. So, for a machine to discover in ethnography it must make this distinction and be able to recognise cases where presentation differs from meaning.

2. Once this distinction is made and instances are identified in which meaning (seems to) differ from presentation, an interpreter needs a method for determining meaning.

We do not need to overcome the indeterminacy of translation or interpretation here: partial interpretation or partial grasp is perfectly fine in ethnography as an intermediate step towards understanding. But some way of getting from presentation to meaning is necessary, perhaps by means of a principle of charity and some informed guesses (Stuart, 2015). This is especially difficult where metaphors, loose speaking, body language or implicature are involved.

Next, meaning is only ever meaning *for*. There are no absolute meanings, or meanings in vacuo. An action might have one meaning for the actor, and a different meaning for the researcher, who looks at it in a different way. Because of this,

3. An interpreter must be able to identify the subject for whom something has a given meaning.

Without being able to say *who* means what, a machine interpreter cannot interpret, not least because the properties of the specific agent are needed to inform the interpretation.

To understand human behaviour, we must understand not only the meanings attributed by actors to events and objects, but also the purposes for which actions are performed and the normative constraints that govern those actions (Winch, 1958, p. 77). This is necessary if we are to give a full explanation of any behaviour: the purpose of intentional action is to achieve some end, which is desired for some reason. Therefore, in order to perform ethnographic interpretation,

4. An interpreter must be able to tell the difference between actions performed intentionally and unintentionally, and identify what the reasons for action are.

Sometimes we can discover someone's intentions simply by asking. But to interpret the answers we receive again requires knowledge of intention, because we must know whether our subject intends to be deceptive before we can consider taking their answers at face-value. In other words, to uncover someone's intentions by asking, we must already be able to interpret intentions. A second difficulty is that we cannot determine what a subject intends based on observation alone. Contributions of irrationality and luck must be recognised, otherwise, we interpret a gambling addict as intending to lose money, and people acting under cognitive biases in general as intending to ignore pertinent evidence or deceive themselves. Finally,

5. An interpreter must observe and track the differences between their worldview and the worldviews encountered in the field.

To understand someone, we must allow that they might not mean what we mean, see things as we do, desire what we desire, attribute the same level of importance to the same things, and so on. Because of this it is crucial for ethnographers to know what their own worldview is, so that they can tell when and how it informs their interpretation of the worldviews under study. "Do *they* mean *A* by *B*, or do I only think so because *A* is what *I* would mean by *B*?"

In sum, we have five abilities required for an agent to interpret in the most difficult cases of ethnographic discovery: the ability to (a) distinguish presentation from meaning, (b) identify meaning, (c) identify the "owner" of a meaning, (d) identify reasons for behaviour (while leaving room for irrationality and luck) and (e) distinguish, track and translate worldviews. There are surely other relevant abilities, but at least these five are necessary.

Can machines possess these abilities? Instead of pretending to know what future machines will be capable of, I want to say what they would have to be like if they were to possess them. Specifically, I want to argue that each ability requires at least the faculty of imagination. Imagination has no commonly accepted definition, but the basic idea is the ability to interact cognitively with objects and states of affairs not currently present to sensory experience (see Stuart forthcoming). Let us go in order.

1. To distinguish between presentation and meaning, an agent must recognise that there are always several possible meanings we could attribute to any given presentation (and vice versa). Such recognition requires looking beyond the presentation, in other words, we must conjure and consider states of affairs not currently present to experience. To distinguish between the statement "I'm fine" and the actual meaning someone intends with that statement, we must be able to imagine that the person could mean different things by that statement.
2. To identify meaning, the machine must be able to present to itself options for semantic ascription other than what is immediately inferable from the data alone, and choose the best option. Sometimes this is a straightforward practice that could be made algorithmic. But at some point we hit bedrock, and to break through we require a special sort of experience and acquaintance. Consider an emotion term like "shame". This

can only be explained by reference to other concepts which in turn cannot be understood without reference to shame. To understand these concepts we have to be in on a certain experience, we have to understand a certain language, not just of words, but also a certain language of mutual action and communication, by which we blame, exhort, admire, esteem each other. In the end we are in on this because we grow up in the ambit of certain common meanings. But we can often experience what it is like to be on the outside when we encounter the feeling, action, and experiential meaning language of another civilization.

> Here there is no translation, no way of explaining in other, more accessible concepts. We can only catch on by getting somehow into their way of life, if only in imagination. (Taylor, 1971, p. 13)

In other words, many basic pieces of the human semantic puzzle can only be grasped by taking part in common actions, values and experiences. Such participation is ultimately the source of many of our own meanings (Winch, 1958, pp. 81ff), though as Taylor mentions, this participation can also take place in imagination. For example, I possess many important concepts that I could not have gained through actual participation in the home-world of those concepts, because those worlds are fictional or in the past. It is therefore only through exercises of imagination that some instances of semantic understanding can be had, and this will be especially true for machines that cannot (yet) experience many of the things humans do. In any case, even when we have all the relevant experience, we still need to be able to come up with reasonable guesses about what someone means, and find ways to test those hypotheses (Stuart, 2015). And this requires imagination because to test hypotheses we must imagine different experimental setups (in non-trivial cases) and decide which would be more effective for testing by reasoning through possible outcomes of these tests. In other words, we must reason through states of affairs that do not (yet) exist.

3. To identify the owner of a meaning, the machine must be capable of taking up the perspective of an agent to see if a given meaning attribution is reasonable. Taking up a different perspective requires a cognitive departure from our present experience of objects and events, and this requires imagination.
4. The only way to identify someone's intentions (without being told what they are) is to imagine that you have the personal and contextual properties of the agent, and then ask yourself what reasons you would have for acting if you were them. In other words, the ability to interpret others depends both on the ability to interpret yourself (Jackman, 2003) – which requires seeing that your own mental actions have more than one possible meaning – *and* the ability to convert yourself mentally into an approximation of someone else. Both of these abilities were discussed above, and both require imagination.

Finally,

5. Tracking the differences between one worldview and another and establishing semantic links that would enable translation between them requires experience of both worldviews. However, we can only occupy one substantial worldview at a time (otherwise we would have to attribute conflicting properties to the same object). So, to determine and compare worldviews, we must be able to distance ourselves from our current worldview, get into another, and then switch back and forth to make comparisons. And this requires presenting the same objects and events to ourselves from different perspectives, which is to cognise objects and states of affairs otherwise than they are given to us.

Imagination is what enables us to recognise that there are several options for what someone might mean, hypothesise a number of plausible candidates, choose ways to test those candidates, and participate in the otherwise inaccessible action-worlds of others and thereby gain new concepts. It helps us put ourselves in another's position or worldview by seeing ourselves acting under different constraints with some of our existing properties strengthened, and others diminished or removed. Each of the five abilities needed to interpret in difficult cases requires cognitive interaction with objects and states of affairs not currently present to sensory experience. Imagination is therefore a fundamental capacity underlying ethnographic interpretation.

4.5   Conclusion

I have discussed the possibility of ethnographic machine discovery and I have argued that interpreting human behaviour and natural language systems of meaning requires imagination. A fortiori, imagination is necessary for producing some of the novel interpretations that solve significant problems in social science. Therefore, some discoveries in social science are only possible if the discoverer possesses imagination. This implies that for machines to be able to discover in social science to the same extent that humans can, they will require imagination algorithms.

Could such algorithms exist? That is, could a machine cognitively interact with objects and states of affairs that are not currently available to their sensory "experience"? Under some interpretations, yes. Computers can propose counterfactual hypotheses to make certain inferences. Logic software does this for *reductio ad absurdum* proofs and conditional derivations. But this is not the same as entertaining something that is not present, e.g., something fictional, since in the case of the logic program, the machine is interacting only with symbols that *are* present to its "experience". Perhaps we could reserve (sense) "experience" for machines that have more human forms of data input, like sight and hearing, but this seems unduly restrictive since most machine discovery systems do not currently have such input.

Concerning more substantial senses of imagination, like those required for perspective shifting and empathy, things are even murkier. I conclude therefore on what I think is a surprising note. The necessary conditions for scientific discovery (conceived of as an action) include providing novel interpretations that solve significant theoretical scientific problems, and in order to say whether machines can produce such interpretations we first need a better understanding of the imagination and what cognitive powers are required for its operation. Unfortunately, philosophers and cognitive scientists are still very far from possessing such an understanding.

To conclude, those who feel skeptical *or optimistic* about the extent to which machines can discover in science might profitably focus that skepticism (or optimism) on the nature and possibility of imagination algorithms. And to do this, we require a better understanding of the nature and cognitive requirements of imagination in humans, and imagination in general.

Acknowledgments Thanks to the organisers and participants of the conference "Scientific Discovery in the Social Sciences" at the London School of Economics, as well as Nancy Nersessian, Marco Buzzoni, Markus Kneer, Maël Pégny and Peter Sozou for comments on earlier drafts of this paper, as well as Susan Staggenborg (and Nancy Nersessian again) for generosity in sharing their knowledge of social scientific methodology. This work was funded by a postdoctoral fellowship from the University of Pittsburgh, and a postdoctoral fellowship from the Social Sciences and Humanities Research Council of Canada.

References

Achinstein, P. (2001). *The book of evidence*. Oxford, UK: Oxford University Press.

Boden, M. A. (2004). *The creative mind: Myths and mechanisms*. London: Routledge.

Bradshaw, G. L., Langley, P., & Simon, H. A. (1980). BACON4: The discovery of intrinsic properties. In *Proceedings of the third national conference of the Canadian Society for Computational Studies of Intelligence*, pp. 19–25.

Bradshaw, G. L., Langley, P., & Simon, H. A. (1983). Studying scientific discovery by computer simulation. *Science, 222*, 971–975.

Burawoy, M. (1991). *Ethnography unbound*. Berkeley, CA: University of California Press.

Burawoy, M. (1998). The extended case method. *Sociological Theory, 16*, 4–33.

Burawoy, M. (2000). *Global ethnography*. Berkeley, CA: University of California Press.

Charmaz, K. (2001). Grounded theory. In R. M. Emerson (Ed.), *Contemporary field research: Perspectives and formulations* (2nd ed., pp. 335–252). Prospect Heights, IL: Waveland Press.

Coffey, A., & Atkinson, P. (1996). *Making sense of qualitative data: Complementary research strategies*. Thousand Oaks, CA: Sage.

Corbin, J., & Strauss, A. (1990). Grounded theory method: Procedures canons, and evaluative criteria. *Qualitative Sociology, 13*, 3–21.

Dzeroski, S., Langley, P., & Todorovski, L. (2007). Computational discovery of scientific knowledge. In S. Dzeroski & L. Todorovski (Eds.), *Computational discovery of communicable scientific knowledge*. Berlin, Germany: Springer.

Gillies, D. (1996). *Artificial intelligence and scientific method*. New York: Oxford University Press.

Giza, P. (2002). Automated discovery systems and scientific realism. *Minds and Machines, 22*, 105–117.

Glaser, B. (1978). *Theoretical sensitivity*. Mill Valley, CA: Sociological Press.

Glaser, B., & Strauss, A. L. (1967). *The discovery of grounded theory: Strategies for qualitative research*. Chicago: Aldine.

Hudson, R. G. (2001). Discoveries, when and by whom? *The British Journal for the Philosophy of Science, 52*, 75–93.

Jackman, H. (2003). Charity, self-interpretation, and belief. *Journal of Philosophical Research, 28*, 143–168.

Kanter, R. (1977). *Men and women of the corporation*. New York: Basic Books.

Katz, J. (2001). Analytic induction. In N. J. Smelser & P. B. Baltes (Eds.), *International encyclopedia of the social and behavioral sciences* (pp. 480–484). Amsterdam, The Netherlands: Elsevier.

Kocabas, S., & Langley, P. (1998). Generating process explanations in nuclear astrophysics. In *Proceedings of the ECAI-98 Workshop on Machine Discovery* (pp. 4–9). Brighton, UK.

Kuhn, T. S. (1962). *The structure of scientific revolutions*. Chicago, IL: University of Chicago Press.

Kulkarni, D., & Simon, H. A. (1990). Experimentation in machine discovery. In J. Shrager & P. Langley (Eds.), *Computational models of scientific discovery and theory formation*. San Mateo, CA: Morgan Kaufmann.

Lane, P., Sozou, P., Addis M., & Gobet, F. (2014). Evolving process-based models from psychological data using genetic programming. In R. Kibble (Ed.), *Proceedings of the 50th Anniversary Convention of the AISB*.

Langley, P. (1981). Data-driven discovery of physical laws. *Cognitive Science, 5*, 31–54.

Langley, P. (2000). The computational support of scientific discovery. *International Journal of Human-Computer Studies, 53*, 393–410.

Langley, P., & Jones, R. (1988). A computational model of scientific insight. In R. Sternberg (Ed.), *The nature of creativity*. Cambridge, MA: Cambridge University Press.

Langley, P., Shrager, J., & Saito, K. (2002). Computational discovery of communicable scientific knowledge. In L. Magnani, N. J. Nersessian, & C. Pizzi (Eds.), *Logical and computational aspects of model-based reasoning*. Dordrecht, The Netherlands: Kluwer Academic.

Langley, P., Simon, H. A., Bradshaw, G. L., & Żytkow, J. M. (1987). *Scientific discovery: Computational explorations of the creative processes*. Cambridge, MA: MIT Press.

Lareau, A. (2003). *Unequal childhoods: Class, race, and family life*. Oakland, CA: University of California Press.

LeCompte, M. D., & Schensul, J. J. (1999). *Journeys through ethnography: Realistic accounts of fieldwork*. Boulder, CO: Westview Press.

Lenat, D. B. (1977). Automated theory formation in mathematics. In *Proceedings of the fifth international joint conference on artificial intelligence* (pp. 833–842). Cambridge, MA: Morgan Kaufmann.

Lenat, D. B. (1982). AM: Discovery in mathematics as heuristic search. In R. Davis & D. Lenat (Eds.), *Knowledge-based systems in artificial intelligence*. New York, NY: McGraw-Hill.

Lindesmith, A. (1947). *Opiate addiction*. Bloomington, IN: Principia Press.

Lofland, J., Snow, D., Anderson, L., & Lofland, L. H. (2006). *Analyzing social settings* (4th ed.). Belmont, CA: Wadsworth.

McArthur, D. J. (2011). Discovery, theory change and structural realism. *Synthese, 179*, 361–376.

Miles, M. B., & Huberman, A. M. (1994). *Qualitative data analysis: An expanded sourcebook* (2nd ed.). Thousand Oaks: CA: Sage.

Newell, A., Shaw, J. C., & Simon, H. A. (1958). Elements of a theory of human problem solving. *Psychological Review, 65*, 151–166.

Poincaré, H. (1914). *Science and method*. London: Thomas Nelson and Sons.

Schaffer, S., & Shapin, S. (1985). *Leviathan and the air-pump*. Princeton, NJ: Princeton University Press.

Schickore, J. (2014). *Scientific discovery. Stanford Online Encyclopedia of Philosophy*. Available at http://plato.stanford.edu/entries/scientific-discovery. Accessed 15 Nov 2016.

Schickore, J., & Steinle, F. (Eds.). (2006). *Revisiting discovery and justification: Historical and philosophical perspectives on the context distinction*. Dordrecht, The Netherlands: Springer.

Schindler, S. (2015). Scientific discovery: That-whats and what-thats. *Ergo, 2*, 123–148.

Shrager, J., & Langley, P. (Eds.). (1990). *Computational models of scientific discovery and theory formation*. San Mateo, CA: Morgan Kaufmann.

Simon, H. A. (1977). *Models of discovery*. Dordrecht, The Netherlands: Reidel.

Simon, H. A. (1979). *Models of thought*. New Haven, CT: Yale University Press.

Snow, D., Morrill, C., & Anderson, L. (2003). Elaborating analytic ethnography linking fieldwork and theory. *Ethnography, 4*, 181–200.

Spangler, S., Myers, J. N., Stanoi, I., Kato, L., Lelescu, A., Labrie, J. J., ... Comer, A. (2014). *Automated hypothesis generation based on mining scientific literature*. Association for Computing Machinery's Digital Library.

Strauss, A. (1987). *Qualitative analysis for social scientists*. New York: Cambridge University Press.

Strauss, A., & Corbin, J. (1990). *Basics of qualitative research: Grounded theory procedures and techniques*. Newbury Park, CA: Sage.

Strauss, A., & Corbin, J. (1994). *Grounded theory methodology: An overview*. In N. K. Denzin & Y. S. Lincoln (Eds.), *Handbook of qualitative research* (pp. 273–285). Thousand Oaks, CA, USA: Sage Publications, Inc.

Stuart, M. T. (2015). Philosophical conceptual analysis as an experimental method. In T. Gamerschlag, D. Gerland, R. Osswald, & W. Petersen (Eds.), *Meaning, frames and conceptual representation* (pp. 267–292). Düsseldorf, Germany: Düsseldorf University Press.

Stuart, M. T. (Forthcoming). Towards a dual process epistemology of imagination. *Synthese.* https://doi.org/10.1007/s11229-019-02116-w.

Taylor, R. (1971). Interpretation and the sciences of man. *The Review of Metaphysics, 25*, 3–51.

Valdés-Pérez, R. E. (1995). Machine discovery in chemistry: New results. *Artificial Intelligence, 74*, 191–201.

Winch, P. (1958). *The idea of a social science and its relation to philosophy.* London: Routledge.

Znaniecki, F. (1934). *The method of sociology.* New York: Farrar and Rinehart.

Żytkow, J. M., & Simon, H. A. (1986). A theory of historical discovery: The construction of componential models. *Machine Learning, 1*, 107–137.

Chapter 5
The Structure of Scientific Fraud: The Relationship Between Paradigms and Misconduct

Ben Trubody

Abstract This chapter argues that the level of difficulty in committing scientific fraud is a route to analysing the similarities and differences between the sciences. In *The Structure of Scientific Revolutions* Kuhn presents a paradigmatic theory of scientific change. "Paradigms", I argue, set a limit for things that pretend to be scientific, where the possibility and potential for "fraud" is dependent upon the strength or weakness of the paradigm. For the dishonest scientist two types of expertise become useful: (a) "contributional expertise" and (b) "interactional expertise". The weaker the paradigm is, the more these two types of expertise begin to blur; what constitutes an act of contribution becomes unclear. I highlight a criterion of "reasonableness" and "significance" as being key to "contribution". A claim that is unreasonable or trivial will either not be taken seriously, or draw too much critical attention, both unsuitable for fraud. What is deemed "reasonable" or "significant", however, is relative to the field of practice: in some sciences, different practitioners are allowed to hold fundamentally contradictory positions, whereas in others rejection of a widely accepted belief would be taken to signify poor practice.

Keywords Anaesthesiology · Cold fusion · Contributional expertise · Interactional expertise · Kuhnian paradigm · Scientific fraud · Scientific misconduct · Semi-conductor · Social psychology

5.1 Introduction

What separates alchemy from chemistry or astrology from astronomy? As received wisdom has it, on the one hand, we have science aligned with truth-seeking, theory-testing and critical thinking, and on the other hand, we have pseudoscience, with its mistaken beliefs, sloppy methodology, and wishful thinking (Pigliucci & Boudry, 2013). Scientific fraud, however, challenges these distinctions. It is neither a non-

B. Trubody (✉)
School of Liberal and Performing Arts, University of Gloucestershire, Cheltenham, UK

© Springer Nature Switzerland AG 2019
M. Addis et al. (eds.), *Scientific Discovery in the Social Sciences*,
Synthese Library 413, https://doi.org/10.1007/978-3-030-23769-1_5

science nor a pseudoscience; at its best it is indistinguishable from science, waiting for someone to unmask it.

How does one then commit fraud in a practice known for its rigour and standards of testing? The first principle of "fraud" offered here is that the "fraudster" should make a claim that is neither too radical or novel, nor too banal or trivial. It has to balance being reasonable enough to be considered a scientific contribution, but not so significant that critical attention will be drawn to the claim. For example, claiming to have invented a perpetual motion machine is both unreasonable and potentially highly significant. As the laws of energy conservation are well established it would not take long to disprove or at least bring into severe doubt the veracity of the claim.

Whilst any practice that seeks to make empirical or objective truth claims will contain erroneous knowledge, it is generally assumed that it does so unknowingly. The possibility of honest error is an accepted part of the scientific method. However, there are people who use the standards, norms and expectations of science in order to present a dishonest façade of genuine research. How easy or difficult this is, I argue, will tell us something about the state of that "science". Using the Kuhnian ideas of "paradigm" and "normal science", I argue that these not only set the limits for what a science is, but also for things that pretend to be of that science. What exactly a "paradigm" is and how much explanatory worth it has have been debated ever since Kuhn first popularised it (Richards & Daston, 2016). However, it may be reasonable to give as much emphasis to the tacit background conditions of science and knowledge as to the explicit foreground of representationalism and epistemology (Rouse, 2002). Paradigms at their strongest become accepted as almost identical with reality, making it transparent, where scientists simply observe nature. When wood burns we do not "see" spirits or phlogiston escaping, but rather we experience combustion through oxidation. When Robert Plot examined a large femur bone he "saw" the leg bone of a gigantic human rather than the world's first dinosaur bone. Given what else was believed to be true or possible at the time the notion of a giant human was more reasonable than the existence of a previously unknown, massive prehistoric animal as his discovery predated the theory of evolution. Thus, paradigms lend interpretation to our experiences where we "see" one thing and not another as meaningful. Phenomena that are not subject to evolutionary theory are not allowed to be entertained as meaningful by modern biologists; any biologist that acts otherwise is regarded as a bad biologist, or as someone not doing biology. Here, the paradigm limits interpretation. Conversely, where there are multiple competing paradigms there is far greater scope for interpretation; more things are potentially meaningful. In the social sciences, for example, two practitioners can hold fundamentally contradictory theories yet can both be recognised in their field. Paradigms then set the boundaries for what one can meaningfully do or say scientifically, which in turn sets limits for fraud. These limits are the parameters for what is *reasonable* and *significant* for the field, which we might term *contribution*. The paradigm tells the scientist what constitutes an act of contribution. It distinguishes the trivial from the non-trivial.

To successfully perpetrate fraud, a claim should neither be too radical, as this will either draw lots of attention from the relevant community of experts or not be taken seriously at all, nor too trivial, as it will not be recognised as a worthwhile contribution. Like Goldilocks, it has to be "just right" for the field in question. I argue that this "Goldilocks criterion" becomes easier to fulfil the less dominant the paradigm. "Fraud" also involves both "contributional" and "interactional" expertise (Collins & Evans, 2007). The first is to know how to contribute; it is the physical doing of a practice, where skills are required. The other is its social form, i.e. communication of what has to be done. As the paradigm weakens so too does the delineation between contribution and communication. Fraud becomes easier to commit as more things can be regarded as an act of contribution. Other limitations to fraud are the complexity of the objects under study and the level of confidence in the theories that postulate them. In domains where objects are simple and confidence is high fraud is short-lived as contribution is well-defined making testing of claims easier. Where objects are complex or vaguely defined and confidence is low more things become acceptable as being part of that science making it harder to rule out competing interpretations. What counts as a problem, a methodology, or evidence are all contestable. As there is no dominant paradigm to tell the scientist how the world is the field becomes much more ambiguously pluralistic. Here, "contribution" is much harder to define as there is no consensus on how one makes a contribution or even what one is exactly contributing to. Moreover, it becomes harder to tell radical and moderate claims apart. Such conditions lead to conflation between genuine contribution, bad science and deliberate acts of misconduct as they all appear alike.

5.2 Fraud and Scientific Misconduct

"Fraud" is a type of "scientific misconduct" which could include plagiarism, duplication, manipulation and fictionalisation of data, and "ghost" co-authoring. Ideally, suspect research would be weeded out by the scientific method: falsification by conjecture and refutation. Science, however, is also a social activity involving, among other things, research audit policies, financial incentives, peer-review and whistle-blowing. What should be an open process reliant upon an interconnected peer community has, with the expansion and anonymity of the internet, become more closed. The rise of the "publish or perish" culture of modern academia has led to a supply of and demand for dubious journals, institutes and "peers" who all act as a gateway to research publication and knowledge production (Qiu, 2010; Trubody, 2016). Martin (1992) lists types of scientific misconduct that are not illegal, but remain suspect, in areas such as the selection of data. Medawar (1963) considered the scientific paper itself to be fraudulent, in the sense that how the finished article is presented is not faithful to how science is actually done. Feynman (2001) wrote about the ability of scientists to "fool themselves" with respect to which results they take seriously and which they ignore. He points to the Millikan "oil drop experiments" and the changing value for the charge of the electron. His question is: Why did the reported value of the charge on an electron increase incrementally over time? Why not discover its actual value right away given everything needed for its determination already existed? Feynman (2001) said:

> It's a thing scientists are ashamed of – this history – because it's apparent people did things like this: When they got a number that was too high above Millikan's, they thought something must be wrong – and they would look for and find a reason why something might be wrong. When they got a number closer to Millikan's value, they didn't look so hard.

Today, we see the increasing influence of the professionalisation of science, where private companies can legally withhold the results of clinical trials and organisations can sue over challenges to the efficacy of their claims (Singh & Ernst, 2008). These are all currently permissible ways of acting in science, which one may use in order to mask phoney research. "Misconduct" may then be hidden by the *methodology* (e.g. study difficult/impossible to replicate), *the type of claim* (e.g. a prediction that is very hard/impossible to test or falsify), *social expectation* (e.g. fear of challenging authority) and *institutional norms* (e.g. audit policies, intellectual property rights). Rewriting experiments to, for example, make changes to data selection, omit results and withhold findings for fear of intellectual theft are all, whether desirable or not, part of science. "Fraud", as an intentional act to deceive, is an after-the-fact event. We can never know someone's intentions, but we can forensically analyse what is probable, sometimes aided by admissions of guilt. Nominally, in science we take on trust that the research has been conducted honestly: even if the person is mistaken, the mistake is honest. A metric then for misconduct is "retraction", where an article previously published as "knowledge" or "contribution" is withdrawn from publication, no longer endorsed by the relevant community.[1] Again another problem with the proliferation that the internet allows is the circulation of bogus research, in that a paper may be retracted but the "research" continues to be cited in papers many years later. Whilst honest human error is common to all fields (Decullier, Huot, Samson, & Maisonneuve, 2013), I wish to draw on examples of how pathological a claim can get whilst, for a time, remaining congruent with the field. My claim is that the stronger the surrounding paradigm the quicker the fraud will be detected. The professionalisation of science, however, helps immunise claims against scrutiny, meaning that they persist longer than would otherwise be the case.

5.3   Kuhn, Paradigms and Science (Misconduct)

Kuhn (1996) in the *Structure of Scientific Revolutions* developed a number of concepts for analysing the historical transition of science, as well as critiquing the abstract way in which science had been treated within the philosophy of science. "Paradigms" began as being central to *Structure*, but eventually became displaced

---

[1] It is unhelpful for studies of paper retractions that journals do not always declare why a paper was retracted.

by "incommensurability" and a wider "linguistic turn" (Gattei, 2008; Kuhn, 1993). This downplaying of the role of "paradigms" may be due in part to their perceived explanatory worth. Masterman (1999, pp. 80–81) identified 21 different ways the term gets used in *Structure,* labelling it a "crude analogy". Kuhn's own mentor, James Bryant Conant, worried over the vagueness of the term, making Kuhn the guy who "grabbed on to the word 'paradigm' and used it as a magic verbal wand to explain everything" (Cedarbaum, 1983, p. 173).

Firstly, I think the vagueness with which "paradigms" are discussed is unavoidable as the term seeks to refer to both the explicit and tacit features of science: its methodology and concepts as well as the socio-historical grounding of scientific knowledge. This is alluded to in the postscript of *Structure* by Kuhn's later inclusion of Polanyi's "tacit" (Kuhn, 1996, pp. 191–198). So, whilst paradigms do have an explicit dimension, i.e. past exemplars, they also have a tacit background context. This might be identified as the culture or socialisation of the scientist, which leads them to experiencing the world one way rather than another. "Paradigms" then are interpretations of the world, which aim at a one-to-one correspondence between what we say about the world and how it really is. It is only when paradigms go into crisis that this interpretive aspect comes into focus. Even though it is rare, when paradigms do undergo a crisis it provokes feelings of ambiguity, uncertainty and vagueness. It becomes uncertain what counts as evidence, an object of enquiry, or even a meaningful question. Here the field opens up and returns to an almost philosophical state where the fundamentals have to be reconsidered.

By contrast, where there are multiple paradigms, collective agreement over the meaning of things becomes impossible, forcing the science(s) to remain in a state of immaturity. Kuhn argued that paradigms vary in appearance, from modification in technology use to supplanting whole world views. In both cases, they alter what is intelligible to say, what questions get asked, what standards we might appeal to, and what things we can consider to reasonably exist. Paradigms provide concrete meaning for problems, concepts and ways of acting, that otherwise would not be taken seriously. This can manifest itself as "normal science", a way of proliferating the paradigm. The shared tacit agreement that a paradigm brings, where fundamental questions are not an issue, means research and experimentation continue to an almost esoteric level (Kuhn, 1996, pp. 24–25). In the process of extending the reach of the paradigm anomalies begin to accumulate, gradually undermining its explanatory power. From here the paradigm can be persisted with until either a more comprehensive theory is found, or it can coexist with other paradigms removing it from the centre of scientific enquiry. The paradigm may also fade out altogether due to it ceasing to produce research puzzles/solutions, lessening its appeal to would-be followers.

Unlike "normal science", multi-paradigmatic sciences allow for dispute at a fundamental level. Due to the complexity of phenomena involved, the uncertain ontological status of its objects and the theories that posit them, scientists come to disagreement much quicker or simply fail to see the point of what others are doing. Economics, for example, has at least nine fundamental schools of thought, all differing over what its objects of study are and how it should be done (Chang, 2014).

Here, it is an accepted part of doing economics that one can take a fundamentally contradictory position to a fellow economist and both still be doing economics (even share a Nobel Prize).[2] Now take the same type of fundamental dispute in biology: Could someone meaningfully entertain the idea that evolution does not happen and still be doing modern biology? For sociologists, psychologists, economists and even philosophers, due to there being no dominant paradigm, the "world" has no fixed interpretation as to "how things are", which brings about a foundational instability preventing "normal science". Given this lack of dominant interpretation it becomes unclear what is *unreasonable* to claim, what is *insignificant* and thus what *contributing* to that field is.[3] This uncertainty feeds the possibility and potential for fraud and misconduct in general.

As paradigms cover both explicit and tacit aspects, the tendency for philosophers of science is to dwell upon the explicit component, be it discovering a logico-semantic structure of theories (Laudan, 1977; Suppe, 1977) or the cognitive content of paradigms (Bird, 2012). Whilst this is partly what a paradigm is, Kuhn also indicates that those who only seek a formal explication of a paradigm will only have partial success (Kuhn, 1996, p. 43), for it ignores what is "tacit", which is essentially socio-historical. Dreyfus (1980) argues that the background tacit aspect of paradigms does not "consist in a belief system, a system of rules, or in formalised procedures; indeed, it seems the background does not consist in representations at all" (Dreyfus, 1980, p. 4). Why this is relevant is that both the tacit and explicit components limit the scope of fraud. Explicitly, fraud has to appear to be conducted within the methodological norms of the field where it can blend in. Tacitly, it also takes on the socio-historical content of that science in that what gets mimicked or faked is itself historically bounded. Here, one cannot think outside the assumptions, errors and biases of the time, as this would draw attention to the claim. For example, the types of fraud committed in the nineteenth century concerning spiritual mediums will no longer attract the attention of serious scientists like they did back then. Science today has virtually eliminated the "supernatural" as a meaningful object of investigation. Those that do investigate, or hold certain occult forces as scientifically sensible are usually ostracised by the scientific community.[4] Arguably the spiritualism or phrenology of the past has been replaced by equally occult forces today, be it the "mind as computer" or "genetic determinism". Whilst it might seem sensible to compare the mind to a computer or DNA with digital coding, the metaphorical articulation of scientific content is always limited historically by whatever the most advanced forms of technology were at the time and the state of philosophical debate surrounding those concepts (Tallis, 2004, 2012). So, if one were to commit fraud today in the cognitive or genetic sciences, one would play to

---

[2]Fama, Hansen and Schiller all shared the 2013 Nobel Prize for Economics although their theories are in direct contradiction with each other over the efficiency of markets.

[3]Currently psychology is undergoing a "reproducibility crisis" where psychologists cannot agree what reproducibility means (Baker, 2016).

[4]The Nobel Prize winner Brian Josephson is a good example of this (Stogratz, 2004, pp. 150–152).

these metaphors and models rather than offer an alternative. It is also interesting to see how the biases, assumptions and metaphors of the past impacted on fraudulent efforts. "Piltdown man", for example, was not identified as a hoax straight away, partly because the forensic technology did not exist, but also because it played to the biases and errors of the day, such as cranium size to jaw ratio, the size of canine teeth and crucially locating Britain/Europe as the cradle of civilisation and not Africa (Lewin, 1997).

Next, I will briefly cover a range of case studies involving fraudulent or suspected fraudulent activity. From the case studies, the relationship between paradigm and fraud will hopefully show how the potential for fraud may be supported or undermined by the surrounding paradigm(s). It should also be noted how the professionalisation of science may be in antagonism with science as a practice in making claims open to scrutiny. I begin with the phenomenon of "cold fusion". Given what else would also have to be true in order for cold fusion to be genuine, it makes the claim both unreasonable and highly significant. From here, I will move through the "hard" sciences into the more statistical based sciences, ending with the "softer" social sciences.

5.4   Andrea Rossi: Cold Fusion

Cold fusion is the notion that nuclear fusion can take place without the very high temperatures assumed to be necessary. It is normally associated with the Fleischmann–Pons experiment and has persisted for at least three reasons: (a) *epistemic* – experimental anomalies make it hard to totally ignore; (b) *social* – the potential significance if it were proved to be real; and (c) *institutional* – the stigma around cold fusion means it does not get funding and research papers are hard to publish. As a result, research tends to be privately backed by speculative investors hoping to be at the forefront of energy science. Due to the potential ramifications, sharing or providing access to data, methods and equipment is highly restricted. From 2011 the entrepreneur Andrea Rossi and the late physicist Sergio Focardi worked on the possibility of "cold fusion" that exploits a phenomenon known as "Gamow's window".[5] Rossi is a convicted fraudster (Ritter, 2012), which by itself does not make the claims false, but should raise suspicion.[6] Rossi's "E-Cat" technology claims to fuse hydrogen and nickel into copper at room temperature via a proprietary catalyst that releases energy. E-Cat technology now has an international patent bought by hedge-fund investors Cherokee Partners and Industrial Heat LLC

---

[5]Other notable attempts are Brilliant Light Power Inc., whose founder Randell Mills claims to have harnessed a new source of energy he calls the "hydrino", which as of 2006 has attracted over \$60 million in private investment (Morrison, 2008).

[6]Rossi allegedly wrote his Master's thesis on the relationship between Husserlian phenomenology and Einsteinian relativity. Whether there is a link between Rossi's background in the philosophy of science and his ability to create doubt over the impossibility of his claims is an interesting prospect.

for an undisclosed amount, but a current lawsuit involving Rossi and Cherokee Partners et al. suggests a figure of $100 million (Rossi and Leonardo Corporation v. Darden et al., 2016). Rossi's claim is essentially that E-Cat produces more energy than it consumes. This is both highly significant and unreasonable; for example, critics have argued that were the proposed method to work as claimed, it should have created mortally high levels of radiation.

Just because a phenomenon is improbable does not make it false, but it does make it hard to test. If one is dealing with a rare event, one has to appeal to a small number of isolated cases for evidence. Unlikely things, by their nature, do not lend themselves to methods where a quality like reproducibility is desirable, all of which is to the fraudster's advantage. Rossi, however, is not the first to make the claim. Julian Schwinger (1991) worked on the theoretical possibility for "cold fusion", where he states that "reproducibility" is fine for areas of established science, but an inappropriate criterion for fringe research or novel phenomena, which would actually be a barrier to new discovery. Even for Schwinger, scientific journals made it very hard for him to publish papers without heavy editing or redaction (Mehra & Milton, 2000, p. 552). Ever since then "cold fusion" phenomena have sporadically been reported, adding doubt as to how unlikely it really is. For Rossi, such doubt is the perfect cover for not reproducing results. Some may point to his patent as evidence that he has a genuine discovery; however, whether or not a device works is irrelevant to its patent as it can fulfil a "prophetic" requirement that given certain theoretical conditions, a device *could* work. For an area of research that is potentially as lucrative as free energy the gamble of financing seems to be worth the investment. How then, if this is a fraud, does one manage to keep alive a radical claim that goes against the majority of the scientific field? As with negative claims about man-made climate change or the link between smoking and health risk, it is partly the ability to create and use doubt (Oreskes & Conway, 2010). The lack of interest from research programmes suggests that the field is not worth pursuing. However, this lack of funding and interest can also be blamed for the slow progress of the field. Scientists here have had to become more entrepreneurial in attracting private investment. Equally, the professionalisation of science has meant values and principles of "business" not "science" are being used to conduct and evaluate research. Here the raw data, technology and methods are closely guarded to prevent intellectual theft, where "verification" is behind closed doors, possibly involving a conflict of interest, with testing tightly stage-managed. This closed organisation only furthers speculation and doubt. The "Lugano E-Cat Report" (2014), for example, asks: how independent were the principal investigators? Why has the report not been published in any respected science journals? What exactly was the "chain of custody" for the nickel powder charge and after-test ash? How much of the data was due to measurement errors? Why have no independent institutions trumpeted the findings? Whilst the excess heat measured in Rossi's closed tests could be from a type of fusion, the simplest explanation is either a mis-connected earth wire or hidden external device (Siegel, 2016). So, while cold fusion is possible, it is not probable. This case makes a virtue of unlikely events and a lack of strong evidence, revels in outliers and seems to embrace a kind of "secret knowledge", where mainstream science is a cover-up or mouthpiece for the establishment. The apparent threat of intellectual theft means Rossi's work is closely guarded, preventing independent testing. The negative reaction to "cold fusion" from the peer community is then explained by it not being in the interests of "Big Business" who have interests in existing energy sources.

Currently, Rossi is suing Industrial Heat et al. for misappropriation of intellectual property (Rossi and Leonardo Corporation v. Darden et al., 2016). One interpretation is that, if the matter has gone to court, then there must be something worth fighting over; another is that Rossi was forced into suing after an alleged failed year-long test that would have had Industrial Heat et al. sue him first for fraud. This way Rossi can portray himself as the victim. Given my criteria of *significance* and *reasonableness* and the paradigm of low energy nuclear physics, claims of "cold fusion" are too contrary to the paradigm and too significant given the scientific, financial and environmental implications. This may then be an example of how to defraud private investors, but not the scientific community.[7] As the saying goes, extraordinary claims require extraordinary evidence. To contravene this maxim might be acceptable for pseudoscientific fraud – crystal healing and miracles – but not for full blown scientific fraud.

5.4.1 Hendrik Schön: Organic Semi-conductors

The physicist Hendrik Schön was awarded the Otto-Klung-Weberbank and Braun-schweig Prizes and the Outstanding Young Investigator Award of the Materials Research Society (2001–2002) for breakthroughs with organic semi-conductors. In 2001, Schön claimed to have invented a way of using organic dye molecules to create an electrical circuit which when prompted by an electric current behaved as a transistor. During this period, he published a paper, on average, every 8 days in high-ranking journals. Whilst experimenting with organic materials, he claimed to have observed unprecedented "on/off" behaviour, amounting to the world's first organic electrical laser and the world's smallest transistor. His results, in most cases, confirmed prior theoretical predictions (Reich, 2009). His findings were heralded despite no one else replicating them. Eventually, anomalies in his research were pointed out at the peer-review level, such as duplicated graphs and data for different phenomena, which he explained as accidents in data submission (Beasly, Datta, Kogelnik, Kroemer, & Monroe, 2002). There was further failure to replicate his molecular transistor using his method of nano-lithography, which also brought further duplicated data to light. On formal investigation of his work, all his notebooks and computer files containing the "raw data" had been destroyed because he claimed to not have the hard-drive storage space. From October 2002 to March

---

[7]The case was settled after 4 days for an undisclosed amount with the defence accusing Rossi and engineer Penon of fabricating results, which could not be proved in court (Lewan, 2017).

2003, 28 articles authored by Schön were retracted. He was found guilty of having "substituted data", "unrealistic precision of data" and "results that contradict known physics" (Beasly et al., 2002). Schön used his knowledge of theory to generate fictional data sets, arguing he did so only to draw attention to behaviour that really was observed.

Most of Schön's work was not contrary to his field, but an exaggerated version of known and suspected effects. His rate of publication was congruent with an important new discovery, and his position at the prestigious Bell research facility also lent authenticity. As Kaiser (2009) notes, "[Schön] worked with a particular idea of what real or legitimate knowledge claims should look like. He sought to make his fakes fit in rather than stand out, massaging his data to better match established predictions". Counter-intuitively, the peer review process actually aided Schön by having the reviewers make suggestions about what would have to be altered in order for sceptical people to be convinced. Reich (2009) also argues that as "big money" was involved, scientists were too busy coat-tailing the new discovery to seriously scrutinise the original claims. The financial pressures Schön's research facility was under also suggests that managers and administrators do not look too hard at a scientist who claims to be producing ground-breaking research. In total his fraud lasted 2 years. Had Schön stuck with low-level claims in an emerging field, his activities may have gone disguised longer; but possibly because of how easy it was to get published, the potential for rewards and fame with a lack of oversight meant his claims escalated to a point that they were hard to ignore. His "findings" were reasonable enough to not be initially questioned and potentially significant enough that they should be allowed to happen. Possibly because of how easy it was for him, the execution of his claims got lazier, duplicating graphs in different articles for different materials and producing data sets that fit "too well" with his predictions. In a field such as organic physics, duplicated graphs and data that fit "too well" stick out more than the extravagance of the claim, as this is not what other physicists experience when doing the research. There are, however, other fields of study where data may well be statistically significant, but scientifically meaningless, where the phenomena involved are more complex, bringing about greater scope for the interpretation of results, and where all of this is still recognised as doing science, which makes fraud easier still to perpetrate.

5.4.2 Fujii and Reuben: Anaesthesiology

Yoshitaka Fujii specialised in the management of post-operative nausea and vomiting, focusing on the drug granisetron. From 1993, over the next 19 years, he published 249 papers, 183 of which have been retracted whilst others remain suspect (Carlisle, 2016; Cyranoski, 2012). It took until 2000 for the journal *Anaesthesia & Analgesia* to suggest that his data was "too nice", but this was quickly overlooked. One way that Fujii evaded detection was that he would submit articles to journals whose specialism was outside anaesthesiology, and therefore less well placed to judge the claims. Anaesthesiologist Daniel Jolley (2012) notes that Fujii's area of research was neither exciting nor celebrated, none of his research was ground-breaking and few of his articles were widely cited. Nor did Fujii receive awards or prizes for any of his studies. He was thoroughly average. His claims were not significant enough to draw much interest, but were reasonable enough to be published. He was eventually caught due to the consistently "nice fit" of his data. In a field that already includes things like unconscious data bias, weak methodology, questionable P values, as well as low level scientific misconduct, Fujii's efforts did not really stick out. On the whole, he tended to over-estimate the effects of certain drugs, but to what degree is uncertain, as it would seem that more fraudulent data and papers upon which other research is based are still in circulation (Carlisle, 2016, p. 167).

The anaesthesiologist Scott Reuben has 25 fraudulent articles retracted to date, as well as a six-month prison sentence, 3 years supervised release and financial penalties (Thirlwell, 2014, p. 457). His research focused on COX-2 inhibitors "Vioxx" and "Celebrex". Reuben claimed to have conducted experiments utilising the environments of operating theatres, which ordinarily give ample opportunities for clinical research to be done under minimal supervision. Reuben used his knowledge of the clinical setting, as well as a lax research audit policy, to never actually conduct any research. His first fraudulent paper appeared in 1996, but it took until 2008 for any of his criminal activity to come to light, despite publishing faked research of "significance". As with Fujji, it is the length of perpetrated fraud that might be more telling of a science that, due to the statistical nature and complexity of its objects, accommodates greater interpretations. Reuben started by publishing the results of clinical trials with added fictional patients, increasing the weight of clinical evidence. The majority of Reuben's "research" showed augmented analgesic effects for the drugs Vioxx and Celebrex, research paid for by pharmaceutical companies. The drug Vioxx (owned by Merck and Co.) has been linked to 40,000 deaths in the US (Fraser, 2014, p. 238). It was recalled on safety grounds over long term, high-dosage being associated with heart attacks and strokes. Owners Merck were taken to court over suppression of data linking the drug to heart problems and promoting Vioxx for conditions that had not been FDA approved. Bextra, another drug Reuben's fictional work endorsed, was also pulled from the market over a similar health risk. After Vioxx and Bextra were pulled, this led to a surge in sales for the painkiller Celebrex, another drug Reuben had made-up positive results for, which was owned by rival drug company Pfizer. Reuben received five research grants from Pfizer between 2002 and 2007 and was a paid member of the company's speaker bureau. None of this research was FDA nor IRB approved (Borrell, 2009). The involvement of "Big Pharma" in funding Reuben's research suggests that he was financially incentivised to convince orthopaedic surgeons to shift from the first generation of nonsteroidal anti-inflammatory drugs to the newer, propriety COX-2 inhibitors.

Reuben's work began to come under scrutiny when several anaesthesiologists noticed his studies never showed any negative results for the drugs he was investigating; however, like Fuji's these were soon forgotten. It took a routine audit by his employer Baystate Medical Centre, which found he had not received ethical approval for two of his "studies" (Borrell, 2009). It was partly chance that his work got selected, but apart from a few people questioning the statistical consistency of his work, the content of his research went unquestioned for 12 years. We may want to say that Reuben's efforts go against my criteria of "significance" as all his results were positive, upon which wider research was based. However, in a field that is largely statistical, where researchers have pressure applied by investor interests, messy or inappropriate methodologies are used and low level scientific misconduct (e.g. data selection bias) may well be a silently (perhaps tacitly?) accepted practice, it is not uncommon for studies to turn out results of high statistical significance which are essentially meaningless (Glasser & Duval, 2014). Even though Reuben had found favourable results for new drugs, his work did not attract wide citation; other researchers also found positive results, whilst others found the opposite (Redman, 2013, p. 95–98). Here, a term like "contribution" starts to be problematic. This situation is problematised further by the professionalisation of science, where financial incentives can skew the objectivity of research, and the need to publish for job security, along with the demands of journals for "exciting" or "dramatic" articles, means data bias is quietly encouraged. With positive results twice as likely to be published as the null hypothesis/negative results meta-studies have suggested that most published findings of this type are probably false (Ioannidis, 2005). Colquhoun (2014) states that scientific papers which give statistical significance for reported findings very rarely have the shortcomings of their methods highlighted, where a test for screening Alzheimer's in healthy bodies with 95% specificity and 80% sensitivity can still be wrong 86% of the time.

Again, what got Fujii and Reuben caught was not so much what they claimed as how they claimed it, in that their data was "too good". However, "too good" here does not immediately stand out, for the complexity of the objects of study and the lack of reliable conclusions that can be drawn from statistical analysis, means that in the short term the "reasonableness "and "significance "of the research is hard to determine. It is accepted that drug trials can show positive and negative results, without them seeming contradictory. There are, however, practices where the ontological status of objects is less well defined than clinical trialling, where the boundaries of multiple-competing paradigms blur; incommensurable positions may then be taken without the field being brought into disrepute. Here, "reasonableness", "significance "and "contribution "are all open to interpretation, meaning fraud and misconduct are easier still.

5.4.3   Diederik Stapel: Social Psychology

Diederik Stapel graduated "cum laude"from Amsterdam University in 1997, winning the ASPO Thesis Prize. He gained a professorship at Groningen within 3 years, then at Tilburg where he established the Institute for Behavioural Economics Research. In 2010 he was made professor and Dean of the faculty. He received numerous awards for his work in experimental social psychology (e.g. Jos Jaspars Early Career Award and Career Trajectory Award) as well as supervising multiple PhDs that expanded upon his research (Witkowski & Zatonski, 2015, p. 44). Among his findings were the discoveries that meat-eaters are more selfish than vegetarians and that chaotic environments promote stereotyping and discrimination. In 2011, an inquiry into Stapel's work found him guilty of manipulating and falsifying data and plagiarism, as well as never letting his students ever complete an experiment. Again, he was caught not because of what he claimed, but how he went about practising science, never allowing students access to raw data, gradually raising suspicion. Had Stapel forged raw data, his fraud could have gone on indefinitely. To date he has 54 paper retractions with others outstanding, as he cannot remember which experiments were real or which were imaginary, as well as multiple doctoral theses that were based on imaginary data (Ibid., p. 44). Stapel's method was to collaborate with a colleague and devise an imaginary experiment, the hypothesis, explanation and so on, as just an academic exercise. He would then invent data to fit this hypothetical set-up, then present it to his students to write up, normally resulting in a publication. For an early-career researcher the opportunity to co-author a paper with a renowned academic is readily welcomed.

In the ensuing investigation there was a lot of "after-the-fact" analysis that said his results were "too good", where effects were large; missing data and outliers were uncommon; and hypotheses were rarely refuted. Yet at the time this did not stop journals, academics and the media from accepting his work (Markowitz & Hancock, 2014). How credible are social psychology "findings"? There is currently a "reproducibility crisis" within psychology where the majority of reported experimental effects are unreproducible. Moreover, scholars cannot agree on what "reproducibility" means in psychology (Baker, 2016). This claim has been backed up by many meta-studies of the field showing misreporting, falsifying data and significant statistical errors (Aarts et al., 2015; John, Loewenstein, & Prelec, 2012; Wicherts & Bakker, 2014). Do fellow psychologists read the results of social psychology experiments with an understanding of just how easy it would be to make things up, and the lack of checks to ensure reliability of psychological research? Stapel, in his memoirs, revealed the complete lack of oversight of his work: due to his reputation, people just let him do what he wanted (Stapel, 2013, p. 64). The fact that Stapel got away with this level of fraud at at least three different universities should say something not only about the integrity of Stapel as an academic, but also the state of the field. The Levelt Report (2012), which investigated Stapel's activities, described a "lack of (fixed and clear) standards" regarding the protocols of Stapel's work, which may also be a wider feature of the field in general. The report said

> virtually nothing of all the impossibilities, peculiarities and sloppiness mentioned in this report was observed by all these local, national and international members of the field, and no suspicion of fraud whatsoever arose.

This is symptomatic of a field that lacks a dominant paradigm, where it is much harder to tell moderate and radical claims apart. This also affects how one thinks about contribution, given the ambiguity of the reasonableness and significance of the claims. In dealing with social phenomena, many more things become possible and hence could be meaningful. Maybe carnivores are more selfish than herbivores? In a field where very few fundamentals are agreed upon, researchers can hold contradictory positions, fabricated and genuine research can become indistinguishable, and talking about and doing the research readily overlap. As we struggle to discern radical from moderate, significant from insignificant and reasonable from unreasonable ways of practising the science, it is difficult to separate genuine contribution, bad science and misconduct.

5.5 Conclusion

I have argued that the case studies here can be analysed in terms of Kuhnian "paradigms" in what the practice allows you to meaningfully claim. Due to the strength or weakness of the paradigm this will set the boundaries for reasonableness, significance and what an act of contribution is. In a field that has a dominant paradigm and accompanying "normal science" all these criteria are easy to discern. Moderate and radical claim are easy to distinguish, while in the case of fraud it is harder to maintain a balancing act between novelty/significance of a claim and its reasonableness. Where the paradigm is strong, epistemic and social expertise are required in order to perpetrate fraud. Here, it is not just what is claimed that has to be measured, but tactics that utilise the norms and expectations of the field in order to mask bogus work. As we approach the more statistically-based sciences, like medicine and drug trialling, claims become more diverse, as the phenomena under investigation become more complex and their ontological status less well-defined. Here "contribution" starts to become fuzzy, as the criteria of significance and reasonableness also widen in meaning. As "contribution" becomes more ambiguous, more types of research and claims become acceptable as potentially belonging to that field. Here, results can be "ordinary", "unextraordinary" or even "significant", and still not mean anything, as it is part of the tacit understanding that goes with data selection, confirmation/publication bias, conflicts of interest and the sloppiness/unreliability of methods. These conditions also give fraudsters a greater window of opportunity, as what really is an act of contribution will only be found out by the overall practice of "good" science in the field, i.e. meta-studies. Moving into fields where "reasonableness", "significance" and "contribution" are almost impossible to discern, where most acts *could* be viewed as a type of contribution, fraud is easy to commit. Due to the lack of a ruling paradigm most claims become meaningful. It is at this point we may ask whether it is a science at all.

References

Aarts, A. A., Anderson, J. E., Anderson, C. J., et al. (2015). Estimating the reproducibility of psychological science. *Science, 349*, aac4716–aac4718.

Baker, M. (2016). 1,500 scientists lift the lid on reproducibility. *Nature, 533*, 452–454.

Beasly, M. R., Datta, S., Kogelnik, H., Kroemer, H., & Monroe, D. (2002). *Report of the investigation committee on the possibility of scientific misconduct in the work of Hendrik Schon and coauthors*, APS. http://publish.aps.org/reports/lucentrep.pdf. Accessed 15 Apr 2016.

Bird, A. (2012). What can cognitive science tell us about scientific revolutions? *Theoria, 27*, 293–321.

Borrell, B. (2009). *A medical Madoff: Anesthesiologist faked data in 21 studies*. Scientific American   http://www.scientificamerican.com/article/a-medical-madoff-anesthestesiologist-faked-data. Accessed 6 Feb 2016.

Carlisle, J. (2016). Post operative nausea and vomiting research: Methodology, assessment and strength of research. In T. J. Gan & A. S. Habib (Eds.), *Postoperative nausea and vomiting: A practical guide* (pp. 156–169). Cambridge, MA: Cambridge University Press.

Cedarbaum, D. G. (1983). Paradigms. *Studies in the History & Philosophy of Science, 14*, 173–213.

Chang, H. J. (2014). *Economics: The user's guide*. London: Pelican.

Collins, H., & Evans, R. (2007). *Rethinking expertise*. Chicago: Chicago University Press.

Colquhoun, D. (2014). An investigation of the false discovery rate and the misinterpretation of p-values. *Royal Society Open Science, 1*(3), 140216. https://doi.org/10.1098/rsos.140216.

Cyranoski, D. (2012). Retraction record rocks community. *Nature, 489*(7416). http://www.nature.com/news/retraction-record-rocks-community-1.11434. Accessed 17 Feb 2016.

Decullier, E., Huot, L., Samson, G., & Maisonneuve, H. (2013). Visibility of retractions: A cross-sectional one-year study. *BMC Research Notes, 6*, 238. https://doi.org/10.1186/1756-0500-6-238.

Dreyfus, H. (1980). Holism and hermeneutics. *The Review of Metaphysics, 34*, 3–23.

Feynman, R. (2001). Cargo cult science: Some remarks on science, pseudoscience, and learning how to not fool yourself. In J. Robbins (Ed.), *The pleasure of finding things out: The best of the short works of Richard P. Feynman* (pp. 205–216). London: Penguin Books.

Fraser, D. A. S. (2014). Why does statistics have two theories? In X. Lin, C. Genest, D. Banks, et al. (Eds.), *Past, present, and future of statistical science* (pp. 237–254). Boca Raton, FL: CRC Press.

Gattei, S. (2008). *Thomas Kuhn's "linguistic turn" and the legacy of logical empiricism: Incommensurability, rationality and the search for truth*. Aldershot, UK: Ashgate Publishing Limited.

Glasser, S. P., & Duval, S. (2014). Meta-analysis, evidence-based medicine, and clinical guidelines. In S. P. Glasser (Ed.), *Essentials of clinical research* (pp. 203–223). London: Springer.

Ioannidis, J. P. A. (2005). Why most published research findings are false. *PLoS Medicine, 2*(8), e124.

John, L. K., Loewenstein, G., & Prelec, D. (2012). Measuring the prevalence of questionable research practices with incentives for truth-telling. *Psychological Science, 23*, 524–532.

Jolley, D. (2012). Fujii, anesthesia & research fraud. *Gas Exchange*. http://gasexchange.com/articles/fujii-anesthesia-research-fraud/. Accessed 26 June 2016.

Kaiser, D. (2009). Physics and pixie dust. *American Scientist, 97*, 469–478.

Kuhn, T. S. (1993). Afterwords. In P. Horwich (Ed.), *World changes: Thomas Kuhn and the nature of science* (pp. 311–341). Cambridge, MA: MIT Press.

Kuhn, T. S. (1996). *The structure of scientific revolutions* (3rd ed.). Chicago: University of Chicago Press.

Laudan, L. (1977). *Progress and its problems: Towards a theory of scientific growth*. Berkeley, CA: University of California Press.

Lewan, M. (2017). Here's the settlement – Getting the license back was Rossi's top priority. *An Impossible Invention*, https://animpossibleinvention.com/2017/07/18/heres-the-settlement-getting-the-license-back-was-rossis-top-priority/. Accessed 22 July 2017.

Lewin, R. (1997). *The bone of contention: Controversies in the search for human origins*. Chicago: University Press.

Markowitz, D. M., & Hancock, J. T. (2014). Linguistic traces of a scientific fraud: The case of Diederik Stapel. *PLoS One, 9*(8): e105937. https://doi.org/10.1371/journal.pone.0105937. Accessed 18 Apr 2016.

Martin, B. (1992). Scientific fraud and the power structure of science. *Prometheus, 10*, 83–98.

Masterman, M. (1999). The nature of a paradigm. In I. Lakatos & A. Musgrave (Eds.), *Criticism and the growth of knowledge* (pp. 59–90). Cambridge, MA: Cambridge University Press.

Medawar, P. B. (1963). Is the scientific paper a fraud? *The Listener, 70*, 377–378.

Mehra, J., & Milton, K. A. (2000). *Climbing the mountain: The scientific biography of Julian Schwinger*. Oxford, UK: Oxford University Press.

Morrison, C. (2008, October 21). Blacklight power bolsters its impossible claims of a new renewable energy source. *The New York Times*. http://www.nytimes.com/external/venturebeat/2008/10/21/21venturebeat-blacklight-power-bolsters-its-impossible-cla-99377.html. Accessed 28 Mar 2016.

Oreskes, N., & Conway, E. M. (2010). *Merchants of doubt: How a handful of scientists obscured the truth on issues from tobacco smoke to global warming*. New York: Bloomsbury Press.

Pigliucci, M., & Boudry, M. (Eds.). (2013). *Philosophy of pseudoscience: Reconsidering the demarcation problem*. Chicago: The University of Chicago Press.

Qiu, J. (2010). Publish or perish in China. *Nature, 463*, 142–143.

Redman, B. K. (2013). *Research misconduct policy in biomedicine: Beyond the bad-apple approach*. Cambridge, MA: MIT Press.

Reich, E. S. (2009). *Plastic fantastic: How the biggest fraud in physics shook the scientific world*. New York: Palgrave Macmillan.

Richards, R. J., & Daston, L. (2016). *Kuhn's structure of scientific revolutions at fifty: Reflections on a science classic*. Chicago: University Chicago Press.

Ritter, S. K. (2012). Reviving cold fusion. *Chemical & Engineering News, 90*, 42–44.

Rossi A, Leonardo Corporation v. Darden T, John T. Vaughn, Industrial Heat, LLC, IPH International and Cherokee Investment Partners, LLC. (2016). Case 1:16-cv-21199-CMA Document 1. http://www.e-catworld.com/wp-content/uploads/2016/04/Leonardosuit01-main.pdf. Accessed 15 July 2016.

Rouse, J. (2002). Kuhn's philosophy of scientific practice. In T. Nickles (Ed.), *Thomas Kuhn* (pp. 101–121). Cambridge, MA: Cambridge University Press.

Schwinger, J. (1991). Cold fusion: Does it have a future? In M. Suzuki & R. Kubo (Eds.), *Evolutionary trends in the physical sciences: Proceedings of Yoshio Nishina centennial symposium, Tokyo, 5–7 December 1990*. Berlin, Germany: Springer.

Siegel, E. (2016). Is cold fusion feasible? Or is it a fraud? *Forbes*. https://www.forbes.com/sites/startswithabang/2016/09/23/is-cold-fusion-feasible-or-is-it-a-fraud/#a982d057a050. Accessed 13 Dec 2016.

Singh, S., & Ernst, E. (2008). *Trick or treatment: The undeniable facts about alternative medicine*. London: Norton.

Stapel, D. (2013). *Ontsporing*. Amsterdam: Prometheus.

Stogratz, S. (2004). *Sync: The emerging science of spontaneous order*. London: Penguin.

Suppe, F. (Ed.). (1977). *The structure of scientific theories*. Urbana, IL: University of Illinois Press.

Tallis, R. (2004). *Why the mind is not a computer: A pocket lexicon of neuromythology*. London: Macmillan.

Tallis, R. (2012). *Aping mankind: Neuromania, darwinitis and the misrepresentation of humanity*. Durham, NC: Acumen.

The Levelt Report. (2012). *Flawed science: The fraudulent research practices of social psychologist Diederik Stapel*. Levelt Committee, Noort Committee and Drenth Committee. https://www.commissielevelt.nl/. Accessed 10 May 2016.

Thirlwell, J. (2014). A history of anaesthesia journals. In E. Eger, L. Saidman, & R. Westhorpe (Eds.), *The wondrous story of anaesthesia* (pp. 443–458). New York: Springer.

Trubody, B. (2016). The seduction of science: How paradigms can lead one astray. In C. Martins & M. J. Damásio (Eds.), *Seduction in popular culture, philosophy and psychology* (pp. 1–32). Hershey, PA: IGI Global.

Wicherts, J. M., & Bakker, M. (2014). Broken windows, mediocre methods, and substandard statistics. *Group Processes & Intergroup Relations, 17*, 388–403.

Witkowski, T., & Zatonski, M. (2015). *Psychology gone wrong: The dark sides of science and therapy*. Boca Raton, FL: Brown Walker Press.

Part II
Discovery in Practice

Chapter 6
Information in Financial Markets

Catherine Greene

Abstract The concept of "information" is central to our understanding of financial markets, both in theory and in practice. Analysing information is not only a critical part of the activities of many financial practitioners, but also plays a central role in the Efficient Market Hypothesis (EMH). The central claim of this paper is that different data can count as information in financial markets and that particular investors do not consider all of the available data. This suggests that firstly, saying the price of a stock *should* be $X once a particular piece of information has been incorporated in the price is only justifiable if we know that this information really is relevant for other investors. Secondly, the EMH is often tested by looking at market behaviour after the release of information; again, this is only justified if we know that other market participants share the view that this is information. The purpose of this chapter is to suggest that there are good reasons for thinking that we do not know this. Finally, this chapter also suggests that bubbles in financial markets are best understood in terms of salience of information, rather than irrationality.

Keywords Arbitrage investor · Asset bubble · Efficient market · Financial market · Fundamental equity · Information · Macro investor · Theoretical value

6.1   Introduction

Finance is a social science that has explicitly applied equations used in the natural sciences, most notably for pricing options. Finance therefore appears to be a good example of the application of scientific discoveries to the social sciences. Despite this, there remain several fundamental concepts that are in need of further analysis. This chapter will focus on the concept of information. The concept of "information" is central to our understanding of financial markets, both in theory

C. Greene (✉)
Centre for Philosophy of Natural and Social Science, London School of Economics and Political Science, London, UK
e-mail: c.m.greene@lse.ac.uk

© Springer Nature Switzerland AG 2019   87
M. Addis et al. (eds.), *Scientific Discovery in the Social Sciences*,
Synthese Library 413, https://doi.org/10.1007/978-3-030-23769-1_6

and in practice. Analysing information is not only a critical part of the activities of many financial practitioners, but also plays a central role in the Efficient Market Hypothesis (EMH). This chapter suggests that there are two ambiguities about what information is. These are, firstly, that there is disagreement about what data counts as information and, secondly, that even when there is agreement about what data counts as information this information can mean different things. If this is accepted it follows both that hypotheses about "theoretical values" of financial assets need further elaboration, and that many tests of the EMH are not, in fact, tests of the EMH at all.

This chapter begins by introducing the role information plays in the EMH. To a great extent, this covers well-trodden ground, but lays a foundation from which more substantive points can be developed. I then adopt Skyrms' (2013) description of information as whatever alters probabilities to show that different investors do not just disagree about the significance of a particular piece of information, but also disagree about what counts as information. The central claim of this paper is that different data can count as information in financial markets and that particular investors do not consider all of the available data. This suggests that, firstly, saying the price of a stock *should* be $X once a particular piece of information has been incorporated in the price is only justifiable if we know that this information really is relevant for other investors. Secondly, the EMH is often tested by looking at market behaviour after the release of information; again, this is only justified if we know that other market participants share the view that this is information. The purpose of this chapter is to suggest that there are good reasons for thinking that we do not know this. Finally, this chapter also suggests that bubbles in financial markets are best understood in terms of salience of information, rather than irrationality.

6.2   The Efficient Market Hypothesis

Eugene Fama (1970) is usually credited with the first formulation of the Efficient Market Hypothesis (EMH), which postulates that the prices of securities traded in financial markets accurately reflect all available information. There are three forms of the EMH. The weak EMH suggests that future security prices are independent of past prices. The semi-strong EMH states that security prices reflect new public information as it becomes available. The strong EMH states that security prices accurately reflect all information, including restricted, or insider, information. Fama himself accepts that the strong EMH is not reflective of reality, but argues that it is a useful benchmark against which to judge real markets. If true, the weak EMH suggests that it should be impossible to make money by taking advantage of trends, or patterns, in security prices, and the semi-strong EMH suggests that it is impossible to benefit from analysing public information. All forms of the EMH have been challenged; firstly, by arguing that people do, in fact, manage to make money both by spotting patterns in security prices, and by analysing public information, and secondly, by questioning the conceptual framework of the EMH. This has relied on demonstrating statistical relationships between past and current security prices and highlighting behavioural features of investors that suggest information is not reflected in security prices in the efficient manner suggested by the EMH. However, I want to take a different tack.

Fama notes that the statement that "prices 'fully reflect' available information is so general that it has no empirically testable implications" (Fama, 1970, p. 384) because this leaves it unclear what it means to "fully reflect" information. His remedy is to specify more precisely the notion of "fully reflecting" information. His focus is therefore on analysing the process of price formation. It is my contention that the concept of "information" is in equal need of more precise specification. The concept of "information" is critical to the EMH, but it is largely taken as given that we know what "information" is. I argue that this cannot be taken for granted. In this chapter I use Skyrms' (2013) description of information and discuss its application to financial markets. Given the focus on "information", the primary concern is with the semi-strong EMH. However, later in the paper I discuss the implication of my conclusions for the weak EMH.

6.3   What Is Information?

Under the usual characterisation of the EMH, information is data that is relevant for the price of a security. The difficulty is with judging what is relevant. Skyrms (2013, ch. 3) provides a framework for understanding information that we can use in this context. His analysis is motivated by the evolution of sender-receiver games where senders transmit signals to receivers, who act on these signals. Biological examples include various groups of monkeys who have unique alarm calls for different predators (Skyrms, 2013, ch. 2). Skyrms says that:

> Information is carried by signals. It flows through signalling networks that not only transmit it, but also filter, combine, and process it in various ways. We can investigate the flow of information using a framework of generalised signalling games. (Skyrms, 2013, p. 33)

This picture fits financial markets particularly well, at least as far as equity markets are concerned. Companies transmit signals, which are information about their financial health, and these signals are received by investors, who combine them with other information, and, sometimes, act on these signals.

Signals transmit information, but what is information? Skyrms argues that information alters probabilities. He says, "The *informational content* of a signal consists in how the signal affects probabilities. The *quantity of information* in a signal is measured by how far it moves probabilities" (Skyrms, 2013, p. 34, italics in original). The following example illustrates the difference between informational content and the quantity of information. We begin with two possible future states (1 and 2), which are equiprobable. Some information, A, moves the probabilities to 9/10 and 1/10 for states 1 and 2 respectively. Other information, B, moves the probabilities to 1/10 and 9/10 for states 1 and 2. This is a symmetrical situation, so A and B contain the same amount of information. However, the content differs, because each piece of information moves the probabilities in an opposite direction. A moves the probability of state 1 up, while B moves the probability of 1 down. He concludes, "The key to information is moving probabilities" (Skyrms, 2013, p. 35). The subtleties of Skyrms' evolutionary models need not concern us here because they are not directly applicable; however, his description of information is relevant and yields some interesting conclusions.

This description of information fits well with financial markets, where investors are dealing with (usually implicit and subjective) probabilities of prices rising or falling. For example, an investor may believe that a company is worth £10 per share. The company then announces a higher level of earnings than expected. After taking account of this information, the investor believes that the company is now worth £10.50 per share. The shares of the company trade on the stock exchange at £9.50 per share before the earnings announcement. At this point the investor might believe that there is a 70% chance that the shares will rise to £10. After the earnings announcement he may revise his beliefs and say that there is a 90% chance that the shares will rise to £10.

Investors have three potential actions they can take with regard to any financial asset; they can buy, sell, or do nothing (if they are already invested this means holding the investment, if they are not already invested this means not buying or selling it). New information will shift investors between these actions. Applying Skyrms' (2013) framework to financial markets suggests an important question, which I will address in the following section. If information moves probabilities, how should this process be described in financial markets? We can see investors as responders to information. However, the interpretation of this information can be subjective, in other words, different investors take the quantity of information in a signal to differ. Information appears and investors adjust their expectation in the light of it, and prices move to reflect these changing expectations. However, what is interesting is that many things may move probabilities. The usual analysis of the EMH assumes that an earnings announcement is, uncontroversially, the sort of thing that moves probabilities. With this overview of Skyrms in hand, I hope to show why this may not be the case.

6.3.1   Your Information Isn't My Information

Investors pursue many different strategies, and buy securities for many different reasons. What counts as information for an investor following one strategy may not count as information for an investor following a different strategy. In other words, an earnings announcement may significantly affect one investor's assessment of the probability of a security price rising, but leave another investor's probabilities unchanged. To be clear, I am not just saying that both investors interpret the significance of the information differently, or that they disagree about the importance of the information; I am also saying that for one investor it does not count as information because it has no informational content in the sense of Skyrms' (2013) framework: it does not move the investor's assessment of the probability of the stock price rising.

I will simplify a variety of investment strategies to illustrate this. Because single stocks are the simplest financial instrument to understand, I will limit my examples to considering the different motivations for buying stocks. In reality, investors using these strategies would use a variety of instruments, and execute their trades in ways that differ from my description. However, I do not believe these simplifications alter the examples in a fundamental way. These investors are pursuing simplified versions of trading strategies used by investment funds and other financial institutions. While real investors may combine these strategies, I have picked these three strategies because they are relatively easily distinguishable. Most fundamental equity investors do not combine fundamental equity investing with macro strategies or the type of arbitrage strategy described here. Nor do users of the arbitrage strategy used here usually combine this strategy with fundamental equity investing or macro strategies.[1]

Fundamental Equity Investor The fundamental equity investor is the one described in the examples above. This type of investor analyses companies with a view to working out what their shares should be worth. To do this, they analyse current financial statements, often meet the companies' management, and model accounting data into the future. They then discount their expectations to get a "present value" for the company. They look for companies' whose listed shares are trading significantly lower or higher than this present value, or companies whose shares look cheap relative to the general market or historical valuations, and buy where the shares are lower and sell where the shares are higher.

This type of investor will care about information relating to the fundamental state of a company. They will not, usually, care about information relating to macro-economics; for example, announcements of UK GDP. In some cases, macro-economic data will be important because it directly affects a company. For example, the fundamental equity investor's model of a company that depends on exports will be affected by changes in exchange rates. However, unless macro-economic data is particularly noteworthy, quarterly GDP data, balance of payments data, and so on do not feature in their models for companies. Many fundamental equity investors see it as a requirement of their job to outperform the benchmark against which they are assessed. This is usually the main equity market index for the country or sector in which they are investing. For the UK it is often the FTSE 100. Given this focus, their concern is with picking UK companies, not worrying about the macro economic situation. As a consequence, GDP announcements (which may count as information for some other investment strategies) will not count as information for

---

[1]A brief, but thorough, overview of the main hedge fund strategies can be found at www.hedgefundresearch.com in the "Hedge Fund Strategy Classification" section. Capocci (2013) provides a more comprehensive analysis.

investors following a fundamental equity strategy. This strategy matches Capocci's Equity non-hedge strategy (Capocci, 2013, p. 275).

Macro Investor A macro investor makes investments based on their expectations for macro-economic conditions. These investors usually invest in many types of securities, including equities, derivatives and debt. For example, they may analyse country A's balance of payments, foreign currency reserves, budget announcements and export data and conclude that, although country A is expected to default on their debt, their macro-economic position is stronger than many other investors realise. In such a situation the macro investor will buy country A's debt. They may buy single equities as part of such trades. For example, if a macro investor is positive on the Greek economy and believes the Greek government will not be forced to exit the Euro zone, then they might buy listed shares of Greek banks. Similarly, a macro investor might have a positive view on commodity prices and, to take advantage of this, buy the shares of Australian mining companies.

A macro investor is concerned with different sorts of information than the fundamental equity investor. They will, primarily, care about macro-economic data. Earnings announcements by specific companies will not affect their reasons for buying an equity as much as information about larger scale data. For example, if a macro investor has purchased a mining company to take advantage of rising commodity prices they will care more about information relating to commodity prices than information relating to earnings. Now, an obvious objection is that, if commodity prices rise, the price of the equity will rise only because the rise in commodity prices will feed through to earnings. However, a macro investor will often believe that the prices of mining companies will rise well before any company level data confirms the impact on earnings; and, importantly, that mining companies as a whole will rise in price. Therefore, distinguishing between mining companies on the basis of profitability, or earnings growth, provides little marginal benefit. Differences in fundamental factors between mining companies will be swamped by the effects of the macro data. To reflect this, the macro investor will often buy all, or a representative sample of, Australian mining companies. This purchase reflects a change in the macro investor's probabilities, based on macro-economic information. Investors following other investment strategies may not alter their probabilities at all following the release of this information. This strategy matches Capocci's Macro strategy (Capocci, 2013, p. 321).

Arbitrage Investor An arbitrage investor aims to take advantage of differences in prices between securities, often ones that are related. For example, a company may be listed on two different stock exchanges, such as the London stock exchange and the Bombay stock exchange. These are shares of the same company, so should, in theory, trade at a very similar price. If they do get out of line, an arbitrage investor will sell the shares that are relatively expensive and buy the shares that are relatively cheap. Arbitrage investors also trade equities against other instruments, such as derivatives, and look for situations where prices move out of a range that is considered "normal". Such investors may also trade "baskets" of stocks, which are groups of shares that historically have been highly correlated with one another.

This type of arbitrage investor will therefore primarily be concerned with information relating to correlations and movements of prices against each other. They may monitor particularly significant macro-economic information and stock specific information. However, this is often so that they can decide whether there are reasons for historic correlations and price relationships no longer holding into the future. Investors using other investment strategies do not alter their probabilities as a result of information relating to correlations and historic relationships between prices; indeed, they may be unaware of this data. This strategy matches Capocci's Relative Value strategy (Capocci, 2013, p. 156).

Skyrms' (2013) characterisation of information in terms of moving probabilities allows me to make an important caveat. I am not arguing that each type of investor *always* cares about entirely separate types of information, but that different types of information affect different investor's assessment of the probability of a security price rising differently. The different investors disagree about the quantity of information in a signal and may change their behaviour, or the way they act, very differently. A few examples should illustrate this.

Let us suppose that the fundamental equity investor, the macro investor and the arbitrage investor have all purchased the listed equity of Company A.

The macro investor has purchased it as part of a basket of stocks because they believe its price will rise when the currency of the home country is devalued. The fundamental equity investor has bought it because the management has recently changed and they believe this will improve the performance of the company. The arbitrage investor has bought it because they have noticed that the share price of this equity has moved out of its historical alignment with another company in the same sector with which it has historically had a high correlation.

These do not just illustrate different investment strategies, but also highlight that the equity of Company A is seen in a fundamentally different way. For each investor the investment is a bet on a different factor. For the macro investor the investment is a bet on currency devaluation, for the fundamental equity investor it is a bet on improved corporate performance within the company, and for the arbitrage investor it is a bet on correlation. For each of these investors the equity of Company A is, in financial terms, a fundamentally different thing. It is a way to profit from different things.

These are the probabilities the various investors place on the equity price rising, based on their differing motivations:

Macro investor: 70% (Buy)
Fundamental equity investor: 60% (Buy)
Arbitrage investor: 75% (Buy)
Next, let us deal with the appearance of different types of information in turn.

Information 1: Over the last month there has been a significant change in the rolling correlation between Company A and the similar company in the same sector. The correlation has moved from 85% to 75%.

Revised probabilities:

Macro investor: 70% (Hold)

The macro investor is not monitoring this information, is unaware of the change and consequently does not alter their probability of the stock price rising. The macro investor makes no changes to their investment.

Fundamental equity investor: 60% (Hold)

The fundamental equity investor is also not monitoring this information, is unaware of the change and consequently does not alter their probability of the stock price rising. The fundamental equity investor makes no changes to their investment.

Arbitrage investor: 45% (Sell)

The expectation that the high correlation between the two stocks would continue was part of the motivation for the arbitrage investor buying the stock. This information is critical so this investor lowers their probability of the stock price rising significantly. The arbitrage investor sells their investment.

Information 2: Specifics about proposed cost cutting by the new management team.

Revised probabilities, and consequent behaviour:

Macro investor: 71% (Hold)

The macro investor will welcome the change, but this information does not relate directly to the reasons they have for owning the equity. Regardless of the specifics of the cost cutting plans, they believe the equity price will be driven by changes in exchange rates. In other words, the exchange rate will drive the performance of Company A, and the other companies they have bought as part of this trade, almost regardless of whether management manage to cut costs in the way they have suggested they will. The macro investor makes no changes to their investment.

Fundamental equity investor: 75% (Buy)

The expected reduction of costs will affect the valuation model that the fundamental equity investor uses and changes their expectations for the equity considerably. The fundamental equity investor buys more of the equity.

Arbitrage investor: 76% (Hold)

Unless the information about cost cutting is likely to change the way the price of this equity performs relative to the related equity, this information is unlikely to change their views significantly. The arbitrage investor makes no changes to their investment.

Information 3: The stock exchange in the country in which Company A is listed is bombed by terrorists.

Revised probabilities:

Macro investor: 30% (Sell)
This is important information for the macro investor due to the uncertainty this type of event creates. They may well try to sell their investment until they know further details about what has happened. The macro investor sells their investment.

Fundamental equity investor: 30% (Sell)
This is also important information for the fundamental equity investor. While it does not, necessarily, relate directly to the fundamentals of the company, it might do so. And until further information is received about the extent of the damage, political implications etc, the fundamental equity investor is also likely to revise their probability of the stock price falling downwards. The fundamental equity investor sells their investment.

Arbitrage investor: 30% (Sell)
The arbitrage investor will also be concerned about this information. Crises can throw historical relationships between stock prices out of alignment as investors (such as the macro investor) sell shares that they own. The arbitrage investor may also try to sell their investments, based on a lower confidence in price activity returning to the historical pattern. The arbitrage investor sells their investment.

The numbers in this example should be taken illustratively. However, this example suggests a number of conclusions. Firstly, depending on how an investor is looking at an investment, many things count as information in the sense that they affect an investor's assessment of probabilities. Secondly, some types of information are information for all investors, such as news of a terrorist attack. Thirdly, some types of information are information for investors pursuing many different strategies, but move their probabilities very differently, such as announcements of cost cutting plans. In this case, the investors disagree about the quantity of information conveyed. Fourthly, some types of information are information only for very specific types of investor, such as information about changing correlation between stocks. In this case different investors disagree about whether the data is information at all.

6.4   Implications

So far, all I have really said is that investors have access to a variety of financial data but that they do not see all of it as information. This is not terribly controversial. However, it does have some important implications. The first is conceptual, the second is methodological. The conceptual implication is that accepting the plausibility of the above example prompts a question about how we are to interpret the requirement of the EMH that prices reflect all available information. The simple answer is that, if the EMH is true, prices should reflect all the various types of information listed above, and any others we can think of. We can understand the actual price of Company A's shares as the net result of all the views about Company

A. In the case of the announcement of cost cutting plans, some investors may believe the plans are realistic, some may believe that, although they are realistic, the management team will fail to implement them. A wide variety of views are possible and these differing views will motivate a wide range of valuations for the equity. The price at which the equity trades will reflect a consensus, or balance between these views.

However, this is problematic. We have shown that many things can count as information for different investors, depending on the strategy they are pursuing. If true, then what the semi-strong EMH says is that markets should adjust to reflect whatever information investors, on average, consider relevant at a particular point in time. This does not say very much, because, over time, what investors consider relevant may change markedly. For example, Rutterford (2004) shows that the methodologies used to value equities are determined primarily by the level of market prices. For example, the idea of a "theoretical value" of an equity only came into use after the South Sea Bubble. Similarly, the information considered relevant to gauging the value of an internet stock changed as prices of those equities rose. The evolution of new investment strategies also gives rise to the consideration of other data as information. Needless to say, there is nothing to guarantee that new valuation techniques will become widespread enough to affect market prices; however, there have been widespread changes in the ways that equities have been valued. Prior to the 1920s equities were valued using dividend yield and book value, reflecting the view that equities are primarily bond-like. Rutterford chronicles the gradual rejection of this view in favour of valuing equities using P/E (price/ earnings) ratios until this became the accepted valuation methodology. A further shift change in valuation methodologies occurred during the technology bubble. Companies with no earnings cannot be valued using P/E ratios, but they can be valued by discounting cash flows (Rutterford, 2004, p. 106-117).

What, then, are we to make of the EMH? When we are clear what information is – let us suppose that we know that earnings announcements are always information in financial markets – then we can say that if the semi-strong EMH is correct, then markets should quickly adjust to the release of earnings announcements. When we are not sure that earnings announcements are always information, then when earnings are announced we cannot say how markets "should" react. Here, an important caveat is needed. It can be responded that, whatever investment strategies are pursued, earnings announcements will always count as information for many investors because they directly relate to the state of companies listed on stock exchanges. This may be true, but what matters is what information is driving the primary buyers and sellers of equities (in other words, those who are influencing the stock price) at a particular point in time. This may be investors who care about earnings announcements, but it could also be arbitrage investors, who do not.

The EMH, without further explication of the notion of "information", is empty in the sense that it gives us no expectation about future market behaviour following the earnings announcement. In other words, any price moves, post the earnings announcement, are compatible with the truth of the semi-strong EMH. Suppose that the market in question is predominantly comprised of fundamental equity investors and arbitrage investors. Further, that the arbitrage investors have more assets under management that the fundamental equity investors. Following the earnings announcement, the price of the equity does not move. It would be wrong to suppose that this should lead us to question the validity of the EMH. This is because although the fundamental equity investors adjust their expectations, and buy more of the equity, thereby fully incorporating the information contained in the earnings announcement their actions are swamped by the buying and selling of the equity by the arbitrage investors who are responding to different information entirely.

The above example also raises a question about how the EMH should deal with potential information. For example, let us suppose that the macro investor's strategy is unique. Given this, suppose that he is extremely successful and retires to a Caribbean island. Once he has left the market, does macro-economic data stop being information for the purposes of assessing Company A? We could say "yes" because, intuitively, if the information no longer moves anyone's probabilities why should we think of it as information? However, it remains potential information, if anyone were to revive the macro fund. Given that it is, potentially, but not actually, information, should efficient markets reflect it? If we answer "no", then the EMH depends on a commitment to a restricted notion of information that is time specific because, over time, investment strategies, and ways of analysing investments, change. If we answer "yes", then the EMH suggests that almost anything counts as information and should be reflected in markets.

6.4.1 Testing the EMH

The majority of studies to test the semi-strong EMH analyse the performance of securities after an announcement, or event, in order to test how quickly the market incorporates this new information. Examples of events that are analysed are dividend announcements, earnings announcements, stock splits, and the effect of Lehman's bankruptcy (see Khan & Ikram, 2010, for a summary). For example, Alexakis, Patra, and Poshakwale (2010) analyse the predictability of stock returns using accounting information. They selected 10 financial ratios and analysed a cross section of 47 companies listed on the Athens Stock Exchange. They conclude that a number of ratios, such as return of equity and price to earnings ratios were predictive of future stock returns. Thus, the prices of these stocks do not reflect publicly available accounting information, and therefore, this market is not semi-strong efficient. Similarly, Lewellen (2004) argues that dividend yield information is predictive of future equity market performance in the US.

Such studies take an announcement, such as notification of a dividend, or release of financial statements, and set out to gauge whether security prices adjust to reflect this information. Clearly, they do not count anything as information. The factors they analyse are the sorts of things in which investors are interested; they relate to the financial state of a company and its equity price. However, they do take it for granted that these things are information that is relevant to judging the price of a security over a particular period in time. In other words, Alexakis et al. assume that return on equity really is "information" in the sense that it is relevant for the price of the equities they are studying during the time period in which they are interested.

This may seem entirely reasonable. It is reasonable because many investors in equities discount future dividends or earnings in order to calculate a "present value" for an equity. They seek to calculate what a company is worth. Given this, the return on equity, or earnings, or cash flow information are obviously relevant for judging the value of a company. However, if the analysis above is accepted, then we cannot take it as given that the most significant investors in a security are the types of investors who view this "information" as information for their strategies. If not, then there is no reason why the market price of a security should reflect this information. The usual conclusion of research suggesting that market prices do not adjust to the release of information is to argue that they are not semi-strong efficient. However, an alternative, and plausible conclusion, is that this was not information for the most influential investors in this security.

In effect, this raises the question of the retiring macro investor. Certain financial ratios, or other information "could" be information. In the same way that exchange rate information could be information. However, if there is no macro investor to take advantage of it, in an important sense it is not information. Similarly, unless we know that the investors participating in a particular market did move their probabilities because of this accounting information, then it remains merely potential information.

An obvious objection is that there are numerous studies which analyse changes in equity prices after earnings announcements (for a recent example, see Olibe, 2016) which illustrate that earnings announcements are information. However, there is also data suggesting that this is not the whole story. Coulton, Dinh, and Jackson (2016) study how investor sentiment is critical to understanding how prices react to information. They say, "The focus of this study is to analyse the impact of economy-wide sentiment on the price formation process" (Coulton et al., 2016, p. 670). They conclude that the speed with which prices respond to information varies with investor sentiment. They write, "Our results challenge the maintained assumption within capital markets research that stock price reactions are independent of the state of the economy. By showing that the price formation process varies depending upon economy-wide sentiment . . . " (Coulton et al., 2016, p. 692). They distinguish between stock specific information and investor sentiment, but we can, instead, characterise this in terms of investor responses to different types of information; data relating to the macro economic situation, and data relating to specific stocks. It is compatible with the framework outlined above that investors consider different data to be more informative at different times. In other words, that macro-economic data moves investors' probabilities to a greater or lesser extent over time, and this affects the extent to which stock specific data moves probabilities.

The point of this chapter is not to suggest that stock specific data is not information, but to suggest that there are many other types of data which may also be information, and which may, sometimes, be the information driving prices. A simple example illustrates the intuition behind this. Suppose that I believe that, based on certain accounting information, the price of Company A's listed shares, which are currently trading at £12, should trade at £15. Then, if over a period of weeks they rise to £15, I cannot say that they rose because my valuation was correct, or that the share price rose because the accounting information became reflected in the price. This is the second methodological implication of the framework discussed next.

6.4.2 Calculating Theoretical Value

When calculating a value for securities an investor tries to work out what the price of a security should be. They may use a variety of methodologies for doing this. When an investor believes that a security price should be different from the price at which it is currently trading, then they are likely to buy, or sell the security on the expectation that the market price will adjust to reflect the information in the investor's pricing model. Let us continue with the example above. Company A releases information about cost cutting plans. Suppose that the company's press release is discussed in the financial press, where most journalists argue that the management will not be able to achieve their cost cutting targets. Suppose that I spend a lot of time with the company's management and believe, not only that they will succeed, but that, when they do, Company A will be in a considerably stronger position than other investors believe. Based on my expectations I believe Company A's shares should trade at £16. They currently trade at £12. I buy Company A shares and wait. Let us suppose that the cost cutting program proceeds in the way that the management team suggested it would. The shares rise steadily to £14. My most obvious explanation of this is that I am right in my assessment on company A, and what the shares are worth.

However, I cannot be sure of this, based on the stock price moves alone. All I have confirmed in this situation is that my assessment of Company A's management and their ability to cut costs is correct. I have not confirmed that the stock price has risen because other investors are adjusting to this information. This is because I have no idea whether the investors responsible for influencing the stock price care about this information. And even if they do care about this information, that they interpret it in the same way. The price of Company A's shares may have risen because investors have reacted to other information entirely. Perhaps even to information of which I am unaware. For example, many macro investors may have bought Company A because of views about the economy in which Company A operates and do not care at all about cost cutting.

To demonstrate that the price of Company A's share price rose as other investors incorporated the implications of the cost cutting plans, I need to show, firstly, that a sufficient number of investors view Company A in the same way that I do; as a fundamental equity investment. Secondly, I then need to show that they did, in fact, change their expectations about the company because of the cost cutting plans. This is not impossible, but complicated by the highly diversified nature of financial markets.

Questioning the status of the theoretical value of financial assets is not new. One recent example is McCauley, who writes that the idea of the "real value" of a financial asset is "not a uniquely defined idea: there are at least five different definitions of "value" in finance theory" (2004, p. 64). These are: book value, the replacement price of a firm, the value calculated by discounting dividends and returns infinitely into the future, the idea of valuation discussed by Modigliani and Miller (1958), and finally, the market price. However, even if investors do manage to calculate a theoretical value for a financial asset "there is no guarantee that the market will eventually go along with your sentiment within your prescribed time frame" (McCauley, 2004, p. 71). McCauley elaborates on this later, suggesting that most investors are looking at noise, which he defines as "useless information" (2004, p. 102), while a few investors (he suggests Soros and Buffet as examples) have "useful information that can be applied to extract unusual profits from the market" (2004, p. 102). In other words, there are different ways of calculating theoretical value. This is not necessarily problematic because, as described above, valuation methodologies have changed over time and, depending on investors' views about investments, different methodologies might be appropriate in different contexts. McCauley's second observation, that markets may not reflect an investor's theoretical value, is the more interesting one, in particular his distinction between "useless" and "useful" information. The difference between the two is that the first does not allow an investor to make profits, while the second does.

My response to this is that McCauley's is not a meaningful distinction because the difference he points to is merely pragmatic. There is no reason why the information used by Soros and Buffet necessarily enables the generation of profits. It is just that the information they use is also seen as information by enough other investors. Discussing the role of hedge funds (including Soros' fund) in the Exchange Rate Mechanism crisis of 1992, Capocci writes, "These funds played the role of leader; their positioning was perceived as a signal that led other players to either take the same positions to make money or avoid taking a position against it" (Capocci, 2013, p. 467). In other words, it is not necessarily that Soros had better, or more useful, information, but that his taking a position in a financial asset was information for other investors in and of itself. Capocci suggests that knowledge of his ownership may have been all the information they needed. However, other investors taking the same positions as Buffet or Soros is consistent with a number of different possibilities. The first is that, as Capocci suggests, investors are copying the purchases and sales made by Buffet or Soros. The second is that they explicitly apply Buffet or Soros' research methodology, which is enabled by the number of books written by these two investors outlining the way they look at financial markets (examples include "Soros on Soros: Staying Ahead of the Curve" by George Soros, and "The Essays of Warren Buffett: Lessons for Corporate America" edited by L. A. Cunningham, which has been reprinted a number of times). Which of these possibilities is, in fact, occurring is not the central concern here because it is the result that is important; if a sufficient number of investors make the same investments they are likely to make profits.

The central point of disagreement with McCauley is therefore that Soros and Buffet do not have "useful" information *per se*, but that the information they have is only useful if it is seen to be so by a sufficient number of investors, either directly by other investors replicating their investments, or indirectly by other investors adopting their methodologies. This implies that a stock has no objective value, which different investors attempt to approximate using different methods. Instead, it suggests that stocks have no objective value, just that investors have differing estimates of what their value is and that some of these estimates are shared more widely among the investment community than others.

6.4.3 Asset Price Bubbles-Responding to Different Information

The literature on bubbles in financial assets is extensive: the IMF Working paper (Scherbina, 2013) and Hüsler, Sornette, and Hommes (2013) both provide a good overview. The final implication of accepting the above description of information in financial markets is that it suggests a non-standard description of bubbles in asset prices. Bubbles are usually described as occasions where prices move away from fundamental values for a significant period of time. This description of bubbles suggests that investors buy stocks at values higher than their intrinsic worth. However, as described above, many investors adopted new valuation techniques for internet stocks because, on traditional P/E based valuations, stocks were extraordinarily expensive. So, we can describe this situation differently, as one where investors respond to different information, such as forecasts about the growth of the internet, the digital economy, and future earnings potential of companies, rather than current earnings. We can also include data on past returns, and the performance of investors who have participated in the bubble, as information. Understood in this light, the high prices paid for internet companies were a response to the data that investors considered informative at the time, not a move away from an intrinsically correct value. This is not to say that decisions to invest were always good ones, because many investors lost a lot of money. But the decisions to pay high prices were poor decisions not because investors paid more than a stock was worth, but because they invested on the basis of information which was no longer seen to be information by other investors. Exactly how investors change their minds about what data is information is an interesting project for further research.

6.5 Conclusion

This chapter has proposed a framework for understanding what "information" is in financial markets. I have argued that information can be understood as data that moves investors' probabilities. Further, that investors following different strategies may consider different data to be information. Accepting this view has a number of implications. It follows from this that traditional ways of testing the EMH are not as conclusive as they often appear to be. It also follows that hypotheses about the theoretical values of financial assets require more confirmation than ordinarily supposed. Finally, and more speculatively, I have suggested that it also motivates a non-standard interpretation of bubbles in financial assets.

References

Alexakis, C., Patra, T., & Poshakwale, S. (2010). Predictability of stock returns using financial statement information: Evidence on semi-strong efficiency of emerging Greek stock market. *Applied Financial Economics, 20*, 1321–1326.

Capocci, D. (2013). *The complete guide to hedge funds and hedge fund strategies.* London: Palgrave MacMillan.

Coulton, J. J., Dinh, T., & Jackson, A. B. (2016). The impact of sentiment on price discovery. *Accounting and Finance, 56*, 669–694.

Fama, E. F. (1970). Efficient capital markets: A review of theory and empirical work. *The Journal of Finance, 25*, 383–417.

Hüsler, A., Sornette, D., & Hommes, C. H. (2013). Super-exponential bubbles in lab experiments: Evidence for anchoring over-optimistic expectations on price. *Journal of Economic Behaviour and Organization, 92*, 304–316.

Khan, A. Q., & Ikram, S. (2010). Testing semi-strong form of efficient market hypothesis in relation to the impact of foreign institutional investors' (FII's) investments on Indian capital market. *International Journal of Trade, Economics and Finance, 1*, 373–379.

Lewellen, J. (2004). Predicting returns with financial ratios. *Journal of Financial Economics, 74*, 209–235.

McCauley, J. L. (2004). *Dynamics of markets: Econophysics and finance.* Cambridge, UK: Cambridge University Press.

Modigliani, F., & Miller, M. H. (1958). The cost of capital, corporation finance and the theory of investment. *The American Economic Review, 48*, 261–297.

Olibe, K. O. (2016). Security returns and value responses around international financial reporting standards (IFRS) earnings announcements. *The International Journal of Accounting, 51*, 240–265.

Rutterford, J. (2004). From dividend yield to discounted cash flow: A history of UK and US equity valuation techniques. *Accounting, Business & Financial History, 14*, 115–149.

Scherbina, A. (2013). *Asset price bubbles: A selective survey* (IMF Working Paper). Institute for Capacity Development. Available at www.imf.org

Skyrms, B. (2013). *Signals: Evolution, learning and information.* Oxford, UK: Oxford University Press.

Chapter 7
The Logic of Scientific Discovery in Macroeconomics

Tobias Henschen

Abstract There have been a number of findings in macroeconomics that appear to be worthy of the title of scientific discovery. A striking fact about these discoveries is that they refer to causal relations, i.e. to relations that permit policy manipulations of one aggregate quantity to influence another. And the problem with causal relations in macroeconomics is that empirical corroboration of specific causal relations is impossible. The present chapter takes this problem to imply that scientific discovery in macroeconomics has been following a Kuhnian logic and not, as many theorists believe, a Lakatosian logic: that scientific discovery in macroeconomics has been driven by ideology and not empirical corroboration. The paper argues further that in macroeconomics, the Kuhnian logic of scientific discovery comes with a high social cost of failed policies, output declines, high inflation and so on, and that the Kuhnian logic can and should be replaced with a macroeconomic variant of Popper's situational logic.

Keywords Causal inference · Falsification · Great depression · Kuhnian paradigm · Keynesian economics · Lakatos programme · Macroeconomics · Neoclassical economics · Situational logic

7.1 Introduction

There have been a number of findings in macroeconomics that appear to be worthy of the title of scientific discovery: the Keynesian discovery that an increase in aggregate demand or the money stock raises employment and aggregate output; the neoclassical discovery that output growth is driven exclusively by technological progress; the neo-Keynesian discovery that an expansionary monetary policy shock

T. Henschen (✉)
Faculty of Philosophy, University of Konstanz, Konstanz, Germany
e-mail: tobias.henschen@uni-konstanz.de

© Springer Nature Switzerland AG 2019   103
M. Addis et al. (eds.), *Scientific Discovery in the Social Sciences*,
Synthese Library 413, https://doi.org/10.1007/978-3-030-23769-1_7

decreases the real interest rate and increases output and inflation etc.[1] What is the logic that these discoveries follow? Theorists find it convenient to describe this logic in Lakatosian terms: Blaug (1976) presents classical and Keynesian economics as scientific research programs (SRPs) and the latter as theoretically and empirically progressive in comparison with the former. Maddock (1984) and Weintraub (1988) characterise neoclassical economics as a theoretically and empirically progressive SRP. And it is only a small step to think of neo-Keynesian economics as an SRP that is theoretically and empirically progressive in comparison with neo-classical economics. But there is a snag in describing the logic of macroeconomic discovery in Lakatosian terms. Empirical progress presupposes empirical corroboration, and it is not so clear whether empirical corroboration is forthcoming in macroeconomics.

A striking fact about scientific discoveries in macroeconomics is that they refer to relations that permit policy manipulations of one quantity to influence another. Keynesians think that manipulations of aggregate demand or the money stock lead to changes in employment and aggregate output. Neoclassicists believe that policy manipulations that promote technological progress lead to an increase in output growth. And neo-Keynesians hold that manipulations in the shape of expansionary monetary policy shocks decrease the real interest rate and increase output and inflation. It is true that macroeconomists are not exclusively interested in relations that permit policy manipulations of one quantity to influence another (they are also interested in relations that allow for explanation, statistical inference or forecast). But tradition and the widespread use of macroeconomic models by policymaking institutions suggest that relations that permit manipulations of one quantity to influence another are of primary importance to macroeconomists. It is therefore not surprising that in macroeconomics, scientific discoveries refer to relations that might be exploitable for policy purposes.

Relations that permit manipulations of one quantity to influence another are relations that philosophers (e.g. Pearl, 2009; Woodward, 2003) and some macroeconomists (e.g. Hoover, 2001) refer to as "causal". Scientific discoveries in macroeconomics may therefore be said to refer to causal relations: the Keynesians discovered that aggregate demand and the money stock are causes of (or causally relevant to) employment and aggregate output; the neoclassicists discovered that technological progress is a cause of (or causally relevant to) output growth; and the neo-Keynesians discovered that an expansionary monetary policy shock is a negative cause of the real interest rate and a positive cause of output and inflation. The problem with causal relations in macroeconomics is that empirical corroboration of specific causal relations is impossible. The only evidence that macroeconomists can provide in support of the hypothesis that X is a cause of Y, and that all sides accept as a neutral arbiter, reduces to a correlation between X and Y. And given the common cause principle, there are at least two further hypotheses

---

[1]Do these findings really qualify as discoveries? The answer is 'yes'. It will turn out below, however, that they qualify as discoveries only in a Kuhnian sense.

that are compatible with that correlation: the hypothesis that Y is a cause of X, and the hypothesis that there is a variable (or set of variables) Z that causes both X and Y.

If empirical corroboration in the Lakatosian sense is impossible, then the logic of macroeconomic discovery has to be described in Kuhnian, not Lakatosian terms. The Kuhnian logic is not as different from the Lakatosian one as is sometimes suggested: just as an SRP has a hard core, a protective belt and a progressive and degenerating phase, a Kuhnian paradigm can fall into and emerge from crisis and is characterised by (theoretical or mathematical) principles that are held on to for long, while the empirical statements and auxiliary assumptions at its periphery are more easily given up in the process of normal science activity. It is likewise mistaken to think that the difference between SRPs and paradigms relates to the time span during which an SRP or paradigm comes into being. The decisive difference between SRPs and paradigms is in fact that in the case of the former, scientific discovery is driven by theoretical and empirical progress, while in the case of the latter it is driven only by theoretical progress and theoretical progress by ideology.

If the logic of scientific discovery in macroeconomics is of the Kuhnian and not the Lakatosian kind, then what drives macroeconomic discovery is ideology. This conclusion is not particularly uplifting. But it at least partly explains why macroeconomists often fail to predict real-economy crises or to propose adequate means of mitigating them when they arrive. Macroeconomists perceive real-economy crises (like an extraordinary decline in aggregate output or rise in inflation) as anomalies, i.e. as violations of the paradigm-induced expectations that govern their normal science activities. They of course respond to these anomalies by adjusting or replacing the paradigm, i.e. by turning the anomalous into something that is to be expected. But it is clear that the adjusted or new paradigm will induce expectations that at some point will be violated by another anomaly again.

In macroeconomics, the permanent alteration of normal science and scientific crisis comes with a high social cost of failed policies, output declines, high inflation etc. It is accordingly questionable whether the Kuhnian logic of macroeconomic discovery is the one that should be followed. But is there a logic that might pass for an attractive alternative? It might appear plausible to claim that there simply is not any such alternative, that there is no way of avoiding the high social cost of failed policies and so on, that the state-of-the-art methods in macroeconomics are the best we have etc. The present paper is nonetheless supposed to speculate about the prospects of replacing the Kuhnian logic with a more viable alternative. And the alternative that it is going to defend is a variant of Popper's situational logic.

Popper's situational logic is sometimes dismissed as "obscure", "inconsistent" or irrelevant to contemporary concerns. And it seems that such dismissals are not entirely unjustified. In the present paper, I shall nonetheless attempt to come up with a consistent interpretation of Popper's writings on situational logic that is not irrelevant to contemporary concerns. I will argue, more specifically, that the high social cost of failed policies etc. could be avoided (or at least attenuated) if scientific discoveries were made as part of a normal science activity, and that Popper's situational logic has the potential to allow for scientific discoveries of that sort if a situational analyst (a scientist applying situational logic) is understood as a scientist who (a) accepts the rationality principle only conditionally (and is therefore protected against anomalies in the shape of patterns of irrational behaviour); who (b) realises that ideologies might lead to preferences for (e.g. Keynesian, neo-classical, neo-Keynesian) models that inadequately capture the situation at hand (and who therefore is able to roll back the influence of ideologies as much as possible); and who (c) can develop tentative models for the situation at hand (and is therefore familiar with adequate models for as many social situations as possible – a familiarity that is acquired through the study of causes that, like shifting liquidity preferences, can be ignored in many situations but have been relevant in earlier situations and might become relevant again). The hope is that this interpretation gives rise to a logic of macroeconomic discovery that might pass for an attractive alternative to the Kuhnian logic.

The interpretation of Popper's writings on situational logic will be presented in the fourth and final section of the paper. The second section will analyse the various attempts to describe the logic of macroeconomic discovery in Lakatosian terms. The third section will argue that the logic of scientific discovery that macroeconomists have been following so far has to be regarded as Kuhnian. A decisive premise in that argument is the claim that the empirical evidence that can be provided in support of causal relations in macroeconomics is in principle too inconclusive to support specific causal relations. The argument in support of that claim is intricate and important. But the present paper can only provide a sketch of that argument. Further elaboration of it needs to await another occasion.

7.2   Keynesian, Neoclassical and Neo-Keynesian Macroeconomics: Programs ...

A Lakatosian SRP is defined as a network of interconnected theories and models that consists of a hard core and a protective belt, and that is theoretically and empirically progressive, while also capable of degeneration (Lakatos & Musgrave, 1970, pp. 132–135). The hard core of an SRP contains its rigid parts: purely metaphysical beliefs and a positive heuristic, i.e. a partially articulated set of suggestions or hints on how to change, develop or sophisticate its more flexible parts. The protective belt contains these more flexible parts: auxiliary assumptions and observation reports that combine with the hard core to form the specific testable theories with which the SRP earns its scientific reputation. An SRP is theoretically progressive if its successive formulations contain excess empirical content over its predecessor, i.e. predict some novel fact; and it is empirically progressive if this excess empirical content is corroborated. But an SRP is not scientific once and for all: it becomes degenerate if it is characterised by the endless addition of *ad hoc* adjustments that merely accommodate whatever new facts become available.

Theorists find it convenient to revert to the idea of a Lakatosian SRP when describing the logic of scientific discovery in macroeconomics. Blaug (1976, pp.

358–60), for instance, describes classical economics and Keynesian macroeconomics as SRPs and the latter as theoretically progressive in comparison with the former. He says that the hard core of the Keynesian SRP is continuous with that of the classical SRP in that it retains the ideas of general equilibrium (with a possible exception for the labour market), perfect competition and comparative statics, and that it departs from it in that it contains the radically new beliefs that macroeconomic aggregates must not be reduced to individual-level agents; that the whole economy consists of three interrelated markets for goods, bonds and labour; that what adjusts to changing economic conditions is output (not prices); and that macroeconomic analysis has to concentrate on the short run and to allow for pervasive uncertainty and the possibility of destabilising expectations.

Blaug maintains that the positive heuristic of the Keynesian SRP points the way to national income accounting and statistical estimation of both the consumption function and the period-multiplier, and that the auxiliary assumptions of its protective belt relate to a number of new conceptions: the consumption function, the multiplier, autonomous expenditures, speculative demand for money etc. Blaug also claims that the Keynesian SRP is theoretically progressive in the sense that it makes novel predictions about familiar facts (its principal novel prediction being output and employment declines in the absence of adequate fiscal policy measures), and that to the extent that the Keynesian SRP is progressive, the classical SRP is degenerate: the explanations that the proponents of the classical SRP provide to account for the Great Depression (the surplus of many government budgets in the 1930s, tight monetary policies between 1929 and 1932, the breakdown of the international gold standard etc.) are *ad hoc* in the sense that they leave the full-employment-equilibrium implications of standard theory intact. Blaug (1976, p. 361), finally, suggests that the post-war history of the Keynesian SRP is one of steady degeneration: first, the Keynesian prediction of output and employment declines began to lose its plausibility; then Harrod and Domar discarded more or less the whole hard core of the Keynesian SRP when developing a primitive theory of growth; and finally Friedman's monetarist counterrevolution arrived.

In a similar vein, Weintraub and Maddock describe neoclassical macroeconomics as a Lakatosian SRP that is theoretically progressive with respect to the Keynesian SRP. Weintraub (1988, p. 214), for instance, maintains that the hard core of the neoclassical SRP consists of the beliefs that economic agents exist, that these agents have preferences over outcomes, that independent agents optimise subject to constraints, that choices are made in interrelated markets, that agents have full relevant knowledge, and that observable outcomes are coordinated and must be discussed with reference to equilibrium states. Weintraub (1988, p. 214) further suggests that the positive heuristic of the neoclassical SRP requires the construction of theories or models that make predictions about changes in equilibrium states, and that presuppose that agents optimise and behave rationally. The protective belt of the neoclassical SRP, by contrast, consists of sequences of neoclassical models like the ones that Weintraub (1988, pp. 215–218) discusses in his case study (game theoretic models of the way in which preferences restrict 2-person household demand). Maddock (1984, p. 294) points out that the neoclassical SRP is theoretically progressive in that it predicts the rationality of expectations and the ineffectiveness of policy even in the short run. It is also clear that at some point the neoclassical SRP entered its stage of degeneration. When Maddock and Weintraub analysed the neoclassical SRP in the 1980s, it had not yet entered this stage. But soon a number of difficulties became visible that could not be dispelled except by the addition of numerous ad hoc adjustments: the difficulty that monetary shocks seem to have real effects, the difficulty that large technology shocks (that according to the neoclassical macroeconomists represent the sole determinants of aggregate fluctuations) rarely become apparent etc.

As far as I can see, there have not been any attempts yet to describe neo-Keynesian macroeconomics as Lakatosian SRP. But such a description seems rather straightforward. The hard core of the neo-Keynesian SRP is continuous with the hard core of the neoclassical SRP except for important differences in their respective programs of micro-foundations: according to the neoclassical program, the economy is perfectly Walrasian (i.e. perfectly competitive with firms acting as price-takers); according to the neo-Keynesian program, by contrast, there are important barriers to price adjustment in the goods and labour market. The positive heuristic of the neo-Keynesian SRP is similar to that of the neoclassical SRP. And the protective belt of the neo-Keynesian SRP contains sequences of models that are very different from the models in the protective belt of the neoclassical SRP. Unlike the latter, the models in the protective belt of the neo-Keynesian SRP predict that a contractionary monetary-policy shock raises the real interest rate and lowers output and inflation, that a positive shock to private aggregate demand raises output and inflation and has no impact on the real interest rate, and that an unfavourable inflation shock raises inflation but has no other effects. These predictions arguably render the neo-Keynesian SRP theoretically progressive in comparison with the neoclassical SRP. Especially since the real-economy crisis of 2008–2009 the neo-Keynesian models used in central banks and other policymaking institutions have often been criticised for failing to account for the seemingly important non-Walrasian features of credit markets or the seemingly important irrational patterns of behaviour of economic agents. It is not yet clear, however, whether these criticisms have heralded the degenerating phase of the neo-Keynesian SRP. Perhaps these criticisms can be met by extending the neo-Keynesian models in appropriate ways.

A striking fact about the above descriptions of the Keynesian, neoclassical and neo-Keynesian SRPs is that a convincing account of the empirical progress of these SRPs is perspicuously absent. Maddock (1984, p. 299) simply admits that while the neoclassical SRP was "theoretically progressive, strong empirical corroboration was not forthcoming". And Weintraub does not even attempt to show that the neoclassical SRP is empirically progressive. All he argues is that in a sequence of neoclassical models (the game-theoretic models mentioned above), some are empirically progressive with respect to others (see Weintraub, 1988, pp. 218–223). Blaug provides a very interesting account of the empirical progress of the Keynesian SRP. He admits that macroeconomists have explicitly subscribed to but rarely practiced Popper's methodology of "sophisticated" falsificationism. But he also argues that the history of economics can be reconstructed as "internal history" in the sense of Lakatos (1971, pp. 91–92).

Lakatos seems to believe that economists have never seriously committed themselves to Popper's methodology (see Lakatos & Musgrave, 1970, p. 179n). Blaug (1976, p. 357), by contrast, defends the claim that economists have explicitly subscribed to but rarely practiced that methodology. He concedes that naïve falsificationism (the idea that a single refutation would be sufficient to overthrow a scientific theory) would leave virtually nothing standing. But he also says that sophisticated falsificationism (the idea that a series of refutations is needed to overthrow a theory) is methodologically suitable for economics. He observes that economists have focused on confirmation instead of (sophisticated) falsification: "empirical work in economics is like 'playing tennis with the net down': instead of attempting to refute testable predictions, economists spend much of their time showing that the real world bears out their predictions, thus replacing falsification, which is difficult, with confirmation, which is easy" (see Blaug, 1976, p. 363). According to Blaug, however, their preoccupation with confirmation does not imply that Keynesian macroeconomics cannot be thought of as empirically progressive with respect to classical economics.

Blaug holds on the contrary that the history of the development of Keynesian macroeconomics can be reconstructed as internal history, i.e. as a series of moves from one SRP to another. As a series of moves from one SRP to another, internal history is decisively different from "external history", i.e. from an account of the historical development of a scientific discipline that does not only consider the normal pressures of the social and political environment that are usually associated with the word "external", but also any failure of scientists to act according to the internal history of their discipline. In his reply to Lakatos, Kuhn insists that "what Lakatos conceives as history is not history at all but philosophy fabricating examples" (Lakatos & Musgrave, 1970, p. 240). But Blaug (1976, p. 356) argues that, in his reply to Kuhn, Lakatos (1971, pp. 116–120) can score a logical victory by claiming that his approach represents an SRP that is progressive in the sense that it leads to the discovery of novel historical facts. What Blaug attempts to show is accordingly that while economists might not have converted to Keynesian macroeconomics on the basis of a consistent application of the methodology of sophisticated falsificationism, the history of the development of Keynesian macroeconomics can be reconstructed in such a way that they could have converted to it on that basis.

7.3   . . . or Paradigms?

It is important to see, however, that Blaug's attempt is bound to fail. It is bound to fail because in macroeconomics, excess empirical content must be thought of as a causal hypothesis (or set of causal hypotheses) that is part of a progressive SRP but not of its degenerate predecessor, and because the empirical evidence that can be provided in support of that hypothesis (or set of hypotheses) is too inconclusive in principle. The methods that macroeconomists can use infer that evidence comprises econometric causality tests (e.g. Hoover, 2001, chapters 8–10) and natural experiments. But econometric causality tests rely on natural experiments in an important sense: conditions that need to be satisfied in order for causal evidence to be forthcoming from econometric causality tests include conditions that need to be satisfied if causal evidence is to be inferred from a natural experiment.[2] And the evidence that can be inferred from natural experiments in macroeconomics typically reduces to correlations. Macroeconomists observing natural experiments sometimes claim that there are additional pieces of evidence: co-occurrences of changes in two variables that they think are causally related, the temporal order of these changes etc. But these additional pieces of evidence usually cannot serve as neutral arbiters among competing causal hypotheses.

If the evidence that can be provided in support of the hypothesis that X (e.g. changes in the money stock) is a cause of Y (e.g. changes in aggregate output) reduces to a correlation between X and Y, then given the common cause principle, there are at least two further hypotheses that are compatible with that correlation: the hypothesis that Y is a cause of X, and the hypothesis that there is a variable (or set of variables) Z that causes both X and Y. In other disciplines, scientists use theory or conduct randomised controlled trials to disentangle causal hypotheses that are observationally equivalent: while in astronomy, for instance, they use theory, in the medical sciences and some microeconomic disciplines (such as labour economics) they use randomised controlled trials (RCTs). In macroeconomics, by contrast, competing pieces of economic theory can be used to support each of the competing but observationally equivalent hypotheses. In macroeconomics, it is moreover impossible to conduct RCTs: it is uncertain whether macroeconomists can manipulate expectations of inflation, aggregate demand etc.; and the random samples that they would have to draw from a population of macroeconomic systems would necessarily be small.

If the evidence that macroeconomists can provide in support of causal hypothesis is too inconclusive in principle, then the difficulty of convincingly accounting for any empirical progress of Keynesian, neoclassical and neo-Keynesian macroeconomics is unsurprising. But the in-principle inconclusiveness of causal evidence in macroeconomics also explains why empirical progress in macroeconomics is impossible, why neither sophisticated falsificationism nor even confirmation come into consideration as logic of scientific discovery that macroeconomists should or even could commit themselves to, and why the Kuhnian logic must be the one that they follow as a matter of fact (whether they want to or not). Here is how Kuhn (1996, p. 52) describes scientific discovery in general: "Discovery commences with the awareness of anomaly, i.e. with the recognition that nature has somehow

---

[2]The conditions that need to be satisfied if causal evidence is to be inferred from natural experiments are basically the four conditions that figure in Woodward's (2003, p. 98) definition of "intervention variable".

violated the paradigm-induced expectations that govern normal science. It then continues with a more or less extended exploration of the area of anomaly. And it closes only when the paradigm theory has been adjusted so that the anomalous has become expected." According to Kuhn, that is, scientific discovery runs through approximately three stages. In its first stage, an existing paradigm is confronted with an anomaly: with one or many instances that call into question explicit and fundamental generalisations of the paradigm (Kuhn, 1996, p. 82), that inhibit applications of particular practical importance (Kuhn, 1996, p. 82), and that cannot be ignored or accommodated by slight modifications in the theory's periphery (Kuhn, 1996, p. 81). In its second stage, scientists turn to "a more or less extended exploration of the area of anomaly": to a philosophical analysis with the aim of re-formulating the theoretical and mathematical foundations of the paradigmatic theory such that the anomalous becomes expected (Kuhn, 1996, p. 88). In its final stage, a new paradigmatic theory is established: a theory that implies as a fact what was earlier seen as anomalous.

It seems that the macroeconomic discoveries mentioned above fit this description very well. All these discoveries involved important re-formulations of the theoretical foundations (or "hard core") of the respective preceding paradigm. And all these discoveries commenced with the awareness of anomaly. In the case of the Keynesian discovery that an increase in aggregate demand or the money stock raises employment and aggregate output, the anomaly was the Great Depression. The Great Depression resulted in levels of (involuntary) unemployment that had been unheard of until then. High (involuntary) unemployment was not to be expected from the point of view of classical economics, because according to classical economics, everyone willing to work at the prevailing wage would be employed. High (involuntary) unemployment also inhibited applications of particular practical importance since classical economics did not imply any causal relations that could be exploited for the purpose of fighting unemployment. From the point of view of Keynesian economics, by contrast, high (involuntary) unemployment was something to be expected under specific conditions. Keynesian economics also recommended an expansionary fiscal or monetary policy as an adequate means of fighting unemployment.[3]

In the case of the neoclassical discovery that output growth is driven exclusively by technological progress, the anomaly was a simultaneous increase in inflation and unemployment in the early 1970s. Before that increase, policymaking institutions had assumed that they could exploit the output-inflation trade-off described by the Phillips curve: that they could have low unemployment by putting up with high inflation and low inflation by condoning high unemployment. But after that increase, there was no way of exploiting that trade-off. While the simultaneous increase

---

[3]It is true that Keynesians first downplayed the role of the supply of money, and that monetarism might accordingly be conceived of as a paradigm of its own. But when Hicks (1937) and Modigliani (1944) developed the IS-LM model, they translated the blurred message of Keynesian prose into the formal language of an elegant model that could also be taken to account for the role of the supply of money. Today, moreover, Keynesians take the importance of monetary policy for granted.

in inflation and employment was not to be expected from the point of view of Keynesian economics, it was to be expected when Lucas (1972) described inflation as a function of output and a weighted average of rational inflation expectations and inflation of the preceding period. But this description, of course, had the important implication of the ineffectiveness of inflation-related policy.

In the case of the neo-Keynesian discovery that an expansionary monetary policy shock decreases the real interest rate and increases output and inflation etc., the anomaly was a continuous increase in inflation from business cycle to business cycle throughout the 1970s. In the absence of any noteworthy monetary policy measures, these high levels of inflation were not to be expected from the point of view of neoclassical macroeconomics. Neo-Keynesian macroeconomics, by contrast, managed to account for them by tampering with the neoclassical program of micro-foundations: by allowing for barriers to price adjustment and other nominal frictions in the goods and labour market. To the mind of neo-Keynesian macroeconomists, the apparent effectiveness of inflation-related policy in the 1980s provided further proof of the adequacy of the neo-Keynesian paradigm. A sharp increase in the federal funds rate in 1981 is believed to have brought inflation under control, though perhaps at the cost of the recession of 1981–2 during which the US unemployment rate rose to almost 11%.

It is too early to judge whether the crisis of 2008–2009 (resulting in unusually high rates of decline in GDP across many countries) has triggered the development of a new paradigmatic theory, or whether it can be accounted for within the neo-Keynesian paradigm, more broadly conceived. Once the crisis was recognised, neo-Keynesian macroeconomists came up with a number of policy measures that (like the execution of stimulus packages and large-scale purchases of government debt and toxic assets) are widely believed to have at least attenuated the crisis. But it is also clear that the crisis was not to be expected from the point of view of the neo-Keynesian paradigm. That paradigm allowed non-Walrasian features like nominal rigidities only for the goods and labour markets, and not for the credit market. And its program of micro-foundations perhaps over-rigidly adhered to the principle of the rationality of economic agents. It is therefore not exaggerated to say that the crisis of 2008–2009 represented an anomaly: a violation of the paradigm-induced expectations that govern neo-Keynesian macroeconomics.

Note that the idea of a Kuhnian paradigm is not very different from that of a Lakatosian SRP. Like the hard core of a Lakatosian SRP, a Kuhnian paradigm includes metaphysical and mathematical principles that remain untouched in times of normal-science activity. Like the protective belt of a Lakatosian SRP, a Kuhnian paradigm contains various auxiliary assumptions and observation reports that are added or removed in times of normal-science activity, where normal-science or problem-solving activity is characterised by a general agreement among scientists about the puzzles that require solution and the general form the solution will take (see Kuhn, 1996, pp. 35–42). And like the positive heuristic of a Lakatosian SRP, a Kuhnian paradigm features a number of strategies that are meant to immunise it against recalcitrant evidence.

Note further that SRPs and paradigms do not necessarily differ with respect to the time span during which they come into being. It is true that in the first edition of *The Structure of Scientific Revolutions*, Kuhn refers to the Copernican, Newtonian, or Einsteinian revolutions to illustrate his logic of scientific discovery. But this does not necessarily mean that in the case of SRPs, the time span during which they come into being covers only a few years, while in the case of paradigms, this time span covers perhaps more than a 100 years. In the second edition, Kuhn (1970, pp. 199–200) makes it very clear that "the only point of calling paradigm-changes 'revolutions' is to underline the fact that the arguments that are advanced to support a new paradigm always contain ideological elements that go beyond logical or mathematical proof". Kuhn (1970, pp. 180–181) also points out that his logic of scientific discovery is just as much directed at minor changes in particular scientific fields, which might not seem to be revolutionary at all to those outside "a single community [of scientists], consisting perhaps of fewer than twenty-five people directly involved in it".

The decisive difference between a Lakatosian SRP and a Kuhnian paradigm relates to the way in which one program or paradigm is replaced with another. According to Lakatos, the replacement of an SRP with another requires that the latter be theoretically and empirically progressive in comparison with the former. According to Kuhn, by contrast, a replacement of one paradigm with another (a paradigm change or scientific revolution) involves a conversion that takes on the form of a religious experience: a conversion that is based on persuasion rather than logic and experiment. In Kuhn's account of paradigm change, this persuasion is of the sociological and ideological kind, i.e. emanating from social factors (like authorities, hierarchies, and reference-groups) and ideologies (or value judgments that influence theorising implicitly). But perhaps one may say that in macroeconomics, ideologies play a particularly important role. Theorists from Marx to Krugman have argued that ideologies influence (macro)economic theorising to a substantial degree.

Marx (2005, pp. 85ff.) has arguably been the first to point to the influence of ideologies when accusing all economists who regard the output of the production process as merchandise, i.e. as a commodity to be carried to the market in order to be exchanged for a commodity of equal value plus a profit, of being sycophants to capitalism, i.e. of being members of a community of scientists who tend to repress the fact that their consciousness is dependent on a particular historical stage in the economic development of their societies (capitalism). Schumpeter (1949) discards historical materialism but continues to locate the origin of ideologies in social class affiliation. Keynes (1938, p. 244) seems to understand the belief that "human nature is reasonable" as ideological when referring to it as "disastrously mistaken". And Krugman (2009) claims that what prevented macroeconomists from predicting the crisis of 2008–2009 was ideology in the shape of an unshakeable belief in perfectly efficient financial markets.

7.4   Popper's Situational Logic: An Attractive Alternative?

If the evidence provided by causal inference methods in macroeconomics is too inconclusive in principle, then empirical progress in the Lakatosian sense is impossible, and then the logic of macroeconomic discovery has to be described in Kuhnian, not Lakatosian terms. The Kuhnian logic of macroeconomic discovery, however, is a descriptive account of the historical development of the macroeconomic discipline and not a normative methodology. One may accordingly wonder whether it is normatively desirable. The fact that macroeconomists adjust or modify the theoretical foundations of the prevalent paradigm only in response to anomalies suggests that the answer is negative. This fact explains why they often fail to predict real-economy crises or to propose adequate means of mitigating them. And this failure comes with the high social cost of output declines, high inflation or failed policies. It is of course questionable whether the prediction of real-economy crises is within human power, or whether the occasional occurrence of a severe crisis is something that we simply have to put up with. For the rest of the paper, however, I shall assume that macroeconomists can improve their ability to predict real-economy crises and to propose adequate means of mitigating them by adopting a different methodology. And I will argue that the methodology that might help them to improve that ability is Popper's situational logic.

Popper's situational logic has not received the best press. Latsis (1983, pp. 132–133) dismisses it as "obscure and unsatisfactory" and "either confused or deliberatively elusive". And Marchionni (2009, pp. 225–226) expresses scepticism over the relevance of situational logic to contemporary concerns. It seems that such dismissals and scepticisms are not entirely unjustified. It also seems that Popper's situational logic is intended to capture the logic of scientific discovery in microeconomics, not macroeconomics. In the remainder, however, I shall nonetheless attempt to provide a consistent interpretation of Popper's writings on situational logic: an interpretation that, I hope, will give rise to a methodology that might pass for a viable alternative to the Kuhnian logic of macroeconomic discovery.

As far as I can see, there are essentially three tasks that Popper assigns to situational logic or "situational analysis", as he also calls it. Its first task is to solve problems of explaining or predicting certain kinds or types of event with the help of constructing models of typical social situations (see Popper, 1967a, pp. 357–358). The kinds of events that it attempts to explain or predict may be the topic of education theory, sociology or any other social science discipline. But Popper (1967a, p. 357; 1967b, p. 102) makes it clear that he is most interested in economics. And given the macroeconomic background of the present paper, we will concentrate on types of events like output declines, rises in inflation etc. The models that situational analysts use in macroeconomics to explain or predict these kinds of events are obviously causal models: models representing causal relations among macroeconomics quantities (or relations that permit manipulations of one aggregate quantity to influence another). And the typical social situations that these models are models of are situations in which the types of event in question result from the behaviour of agents given their environment, goals and beliefs and the validity of what Popper (1967a, p. 359) calls the "rationality principle": the principle that says that all agents behave rationally, and that in economics, coincides with the principle according to which all agents maximise utility.

Commentators have struggled with the status of the rationality principle: is it falsifiable, and is it necessary for explanations and predictions in the social sciences? With respect to its falsifiability, Popper (1967a, pp. 360–361) endorses the position that it "is not treated as subject [. . .] to any kind of tests", and that it "is not universally true" and therefore "false". I think that Hands (1985, p. 87) is right when arguing that this position is only seemingly paradoxical: that the rationality principle "can be false as a *universal* principle and yet unfalsifiable in any *particular* application." This is precisely how the neo-Keynesians, for instance, treated the rationality principle when they tried to account for the high inflation that represented an anomaly to the neoclassical paradigm: none of them would have maintained that it is universally true to say that consumers and firms optimise; they nonetheless decided to retain the rationality principle and to give up the Walrasian features of the goods and labour markets instead.

But Popper (1967b, pp. 102–103) appears to be ambivalent on the question of the necessity of the rationality principle. He states on the one hand that "[a] social science oriented towards [. . .] situational logic *can* be developed independently of all subjective or psychological ideas" (my emphasis); he states on the other that "[t]he method of situational analysis is certainly [. . .] not a psychological one; for it excludes, in principle, all psychological elements and replaces them with objective situational elements. [. . .] The explanations of situational logic [. . .] are rational, theoretical reconstruction." Popper's second statement can be read as a plea for the neoclassical and neo-Keynesian programs of micro-foundations. But it conflicts with the psychological principles underlying Keynesian macroeconomics (for instance, with the three psychological motives for holding money). It is also hard to reconcile with the apparent success of disciplines like behavioural economics or econophysics that at one point might come up with viable alternatives to programs of micro-foundations, or at least provide explanations of types of events (like credit market failures) that are better than the rival explanations implied by the neoclassical and neo-Keynesian paradigms. Hands (1985, p. 87), moreover, suggests that Popper's second statement might be inconsistent with a doctrine that he develops elsewhere (a doctrine called "methodological monism"), and that appears to rule out that a methodological principle (in this case the rationality principle) is available to the social sciences but not to the natural sciences.

The rationality principle is certainly useful as a default principle: as a principle that aids model construction in the absence of any indications of patterns of irrational behaviour. But there are clearly situations in which (a great number of) agents behave irrationally, and modelling these situations requires that the rationality principle be given up.[4] The necessity of the rationality principle for

---

[4]Consider e.g. Lux and Marchesi's (1999) financial-market model of rational fundamentalists and irrational chartists.

explanations and predictions in the social sciences should therefore be rejected: macroeconomists should retain the rationality principle as a default principle; but they should also watch out for situations in which the rationality principle is violated, and in which more recent disciplines like behavioural economics or econophysics provide better explanations than the traditional macroeconomic paradigms. If the necessity of the rationality principle is rejected, then this principle is, of course, no longer unfalsifiable in particular applications.

Commentators have also struggled with the type of explanation or prediction that Popper has in mind. Numerous passages in his work (see 1957, pp. 162–164; 1959, pp. 38–40; 1967b, p. 100) suggest that what he has in mind is explanation or prediction in the sense of the deductive-nomological account of scientific explanation: in the sense of an account that understands the explanation or prediction of an event as the deductive inference of a statement describing that event from premises that include at least one universal law and at least one singular statement (or initial condition). In a footnote, however, Popper (1967b, p. 100n) suggests that "[i]n the social sciences, the premises of the explanation usually consist of a situational model and of the so-called 'rationality principle'." And this suggestion brings up the question whether these premises include any universal laws or initial conditions at all. The answer seems to be negative: the rationality principle does not qualify as a universal law because it "is not universally true" (as Popper has it); as long as situational models are understood as causal models, situational models do not qualify as universal laws either because the variables that figure in the equations of these models can typically attain values under which these equations no longer hold (see Woodward, 2003, pp. 65–66); and situational models cannot be understood as initial conditions either because they are concerned with typical social situations, and not with singular ones.

I think that we have to acknowledge that as long as situational models are understood as causal models, they do not explain or predict in the sense of the deductive-nomological account at all. We will rather have to say that a situational model that includes an equation expressing the statement that X causes Y explains $Y = y$ if that statement is true, and that this statement is true if the equation expressing it is invariant under interventions, i.e. if this equation continues to hold in at least some situations in which a hypothetical or actual intervention changes the value of X (cf. Woodward & Hitchcock, 2003, pp. 13, 15). We will likewise have to say that a situational model that includes an equation expressing the statement that X causes Y predicts $Y = y$ if that statement is true, and that this statement is true if the equation expressing it is invariant under interventions. Note that in this sense, "prediction" is not to be confused with the kind of prediction that is possible if Y probabilistically depends on X. But it is clearly the kind of prediction that is relevant for purposes of policy analysis: the kind of prediction that we make when assessing the consequences of policy interventions on X.

The second task that Popper (1967b, p. 97) assigns to situational analysis is "to fight against the confusion of value-spheres". In accordance with the contemporary distinction between epistemic and non-epistemic values, Popper (1967b, pp. 96–97) distinguishes between scientific values such as truth, relevance, interest, significance, fruitfulness, explanatory power, simplicity and precision and "*extra-scientific* values and disvalues" like human welfare, national defence, national policy, industrial expansion and the acquisition of personal wealth. Popper (1967b, p. 96) concedes that it "is clearly impossible to eliminate such extra-scientific interests and to prevent them from influencing the course of scientific research." But he also thinks that it is possible and important to differentiate "the interests which do not belong to the search for truth and the purely scientific interest in truth. [...] This cannot, of course, be achieved once and for all [...]; yet it remains one of the enduring tasks of [...] scientific criticism" (Popper, 1967b, pp. 96–97). Popper's idea that one of the tasks of scientific criticism is "to fight against the confusion of value-spheres" highlights a remarkable break with his earlier anti-psychologist conviction that "the logical analysis of scientific knowledge [...] is concerned [...] only with questions of [...] the following kind. Can a statement be justified? [...] Is it testable? Is it logically dependent on certain other statements? Or does it perhaps contradict them?" (Popper, 1959, p. 5).

Finally, the third task that Popper (1967b, pp. 98–99) assigns to situational analysis is "to show that unacceptable conclusions can be derived from the assertion we are trying to criticise. If we are successful in deriving, logically, unacceptable conclusions from an assertion, then the assertion may be taken to be refuted." This passage is reminiscent of passages that in earlier writings (see especially Popper, 1959, pp. 52–53) describe the method of falsification. Does this mean that the third task of situational analysis is falsification? There are at least two reasons why the answer has to be negative. The first reason is that falsification in the sense of a criticism of an assertion by deriving unacceptable conclusions from it seems to presuppose the deductive-nomological account of scientific explanation, and that this account was found to be inapplicable to situational analysis. The second reason is that according to Popper (1959, p. 66), the acceptance of a basic statement that contradicts a theory is only a necessary condition of its falsification, that a sufficient condition of its falsification requires that the basic statement corroborate a low-level empirical hypothesis, and that corroboration of a low-level empirical hypothesis is impossible if this hypothesis relates to causal relations causation in macroeconomics.

But what is the third task of situational analysis if it is not falsification? I would like to suggest that the third task of situational analysis is falsification in a different or weaker sense: in the sense of a continuous study of typical situations in which paradigmatic models do not hold. In the case of causal modelling in macroeconomics, this continuous study comes down to the study of causes that can be ignored in many situations but have been relevant in earlier situations and might become relevant again. The hope is that by studying causes of this kind, macroeconomists can improve their ability to explain or predict the type of event in question. In Sect. 7.2, I argued that the evidence provided by causal inference methods in macroeconomics is too inconclusive to support specific causal relations. And if this evidence is too inconclusive to support specific causal relations, then it is also too inconclusive to show that a causal model adequately explains or predicts a particular type of event. But perhaps macroeconomists can develop the skill or expertise to explain or predict types of events. And if they can develop that skill or expertise, then a continuous study of typical situations in which paradigmatic models do not hold certainly facilitates that development.

Consider the example of shifting liquidity preferences (as discussed e.g. in Christiano, Motto, & Rostagno, 2010). Shifts in banks' liquidity preferences represent causes of aggregate output that can be ignored in many situations but have been relevant in earlier situations and might become relevant again. Shifts in banks' liquidity preferences might have been irrelevant during much of "the Great Moderation" (the period of unprecedented macroeconomic stability that lasted from the mid-1980s to 2007). But they had been relevant before (especially during the Great Depression) and became relevant again in 2008. There had been a few studies investigating the impact of such shifts (see e.g. Bernanke, Gertler, & Gilchrist, 1999). During the Great Moderation, however, the vast majority of macroeconomists had taken for granted that these shifts can be neglected. The result of that neglect had been that the vast majority of macroeconomists were surprised by the extraordinary output declines that shattered the world in the wake of the failure of Lehman Brothers in September 2008. And it seems that they would have been better prepared to predict or even prevent these output declines if they had not subscribed to the neoclassical or neo-Keynesian models so blindly, and if they had tried to falsify these models in a weak sense of the term: if they had submitted them to a continuous study of typical situations in which they do not hold.

I agree with Hands (1985, p. 94) that Popper's writings on situational analysis have "very little to offer regarding theory choice". I would like to emphasize, however, that Popper's writings have a lot to say about the choice of models that adequately predict or explain particular types of events. These models are the ones that a good situational analyst would choose, and a good situational analyst is one who accomplishes the three tasks described above sufficiently well: who (a) accepts the rationality principle only conditionally (and is therefore protected against anomalies in the shape of patterns of irrational behaviour); who (b) realises that ideologies might lead to preferences of (e.g. Keynesian, neo-classical, neo-Keynesian) models that inadequately capture the situation at hand (and who therefore is able to roll back the influence of ideologies as much as possible); and who (c) can develop tentative models for the situation at hand (and is therefore familiar with adequate models for as many social situations as possible – a familiarity that is acquired through the study of causes that, like shifting liquidity preferences, can be ignored in many situations but have been relevant in earlier situations and might become relevant again).

References

Bernanke, B. S., Gertler, M., & Gilchrist, S. (1999). The financial accelerator in a quantitative business cycle framework. In J. B. Taylor & M. Woodford (Eds.), *Handbook of macroeconomics*
(pp. 1341–1393). Amsterdam, The Netherlands: Elsevier Science.

Blaug, M. (1976). Paradigms versus research programs in the history of economics. In D. M. Hausman (Ed.), *The philosophy of economics: An anthology* (pp. 348–375). Cambridge, UK: Cambridge University Press.

Christiano, L. J., Motto, R., & Rostagno, M. (2010, May). *Financial factors in economic fluctuations* (ECB Working Paper Series No. 1192).

Hands, D. W. (1985). Popper and economic methodology: A new look. *Economics and Philosophy, 1*, 83–99.

Hicks, J. (1937). Mr. Keynes and the 'Classics'. *Econometrica, 1*, 147–159.

Hoover, K. D. (2001). *Causality in macroeconomics*. Cambridge, UK: Cambridge University Press.

Keynes, J. M. (1938). My early beliefs. In J. M. Keynes (Ed.), *The collected writings of John Maynard Keynes* (pp. 433–451). London: Macmillan.

Krugman, P. (2009). How did economists get it so wrong? *The New York Times* 09/06/2009.

Kuhn, T. S. (1970). *The structure of scientific revolutions* (2nd ed.). Chicago: University of Chicago Press.

Kuhn, T. S. (1996). *The structure of scientific revolutions* (3rd ed.). Chicago: University of Chicago Press.

Lakatos, I. (1971). The history of science and its rational reconstructions. In R.C. Buck & R.S. Cohen (Eds.), *PSA 1970: Boston studies in the philosophy of science* 8 (pp. 91–135). Dordrecht: Reidel.

Lakatos, I., & Musgrave, A. (Eds.). (1970). *Criticism and the growth of knowledge*. Cambridge, UK: Cambridge University Press.

Latsis, S. J. (1983). The role and status of the rationality principle in the social sciences. In R. S. Cohen & M. W. Wartofsky (Eds.), *Epistemology, methodology, and the social sciences* (pp. 123–151). Dordrecht, The Netherlands: Reidel.

Lucas, R. E. (1972). Expectations and the neutrality of money. *Journal of Economic Theory, 4*, 103–124.

Lux, T., & Marchesi, M. (1999). Scaling and criticality in a stochastic multi-agent model of a financial market. *Nature, 397*, 498–500.

Maddock, R. (1984). Rational expectations macro-theory: A Lakatosian case study in program adjustment. *History of Political Economy, 16*, 291–309.

Marchionni, C. (2009). Review: T. Boylan and P. O'Gorman (Eds.), Popper and economic methodology. *Economics and Philosophy, 25*, 223–229.

Marx, K. (2005). Das Kapital. Kritik der politischen Ökonomie. Erster Band. In *Marx-Engels-Werke Bd* (21st ed., p. 23). Berlin, Germany: Dietz.

Modigliani, F. (1944). Liquidity preference and the theory of interest and money. *Econometrica, 12*, 45–88.

Pearl, J. (2009). *Causality: Models, reasoning, and inference* (2nd ed.). Cambridge, UK: Cambridge University Press.

Popper, K. R. (1957/1984). The aim of science. In D. W. Miller (Ed.), Popper selections (pp. 162–170). Princeton, NJ: Princeton University Press.

Popper, K. R. (1959). *The logic of scientific discovery*. Oxford, UK: Routledge.

Popper, K. R. (1967a). The logic of the social sciences. In T. W. Adorno (Ed.), *The positivist dispute in German sociology* (pp. 87–104). New York: Harper and Row.

Popper, K. R. (1967b/1984). The rationality principle. In D. W. Miller (Ed.) *Popper selections* (pp. 357–366). Princeton, NJ: Princeton University Press.

Schumpeter, J. A. (1949). Science and ideology. *American Economic Review, 39*, 345–359.

Weintraub, E. R. (1988). The neo-Walrasian program is empirically progressive. In N. De Marchi (Ed.), *The Popperian legacy in economics* (pp. 213–229). Cambridge, UK: Cambridge University Press.

Woodward, J. (2003). *Making things happen: A causal theory of explanation*. Oxford, UK: Oxford University Press.

Woodward, J., & Hitchcock, C. (2003). Explanatory generalizations, Part I: A counterfactual account. *Nous, 37*, 1–24.

Chapter 8
Discovering Solidarity: Research on Solidarity as a Case of a *That-What* Discovery

Jakub Bazyli Motrenko

Abstract We rarely talk about scientific discoveries in sociology, and usually only in research fields that pursue a positivist ideal of science. This does not mean, however, that it does not make sense to talk about sociological discoveries in fields that do not apply research methods to generate large quantities of new data. In this paper, I analyse the case of research conducted by Polish sociologists on the Solidarity social movement in the 1980s in Poland. Solidarity was a social phenomenon which did not fit within the contemporary model for conducting scholarly research and, as a result, led to a significant theoretical change. I argue that this change is accurately described by the term "*that-what* discovery" taken from Kuhn's article "The Historical Structure of Scientific Discovery" (1962). The purpose of analysing this historical case is to adapt Kuhn's concept to the social sciences framework.

Keywords Constructivism · Intentional value · Polish society · Polish sociology · Solidarity movement · Sociology technology · That-what discovery · What-that discovery

Sociologists[1] almost never talk about discoveries in reference to their own work. While the development of natural sciences occurs in the rhythm of consecutive discoveries, social sciences follow a different path. Collins (1994) argues that, contrary to the natural sciences, the social sciences have never become high-consensus, rapid-discovery sciences. Collins claims that the typically identified causes – such as lack of empiricism, measurement and mathematization, and use

---

[1]This research project on the anti-positivist turn in Polish sociology in the 1970s and 1980s was financed by the National Science Centre, Poland (DEC-2012/05/N/HS6/03944).

J. B. Motrenko (✉)
Institute of Sociology, University of Warsaw, Warsaw, Poland
e-mail: motrenkoja@is.uw.edu.pl

© Springer Nature Switzerland AG 2019
M. Addis et al. (eds.), *Scientific Discovery in the Social Sciences*,
Synthese Library 413, https://doi.org/10.1007/978-3-030-23769-1_8

of the experimental method – did not have a decisive impact on the development of such a pattern, since all of them can be found in sociology, or at least some of its orientations. Despite this fact, sociology has not adopted the developmental pattern characteristic of the natural sciences. For these sciences – Collins argues – the invention of research technologies was supposed to constitute a breakthrough: "they can be regarded as the core of the rapid discovery revolution because they produce the fast-moving research forefront" (Collins, 1994, p. 163). Thanks to technology, and as a result of a conscious manipulation on the researcher's part, more previously inaccessible observation data was generated. Collins briefly summarizes his argument about Galileo and his followers who pushed science into a new direction: "What was discovered was a method of discovery" (Collins, 1994, p. 163). Collins wrote in 1994 that sociological research is still theory-driven: "What we lack is the key possession of the rapid discovery sciences, their nonhuman machinery for generating previously unobservable phenomena" (Collins, 1994, p. 172). He himself was wondering if research on artificial intelligence or studies in microsociology, conducted within the framework of conversation analysis with the use of audio-video equipment, could start generating scientific discoveries (Collins, 1994, pp. 172–173). Today we can speculate that the emergence of Big Data and new statistical techniques for their analysis that are now at the disposal of the social sciences opens the path of developments that Collins talks about (see Alvarez, 2016). This is how I understand the ideas behind some of the papers in this volume.

I agree with Collins's thesis that the organization of social sciences is not oriented towards generating scientific discoveries, and I doubt whether the invention of new scientific technologies would transform sociology to make it resemble natural sciences. Taking into account that, within social sciences, alternative paths of scientific progress have been developed, I remain sceptical as to whether the transformation of sociological tradition in the direction described by Collins is possible. Indeed, the author himself also expresses such doubts (Collins, 1994, p. 175). Nonetheless, in some specialized research areas it is possible to conduct studies using technologies which produce discoveries and this is what research practice looks like in those areas.

In this paper, I argue that the previous way of conducting social research – with the use of tested and "traditional" scientific technologies (observation, interview, records and documents, etc.) – is one that does not generate quick discoveries and consensus. I am interested in those discoveries where something "appears" and "strikes" researchers as new, demanding that they make changes to existing theories. After Kuhn, I call this a "that-what" type of discovery. Since Kuhn's conception was formulated for natural sciences, it requires adaption to make it applicable in sociology. In this article, I undertake this task.

8.1 Why Do We Not Talk About Discoveries in Sociology?

I argue that nowadays we talk about discoveries in sociology less that in the past[2] and I link this situation to the critique of the scientific model for conducting sociological research. The anti-positivist critique concerned, among other things, the question of realism in its relation to social reality and the nomothetic ideal. Those two juxtaposed approaches are, respectively, constructivism and historical particularism. Both stances, though not always explicitly communicated, create the picture of sociological knowledge in the eyes of researchers from this discipline and constitute an important element of its self-understanding. Nonetheless, to put it simply, scientists either discover some "material"[3] reality or some theoretical statements that describe it, ideally in the form of scientific laws. However, since the existence of reality independent of the knower and the relevance of formulating laws to describe reality have both been called into question, talking about discovery no longer makes sense.

The aim of the majority of sociological studies is to analyse concrete phenomena, not theoretical objects abstracted from their temporal and spatial context. Usually, their epistemic aim is not to formulate parsimonious and abstract laws, but to analyse particular cases.[4] They try to grasp the reality of various states, nations or groups in rich detail, rather than creating models detached from observed reality, as is often the case in the natural sciences. Also, when sociology intersects with psychology or economics, researchers conduct experiments modelled on laboratory studies, as well as systematic comparative research to define universal dependent variables. However, this is not what typical research looks like in practice. To describe the world, sociologists define their objects of analyses taking into account their historical variety, regardless of whether they formulate theses about social classes, nations or civilizations. Nonetheless, it is possible to imagine that in order to explain particular cases, a researcher refers to some established general laws – according to a deductive-nomological model of explanation formulated by Hempel (1966). Here, however, an important problem appears: if social laws are not banal, they operate under the *ceteris paribus* provision. To list all factors modifying the operating laws seems a difficult requirement to fulfil. Without it, on the other hand, the law becomes empirically worthless and not exposed to falsification. Discovering laws is not researchers' epistemic aim though it is possible to point to some

---

[2]In my opinion, this single reason makes a conference about discoveries in the social sciences – something that goes against popular thinking – such a daring endeavor worthy of attention, even more so since, as McArthur observes: "discovery does seem to be a central notion in science, and is frequently used and debated among scientists themselves" (McArthur, 2011, p. 362).

[3]I put the word "material" in quotations since I do not refer to the materiality of macro objects such as tables and chairs. However, in some important sense, reality remains independent of our knowledge about objects and it is not merely the creation of our conceptional apparatus.

[4]However, it is possible to find contemporary sociological works concerning laws in sociology – see Cuin (2000), Mitchell (2009) and Demeulenaere (2011).

sociological areas of studies where the effort to find and describe such regularities is undertaken.

Sociologists who want to ground their knowledge in historical facts, like historians studying sources, are in no better situation. Whereas historians can talk about discoveries when they come across a new, previously unknown source, sociologists come across a new problem. In social sciences, talking about discoveries is a problem: the language suggests that a discovery is something incidental, something that we "come across", a new reality. However, the division between knowers and independent reality is permanently questioned by social scientists. Even though it is not always made clear, contemporary sociologists have thoroughly internalized a contructivist attitude that blurs the boundary between the objective world and its description. They pay special attention to studying the social genealogies of social categories, pointing to their roots in culture or politics. Therefore, they question the neutral, extra-ideological scientific origins of these concepts. Historical sources are in no way an exception. Objects are construed by discoverers in the historical process of making a discovery. The return to the classic concept where one comes across a reality and seeks the best possible scientific theory to explain it is regarded as naïve realism.

Hudson (2001, p. 91) summarizes Woolgar's (1989) constructivist stance in the following way: "... to refute Woolgar, one must argue that such perceived objects are non-constructed; they are, I want to say, non-conceptual in a fundamental way; they are "out there", non-conceptualized, waiting to be perceived". If sociologists such as Woolgar challenge the natural sciences by questioning their realist stance on the existence of an autonomous world which researchers try to describe, this applies even more so to the object of a sociological inquiry. The social world is doubly construed – by normal people and by researchers. A particular problem may arise when scientists do not see the connections between the two planes of this construction and claim that their science constitutes the world independently of ideology or culture. Those tendencies are accompanied by a conviction that different theories offer different views on reality and it is impossible to decide on one privileged perspective. This conviction questions one of the criteria of a discovery which insists on the confirmation of its genuineness (that is what the speaker talks about is really taking place). In short, this can be expressed with the slogan: "there are many different truths".

After this general introduction in which I have tried to address the question as to why we rarely talk about discoveries in sociology, I will analyse one of the ways that actually make it possible to talk about discoveries in sociology. My theses will not be directed against the anti-positivist critique, although they may be relevant for the meta-sociological stance.

8.2 "What-That" and "That-What" Discoveries

In the essay entitled "The Historical Structure of Scientific Discovery" published in 1962, Kuhn (1977) argued that a scientific discovery is not a precise event, simple in structure and easy to locate in time. It is not a "Eureka!" moment when a researcher gains knowledge about a new object and all of its complexities. Instead, Kuhn proposed a distinction between two crucial moments in scientific discovery: the moment of discovering **that** something exists and the moment of explaining **what** it is. Given the timeframe and the logic of those two moments, it is possible to identify two types of discoveries: "what-that" and "that-what".

In the case of a "what-that" scenario, scientists predict a discovery of an object by employing some established theories. Alternatively, they can make predictions using some conceptual nexus with which they are well acquainted, e.g. by doing appropriate calculations or performing thought experiments. Kuhn illustrates this type of thinking with examples of the discovery of neutrons, radio waves and various chemical elements. We have clear criteria that help us recognize that we have found the object we were searching for. That is why in retrospect it is easy to define the time and place of the discovery and name the discoverer. In the moment of discovery we already know what was discovered. Taking into account the time order, it is possible to say that the "that" and "what" moments happen at the same time – observation and conceptualisation are not separated in time. What remains a challenge, however, is finding this object in reality, and finding references in the theory. As we know from studying the history of science, this is a complex process which requires the involvement of numerous theories of observation.

The "that-what" discovery is different. In this case, finding a new object precedes the formulation of a theory. The object is shown but not named. Even when researchers come across a new object, they often are not aware that they made a discovery. As examples of this type of discovery, Kuhn discussed oxygen, electric currents and electrons. They came as a surprise since their discovery had not been predicted by existing theories. The discovery of an object involves first a detection of something new and unidentified, and then the conceptualisation of what this something is. It is often problematic to point to the exact place, time and person who made the discovery. I argue that research on Solidarity and the political and social crisis of the '80s constituted a "that-what" type of discovery.

Contrary to Kuhn (1977) and Musgrave (1976), Hudson (2001) argues that discoveries are made by a defined subject ("discoverer") in a defined place and time. Therefore, Hudson formulates three criteria that must be met if we talk about a discovery: (a) the discoverer has to present a base description of the object which would allow for its identification, although the description does not have to be an adequate one from the perspective of later knowledge; (b) the discoverer must do a material demonstration; and finally, (c) the novelty condition has to be met. McArthur (2011), who follows the same path, suggests some minor corrections: first of all, he argues that sometimes the discoverer is the person who presented a base description, even though he or she did not perform a material demonstration.

Secondly, he emphasizes that the base description cannot describe any of the object's features since it should identify "basic interaction properties of measurable quantities (i.e. disposition for law-like behaviour) that are utilised in experimental and detection situations" (McArthur, 2011, p. 373). Both authors – though they do not admit it openly – question Kuhn's idea of dividing discoveries into two categories. They hold that it is impossible to refer to a subject if we do not have its description. As a result, the authors argue, all discoveries are of the "what-that" type. They also defend themselves against the argument that, since contemporary descriptions of theoretical objects are very distant from the scientists' intuitions, these are completely different objects.

Hudson and McArthur claim that it is possible to propose such a conceptualisation that would allow one to determine who the discoverer is. They hold that the discoverer needs to have some, however rudimentary, conceptualisation of the discovered object ("base description"). In other words, the researcher has either a conceptualisation sufficient to establish correspondence to the discovered object, regardless of whether the proposed description is appropriate (Hudson), or a conceptualisation that has to relate to the structural features of the object (McArthur). Otherwise, one can conclude that the object has not been discovered. I do not question the criteria outlined by the authors, nor do I formulate my own. Nowadays, it sounds like a platitude to say that every observation is based on some idea or that it is theory-laden. However, in this paper, I argue that the division made by Kuhn is still valid. The criteria put forward by Hudson and McArthur can only be used *sub specie aeternitatis*. With time, when a consensus regarding the "truthful"[5] conceptualisation would be established, it would also be possible to determine who the actual discoverer was. Kuhn, however, adopts the perspective of researchers themselves who are not at all certain that they made a breakthrough discovery. Certainty is sometimes available to the subsequent generation of researchers. The cognitive situation of those who act on the basis of a given theory is totally different from the situation of those who seek conceptualisation when they encounter new phenomena. Every division into observational and theoretical statements is relative. Still, Kuhn's distinction – recognizing that something exists and then describing what the nature of this something is – does not seem to be meaningless. I use Kuhn's approach because it accounts for the course of an important theoretical change in Polish sociology caused by the emergence of the social movement Solidarity in 1980.

---

[5]I use inverted commas since both authors are perfectly aware that any scientific "truth" can be questioned.

8.3   What Does It Mean to Discover Solidarity?

One might say that Solidarity did not have to be discovered and one would be right: everybody knew of its existence. In August 1980, workers protests broke out in the Lenin Shipyard in Gdańsk as well as other places in Poland. They ended in a series of agreements with communist authorities, which allowed for the creation of independent trade union. Though this was not the first mass workers protest in the People's Republic of Poland, for the first time their postulates went beyond their class interests. Moreover, the communist government made significant concessions, which undermined the very *raison d'être* of its existence. According to communist ideology, the Communist Party should express the interests of the working class. However, this time workers demanded their own political representation, independent from the Communist Party. Events then accelerated: several thousand workers protesting in a few factories became a nationwide social movement numbering, at its peak, 10 million Poles.[6]

A few years later, a Polish popular weekly magazine published a report from the Sociological Congress in Wrocław. The author wrote: "What a horse looks like, everybody knows. Honestly, it was not necessary to go to Wrocław to join the sociologists' Congress to know about the society they were discussing there" (Rykowski, 1986). I argue that the diagnosis of what contemporary society was like could have been formulated due to an important theoretical change which took place in Polish sociology and which was linked to the emergence of Solidarity. If it had not been for this change, sociologists (as well as other people) would only know that something important happened, but they would not know what it was.

Unlike many social phenomena which sociology discovers, and which afterward become part of social consciousness, Solidarity was "visible" from its very beginning. This comes as no surprise, since it was called "a social movement" (cf. Touraine et al., 1983), "a revolution" (see Cirtautas, 1997; Laba, 1991) and "an uprising" (see Gella, 1987; Labuda, 1996). Such phenomena do not go unnoticed by even the least attentive observers. Attempts to determine the causes and character of the processes that started in August 1980 were undertaken by all relevant actors: authorities, trade union activists and experts, journalists, Solidarity's supporters from within and outside of its structures, foreign governments, etc. I am interested in two ways in which Solidarity was problematized by sociologists. I am going to discuss two interpretations. The first one was suggested by Stefan Nowak – one of the most influential Polish sociologists. The second was put forward by one of his students, Krzysztof Nowak (no relation), together with Bakaniuk. Krzysztof Nowak and Bakuniak's article can be regarded as a *synecdoche* of sociology developed at the Institute of Sociology's Methodological Department at the University of Warsaw in the 1980s. This group of people held a prominent place in Polish sociology at the time.

---

[6]A good popular introduction to the history of Solidarity is provided in *Polish Revolution: Solidarity* (first published in 1983), by British journalist and political scientist Ash (2002).

8.4   Values as Intentions

Stefan Nowak's paper (Nowak, 1981) concisely discusses the results of sociological research from the previous quarter century which could explain the rise of a social movement putting forward democratic requests:

> Recent events in Poland, illuminated by 25 years of social research, are shown to stem not from a change in values but from a demand for social institutions more in accord with values consistently held. (Nowak, 1981, p. 45)

The article was not only considered to be a synthesis of 25 years of research, but also a triumph of the project of survey sociology. Although Nowak admittedly acknowledges that sociologists failed to predict the emergence of Solidarity, he proposes understanding it *post factum*. In the summary, he writes:

> From a methodological point of view, it can be said that history has provided strong behavioural validation of our survey data. Those who have been studying values and attitudes in Polish society have been studying social forces of great importance. These forces were at least partly shaped under the influence of the social system, but they have now imprinted themselves in the shape of the system itself and, at least to a certain degree, have caused its transformation. (Nowak, 1981, p. 53)

This diagnosis was formulated only a few months after the formation of Solidarity. Stefan Nowak was observing the unfolding of events in Poland from the American perspective where he had been lecturing at Columbia University for a year. The distance ensured cognitive security and allowed him to analyse reality in a cool and reserved manner, without having to continuously compare ideas and hypotheses with reality. Nowak knew what was happening in Poland, but he was not participating in those events or accessing the data gathered by the two research teams established in his department at the Institute of Sociology in the fall of 1980 and led by his students. Nonetheless, what was needed to integrate this knowledge with previous knowledge was a reformulation of the tenets of the scientific program conducted. I will now discuss Stefan Nowak's theses and compare them with the theses put forward by Krzysztof Nowak and Bakaniuk to demonstrate the discovery made by the latter researchers.

Stefan Nowak indicates that the basic mechanisms of the emergence of the social movement boil down to the following three points:

1. Polish society before 1980 was oriented towards egalitarianism and democracy. Surveys showed that lower positions in the social structure were connected to more egalitarian ideals. A reverse trend could be observed in people's attitudes towards democratic values: the higher the position, the more support for the abolition of restrictions on civic rights and the implementation of leadership that would ensure more people's participation in politics. The only exception to this rule was found among skilled workers who, similarly to the upper classes, valued freedom of speech. The combination of egalitarian and democratic values paved the way for the creation of Solidarity. This sentiment was widely shared by society.

2. Polish society was in poor psychological and sociological shape: people simultaneously expressed apathy and political annoyance. People's frustration was expressed in the outbreak of social discontent. To Nowak, the speed with which people consolidated around a social movement testified to the needs present in the society at that time. The Poles understood Solidarity as a means of fulfilling their needs, both instrumental and emotional.
3. A lack of experienced identities of mezzo-level – between family and friends circles, on the one hand, and the national community, on the other hand – was a feature of Polish society discovered by Nowak in the 70s and famously called a "sociological or social vacuum" (Pawlak, 2015). The rise of social life was supposed to be the effect of the previous lack of a sense of belonging and reliance on wider social circles. Since Solidarity contributed to the reintegration of Polish society, Nowak argued, it satisfied the need to belong and identify with institutions situated between family circle and the national community.

The article written for *Scientific American* addressed the question of the origins of a mass social movement fighting for egalitarian and democratic values and became a platform for social reintegration. Stefan Nowak argued that at the core of contemporary collective action lay value systems that had not changed in years. The values and attitudes discussed in the article were implicit since they could not be manifested in unfavourable political conditions; nonetheless, they became a source of change. The triumph of the survey method was connected to the fact that Nowak discovered them before they became the basis for collective action.

Stefan Nowak designed a new task for his research programme: to investigate the causes of Poles' action based on pre-existing value systems. The new historical situation required shifting the research question. Although Nowak regarded the implementation of Stalinism at the end of the 1940s as a political fact from outside of social system, it was difficult to apply a similar schema to Solidarity. The social movement seemed to be the best exemplification of a self-producing, active society. The explanatory model of the time lost its *raison d'être*. Instead of asking about the origins of attitudes, Nowak demonstrated how they became the basis for historical events. Using the language of variables, one could say that attitudes were no longer dependent variables but independent variables. Nowak was aware that Solidarity, as a significant historical event, could have transformed value systems that, however, must have been preceded by something that could explain the rise of a mass social movement. Nowak held that the answer lay in the pre-existing value systems. The stated values were interpreted as and transformed into intentions for taking action.

8.5   The Empirical Deficit of Survey Sociology

In 1979, just a year before the rise of Solidarity and two years before writing the article for *Scientific American,* Stefan Nowak (1980) published a paper entitled "System wartości społeczeństwa polskiego" (translated a year later as "Value systems of the Polish society"). It became the basis for the text published in the American magazine, which repeated many of its arguments. However, those two texts had different objectives and were differently organized. The older one was not oriented towards explanation but a synthetic description of the state of social consciousness of Polish society at the end of the 1970s. Upon rereading this 1979 article, one realizes that some of Nowak's diagnoses call for explanation. I now consider some important issues.

Stefan Nowak was not able to explain why some of the values Poles said were important to them some 25 years before the rise of Solidarity contradicted the very core of the social movement:

1. open conflict with the authorities: the absence of significant differences in value systems led Nowak to the conclusion that there were no social groups holding opposing views in Poland in the 1970s. Consequently, the emergence of a major social conflict seemed rather unlikely.[7]
2. the fight for universal rights: Nowak argued that Polish society consisted of pragmatists interested – first and foremost – in their own well-being, opting for moral compromises, and not interested in public affairs or the realization of high romantic ideals. He reckoned that Poles fled into privacy and focused on fulfilling their modest, material-oriented goals.
3. the explosion of identification with intermediate level associations between family and friends circles, on the one hand, and the national community, on the other: in 1980–1981 all over Poland, people wanted to organize themselves and shape the reality around them. For Nowak the emerging associations became the measure of the unfulfilled needs, both instrumental and emotional. However, how did people who had not previously contacted one other and had not shared a common identity, suddenly discover they had something in common?
4. religiosity as a symbolic vehicle for the movement's activities: Nowak argued that Polish religiosity was characterized by ceremony and ritual; what it lacked, however, was the intensity of religiously-experienced feelings and the active pursuit of brotherly love. Meanwhile, Solidarity drew abundantly from religious symbolism and ritual. The holy mass and confession were regular practices which integrated the community. Catholic theology and philosophy provided a language to express Solidarity's ideals: revival, forgiveness, social ties, care for fellow human beings, community, living in truth and the transformation of conscience.

The birth of the Solidarity social movement presented some significant challenges to the programme of survey sociology. In science, contradictions between theory and facts are commonplace. Their emergence seldom leads to the rejection

---

[7]In an article published in 1976, Nowak (2009, p. 133) discussed a certain advantage connected to the intergenerational standardization of value systems: "It [the level of the standardization of values in the intergenerational scale] constitutes a premise to predict that in our country there will be no serious intergenerational confrontations".

of theory; on the contrary, contradictions often inform a theory's creative reinterpretation. As Lakatos (1970) pointed out, the degeneration of a scientific programme is a process extended over time; in other words, it does not happen on a day-to-day basis. As long as only the theses that form the protective belt are called into question, the programme stands a chance of assimilating new facts thanks to some creative shifts. It is, however, subject to degeneration when it starts to "drag" behind the facts. It can be rejected when its core theses are called into question and an alternative program is formulated. In this situation, it is not only particular theses that are questioned, but the very foundation of the program itself.

The problems of survey sociology were both intrinsic and extrinsic in character. They were intrinsic since, within this framework, it was not possible to account for changes in individuals' values and actions, especially collective actions, when applying the conceptual nexus of the theory of attitudes. Therefore, the programme was called into question as an explanatory theory. The program also had to face external challenges, since the observation theory (Lakatos would call it "interpretative"), constituting bare facts, was called into question. In the next paragraphs, I will give an example of conceptualizing Solidarity as collective consciousness.

8.6 The Discovery of Solidarity

Bakuniak and Krzysztof Nowak (Bakuniak & Nowak, 1987) convincingly demonstrate what it means to discover Solidarity as a new theoretical object. According to Stefan Nowak's conceptual nexus, Solidarity was not a variable problematized by sociologists. It was also redundant with respect to respondents' opinions. Stefan Nowak suggested that Solidarity was the result of the value system existing in people's minds. In turn, Bakuniak and Krzysztof Nowak claim that Solidarity is not the product of a fixed value structure but a historical process in which people interacting with each other created a certain image of the social world they inhabited and obtained a collective identity.

> [W]hat did August 1980 mean in Poland? We are of the opinion that it is sound to interpret it as the emergence of a civil society. It came about by way of processes of overcoming atomization, the objectivization of a new vision of social reality (in which society was presented in opposition to the state) and the organization of the project of social action that aimed at the realization of the various goals and values of this society (Bakuniak & Nowak, 1987, p. 401).

The authors show two aspects of a social process: on the one hand, there is experience and participation in historic events (direct or symbolic); on the other, there is an intellectual analysis of what is happening (Bakuniak & Nowak, 1987, p. 403). Hence, sociologists have to address the process of the formation of collective feelings within a community, which will become the main actor of the unfolding events, and attempt to reconstruct the definition of the situation, which requires regenerating consecutive interpretations of reality which appeared in the collective consciousness. Bakuniak and Krzysztof Nowak describe the process of the formation of Solidarity's collective identity since 1970, pointing out some important caesuras: workers protests in the town of Radom in 1976, the pilgrimage of Pope John Paul II to Poland in 1979, the July 1980 strikes, and, finally, the protests that broke out a month later in Gdańsk. It is worth noting that such a description, which uses completely new theoretical concepts, sheds new light on the origins of Solidarity. The key term here is social consciousness. The historical process of acquiring social consciousness by Polish society described by Bakuniak and Nowak relied on methodological and theoretical innovations: a survey based on a representative sample was replaced by other means of studying social reality, and the theory of attitudes was replaced by theories from cognitive psychology and phenomenological sociology. The systems of values revealed in survey research were no longer at the centre of the sociologists' interest. Instead, they were interested in the emerging collective actor: a civil society which institutionalized itself in the form of the Solidarity trade union. Nowak accounted for the eruption of social discontent as a confrontation between stable value systems and reality, and reactive attitudes towards the deterioration of the external living conditions. The new conceptualisations, however, emphasised the role of collective processes for creating new cognitive structures, which served as interpretative schemas for making sense of social reality and workers' identity, and – in the long run – the identity of all Poles opposing the communist authorities.

8.7   The Experience of Solidarity

In the 1990s, Krzemiński (1998), a member of Stefan Nowak's student circle, was reconstructing the connections between the methodological stance and the moral philosophy in force at the Institute of Sociology. He pointed out that after 1968 – when the Faculty of Philosophy, including the sociological section, was dissolved in the wake of student protests and replaced by the Institute of Sociology, an independent unit which did not, however, accommodate the dismissed professors and students – there were two formations of different political orientations: pro-Marxist and pro-democratic. To mitigate the unresolved conflict, the community of the Institute of Sociology searched for a collection of values that could restore at least a relative unity. Moral philosophy was based on the methodological premises of positivism. The circumstances mentioned above made it more lasting than the cognitive arguments suggested. The moral compromise based on positivist philosophy was undermined by academics engaged with the democratic opposition movements in the 1970s and eventually dismantled in 1980. The questioning of moral philosophy and positivist methodology was influenced by the experience of participating in the underground opposition movements and later in Solidarity. I am interested in the cognitive, rather than moral, aspect of this experience.

In 1980, sociologists from Krzysztof Nowak's circle were actively engaged in a social movement. They were not external observers, but experts advising the trade union's authorities as well as lecturers at folk universities and animators at different levels of the union's organization. They got to know Solidarity not through theoretical concepts, but through the experience of participation. They "came across" a new world because the phenomena they were studying were public in character. It was, to a large extent, dissonant with the diagnoses formulated by Nowak, which I have already discussed. The reality that previously seemed "natural" (the society as a stable, slowly evolving structure of norms constituted in the first years after World War II, and sometimes rooted in even deeper reservoirs of values), started to be perceived as something created through a complex network of cooperation. All of a sudden, the stable social world became a process, and the new social situation became epistemically problematic. Its novelty in comparison to the previous social experience was striking, routine forms of activity were losing their validity, and alternatives for individuals and society were no longer in place. Personal experience had also become the subject of theoretical reflection. In the following years, it was studied and understood in terms of agency, the fluidity of the social order, social change, playing games with authorities, "the feast of regained language", group dynamics, political mobilization, the role of symbols (especially patriotic and religious symbols), ethos, networks of informal connections and so on.

Nowak's students valued the role of immediate experience. A researcher was considered a better means for gathering data than a questionnaire – it was assumed that through observation and natural conversation he had a better capacity to assess reality than through a standardized research tool. However, such an approach does not replace natural connections with structures imposed by a questionnaire – something they called artificial "entireties" (Marody & Nowak, 1983, p. 28). In the most desirable situation, informants would generate information about themselves and researchers would only record it. According to one of the sociologists, referring to his own research on Solidarity, competent informants "adopted the role of a natural social researcher" (Krzemiński, 2005, p. 16). Researchers did not have any influence on this data. Referring to her informants, a scholar studying Poles' religiosity remarked: "We treat them seriously, as people who can tell us about their lives, and who are responsible for what they are saying" (Grabowska, 1989, p. 155).

However, if sociologists would draw the line at providing accounts of their informants' experiences – as well as their own experiences – they would become naïve realists, who believe that immediate experience grants understanding of the social world. Certainly, as contemporary sociologists wanted to give voice to the Solidarity activists and demonstrate the variety of social views on the same phenomenon, this approach was consistent with Solidarity's pluralistic political philosophy. At the same time, they understood the importance of theory and were looking for ways to conceptualize experience. In Nowak's circle, new theories, originated in western philosophy and sociology, were being discussed as early as the 1970s. In the above mentioned paper by Krzysztof Nowak and Bakaniuk, the major theoretical reference was Berger's and Luckmann's 1966 book *The Social Construction of Reality*. Alongside phenomenology, works in sociolinguistics, cognitive psychology and symbolic interactionism were discussed. Sociologists read the classics (such as Weber) and drew inspiration from philosophy (such as Gadamer, Wittgenstein and

Winch). The beginning of the 1980s marked the encounter between the advanced reception of theoretical concepts, which had been present in Western sociology for two decades, and the experience of Solidarity, which legitimized reaching out for new theories. The discovery of Solidarity, a new type of social reality, meant that researchers had to go beyond presenting accounts of their and their subjects' experiences and structure them in the language of new theoretical perspectives.

8.8 Summary

In this article, I have argued that it is possible to talk about discoveries in social sciences, not only – as Collins (1994) suggests – in the case of new technologies generating huge quantities of data due to using algorithms. In the following paragraphs, I would like to touch on some theoretical themes which require more thought, namely, the concept of experience, determining reference and relative novelty.

1. **Experience**. Suggesting that Solidarity had to be discovered is bound to raise objections. As I have demonstrated, Solidarity did not have to be discovered because it was public and apparent to everybody. The questions concerning the nature and origins of social movements are always addressed in the public space by various subjects: the movement's participants, its opponents and its bystanders. The process of interpretation is closely linked to the personal experience of the participants themselves, regardless of whether they are researchers or not. Scientific language is not free from the influence of such interpretations, but it is autonomous, so it is not restricted to merely presenting accounts of people's experience. Instead, scientific language often goes far beyond recounting people's experiences. There remains the theoretical question of how to describe the relationship between the language of everyday experience, in which sociologists participated, and the sociological language they employed.

2. **Reference**. The second remark is related to the first one. Solidarity is not a physical phenomenon and so speaking in terms of establishing a reference does not seem as obvious as in the case of the objects that we perceive in everyday perception. Moreover, sociology rarely uses the language of ontology suggested by Kuhn's article. Social scientists discover not objects but, at best, patterns or causes. Since we cannot point to something in order to refer to it, we need to somehow conceptualize it. Hudson (2001) used the distinction created by Donnellan (1966), holding that a description can be referential or attributive in character. The criterion referred to in the moment of making a discovery is of the former character: it only enables us to refer to an object, which does not necessarily mean that it accurately describes its very nature. In the case of Solidarity, it is difficult to use any scholarly criteria, since it was accessible to everyday observation. Obviously, the realm of everyday experience is a social construction too, but it seems legitimate to add that sociological theory – even if

it is rooted in everyday experience of the world – has developed its autonomous criteria of validation. Although the experience of Solidarity was part of the scientists' lifeworld, it still required scientific conceptualisation. In addition, it is important to notice that establishing a reference is an act complicated in its very structure, since it is accompanied by a conviction that the referenced object was previously unknown.

3. **Relative novelty**. All discoveries are contextual in character; however, in the social sciences they are more dependent on the time and place they are made than in the natural sciences. Analyzing the discovery of America, Brannigan points to the fact that we recognize Columbus – and not the Vikings or the Phoenicians who probably had reached the shores of this continent before him – as the actual discoverer: "We are more tied to the announcement made by Columbus because of its outcome and the structure of recognition given to it, than to the oral sagas of the Irish and Norse" (Brannigan, 1981, p. 124). The theoretical concepts employed by Polish sociologists were known and used in world sociology (or at least referred to). However, one can argue first of all that they did not previously function in Polish sociology, so it was a discovery for the local scientific field. Secondly, and more importantly, Solidarity can be conceptualised as, for example, a case of a social movement, referring to the general theory of social movements (e.g. the theory of mobilizing resources). In this respect, it is difficult to talk about an original contribution of Polish sociologists to sociological theory. It is justified, however, to discuss theoretical innovations in describing Polish society. As I have demonstrated in the introductory remarks, sociology primarily constructs theories of historical objects, not theories of unrelated phenomena. In this respect, this novelty was not relative to any particular scientific field, but an absolute one. The relationship between those two levels of theorizing historical and abstract items requires further study, and as a result, we need to clarify the concept of novelty, which is a definitional feature of a discovery.

References

Alvarez, R. (Ed.). (2016). *Computational social science: Discovery and prediction.* New York: Cambridge University Press.

Ash, T. (2002). *The Polish revolution: Solidarity.* New Haven: Yale University Press.

Bakuniak, G., & Nowak, K. (1987). The creation of a collective identity in a social movement. The case of "Solidarność" in Poland. *Theory and Society, 16,* 401–429.

Berger, P., & Luckmann, T. (1966). *The social construction of reality: A treatise in the sociology of knowledge.* Garden City, NY: Anchor Books.

Brannigan, A. (1981). *The social basis of scientific discoveries.* Cambridge, UK: Cambridge University Press.

Cirtautas, A. (1997). *The Polish solidarity movement: Revolution, democracy and natural rights. Studies of societies in transition.* New York: Routledge.

Collins, R. (1994). Why the social sciences won't become high-consensus, rapid-discovery science. *Sociological Forum, 9,* 155–177.

Cuin, C. (2000). *Ce que ne font pas les sociologues: Petit essai d'épistémologie critique*. Genève, Switzerland: Droz.
Demeulenaere, P. (2011). Causal regularities, action and explanation. In P. Demeulenaere (Ed.), *Analytical sociology and social mechanisms* (pp. 173–197). Cambridge, UK: Cambridge University Press.
Donnellan, K. (1966). Reference and definite descriptions. *The Philosophical Review, 75*, 281–304.
Gella, A. (1987). *Naród w defensywie. Rozważania historyczne* [A nation on the defensive: Reflections on history]. London: Veritas Foundation Publication Centre.
Grabowska, M. (1989). Wywiad w badaniu zjawisk "trudnych". Przypadek polskiej religijności [Data collection for the study of difficult subjects: The case of Polish religiosity]. In A. Sułek, K. Nowak & A. Wyka (Eds.), *Poza granicami socjologii ankietowej* [Beyond survey sociology] (pp. 141–166). Warszawa, Poland: Uniwersytet Warszawski.
Hempel, C. (1966). *Aspects of scientific explanation and other essays in the philosophy of science*. New York: The Free Press.
Hudson, R. (2001). Discoveries, when and by whom? *The British Journal for the Philosophy of Science, 52*, 75–93.
Krzemiński, I. (1998). Metodologia jako filozofia pozytywistycznej równowagi. Ćwierć wieku w Instytucie Socjologii Uniwersytetu Warszawskiego Warszawskiego [Methodology as a philosophy of positivist equilibrium: A quarter century at the Institute of Sociology of the University of Warsaw]. *Kultura i Społeczeństwo, 4*, 103–119.
Krzemiński, I. (2005). Rzeczywistość miłości [The reality of love]. In M. Grabowska & T. Szawiel (Eds.), *Religijność społeczeństwa polskiego lat 80*. [The religiosity of Polish society in the 1980s]. Warszawa, Poland: Wydział Filozofii i Socjologii Uniwersytetu Warszawskiego.
Kuhn, T. (1977). The historical structure of scientific discovery. In T. Kuhn (Ed.), *The essential tension: Selected studies in scientific tradition and change* (pp. 165–177). Chicago: University of Chicago Press.
Laba, R. (1991). *The roots of solidarity: A political sociology of Poland's working-class democratization*. Princeton, NJ: Princeton University Press.
Labuda, G. (1996). Ruch "Solidarności" w perspektywie historycznej [The Solidarity movement in the historical perspective]. In J. Kulas (Ed.), *Sierpień '80: co pozostało z tamtych dni?* [August '80: What remains from those days?]. Gdańsk, Poland: Wydawnictwo Uniwersytetu Gdańskiego.
Lakatos, I. (1970). Falsification and the methodology of scientific research programmes. In I. Lakatos & A. Musgrave (Eds.), *Criticism and the growth of knowledge: Proceedings of the international colloquium in the philosophy of science, London, 1965* (pp. 91–196). Cambridge, UK: Cambridge University Press.
Marody, M., & Nowak, K. (1983). Wartości a działania (O niektórych teoretycznych i metodologicznych problemach badania wartości i ich związków z działaniem) [Values and actions (On certain theoretical and methodological problems in studying values and their relations with actions)]. *Studia Socjologiczne, 4*, 5–30.
McArthur, D. (2011). Discovery, theory change and structural realism. *Synthese, 179*, 361–376.
Mitchell, S. (2009). Complexity and explanation in the social sciences. In C. Mantzavinos (Ed.), *Philosophy of the social sciences: Philosophical theory and scientific practice* (pp. 130–145). Cambridge, UK: Cambridge University Press.
Musgrave, A. (1976). Why did oxygen supplant phlogiston? Research programmes in the chemical revolution. In C. Howson (Ed.), *Method and appraisal in the physical sciences: The critical background to modern science, 1800–1905* (pp. 181–210). Cambridge, UK: Cambridge University Press.
Nowak, S. (1980). Value systems of the Polish society. *Polish Sociological Bulletin, 2*, 5–20.
Nowak, S. (1981). Values and attitudes of the Polish people. *Scientific American, 245*, 45–53.
Nowak, S. (2009). Niedaleko od jabłoni [The apple doesn't fall far from the tree. In S. Nowak (Ed.), *O Polsce i Polakach. Prace rozproszone 1958–1989* [On Poland and Poles: Diverse works 1958–1989] (pp. 123–134). Warszawa, Poland: Wydawnictwa Uniwersytetu Warszawskiego.

Pawlak, M. (2015). From sociological vacuum to horror vacui: How Stefan Nowak's thesis is used in analyses of Polish society. *Polish Sociological Review, 1*(189), 5–27.

Rykowski, Z. (1986). Lustro społeczeństwa [The mirror of society]. *Polityka, 39,* 7.

Touraine, A., Dubet, F., Wieviorka, M., & Strzelecki, J. (1983). *Solidarity: The analysis of a social movement: Poland, 1980–1981.* Cambridge, UK/Paris: Cambridge University Press/Editions de la Maison des Sciences de l'Homme.

Woolgar, S. (1989). *Science: The very idea.* London: Routledge.

Part III
Formalising Theories in Social Science

Chapter 9
Syntax, Semantics and the Formalisation of Social Science Theories

Maria Dimarogkona, Mark Addis, and Petros Stefaneas

Abstract Selected historical and contemporary aspects of the debate between the syntactic and semantic views of scientific theories are presented. The theory of institutions is an abstract model theory approach which allows representation of both the syntactic and semantic views of scientific theories in a way which is free from dependence upon particular formal languages and logics. The standard definition of an institution, and the logical equivalence of the syntactic and the semantic definitions of a theory over an institution are presented. The value of the theory of institutions for formalising computer science theories is reviewed and the wider methodological implications of this approach are considered. Formalising social science theories in the theory of institutions has a number of benefits including enabling approaches which simultaneously require the use of more than one theoretical vocabulary and permitting transitions between different levels of abstraction.

Keywords Formal theory · Indexed structure · Institution theory · Labelled structure · Learning theory · Logical positivism · Semantics · Software specification · Syntax

M. Dimarogkona (✉)
Department of Humanities, Social Sciences and Law, National Technical University of Athens, Athens, Greece
e-mail: mariadim@ntua.central.gr

M. Addis
Centre for Philosophy of Natural and Social Science, London School of Economics and Political Science, London, UK
e-mail: m.addis@lse.ac.uk

P. Stefaneas
Department of Mathematics, National Technical University of Athens, Athens, Greece
e-mail: petros@math.ntua.gr

© Springer Nature Switzerland AG 2019
M. Addis et al. (eds.), *Scientific Discovery in the Social Sciences*,
Synthese Library 413, https://doi.org/10.1007/978-3-030-23769-1_9

9.1 Introduction

There has been much debate over whether the best approach to the analysis of scientific theories is syntactic or semantic. The focus here will be on methods of formalisation and how this relates to the individuation of theories. The syntactic approach developed by logical positivists became known as the received view (Putnam, 1962). In this approach, scientific theories are sets of sentences in deductive axiom systems containing only logical, mathematical and theoretical symbols with appropriate empirical interpretations of non-logical terms (Carnap, 1939; Nagel, 1961). The syntactic approach was criticised for either ignoring or distorting many aspects of theory construction in science (van Fraassen, 1980) and increasingly fell out of favour as logical positivism waned. It was gradually replaced by the semantic approach to scientific theories which held that theories are classes of model theoretic structures where a model is a structure in which a theory is true (Suppe, 1989, 2000). In this approach the connection between formal structures and empirical terms is usually regarded as one of representation (Suppes, 2002). For a long period, the semantic approach was very largely taken to be the correct one and so there was little discussion of whether the analysis of scientific theories should be considered from a syntactic or semantic perspective. Recently, the debate has returned to prominence in the philosophy of science. Currently, the syntactic approach is still widely considered problematic (Muller, 2010), although work by Halvorson (2013) and others has been gradually making it a more acceptable position. There has been particular focus on the issue of whether in principle syntactic or semantic approaches are unable to describe specific theories (Glymour, 2013; Halvorson, 2012, 2013; Lutz, 2014; van Fraassen 2014). Lutz (2017) plausibly argues that careful examination of the debate suggests that there is little real difference between the syntactic and semantic views of scientific theories. The details of these arguments will not be examined here and instead the focus will be upon developing a framework for formalising scientific theories which is consistent with and supports Lutz's view.

A useful starting point for considering what might shape a suitable formal framework for scientific theories is to examine some criticisms that claim formalisation in syntactic approaches is too dependent on particular logics and languages (Lutz, 2017). An objection is that in the received view deductive axiom systems must be in first order logic and a number of significant scientific theories use the kind of mathematics (such as real number theorems in quantum mechanics) which makes their formulation in this logic completely impractical (Suppes, 2002). However, advocates of the received view such as Carnap (1939) and Hempel (1970) did not require restriction to first order logic and permitted higher order logic in deductive axiom systems (Lutz, 2012). Another more general objection is that the received view conflates a theory with the formulation of a theory in a particular language and that language can largely be disregarded when considering the structure of theories (van Fraassen, 1989, pp. 221 et seq.). Given this latter objection, it would be desirable to have a syntactic approach to formalisation which is not too dependent on particular languages and logics.

Another important consideration for what might shape a suitable formal framework for scientific theories is the significant difference between the use of model theoretic labelled and indexed structures in the formalisation of scientific theories (Lutz, 2017). Labelled structures are essentially dependent on particular signatures and uniquely determine particular signatures. For instance, a standard example of this is a definition of structures as pairs $< A, \mathfrak{J} >$ where A is a non-empty domain and $\mathfrak{J}$ is an interpretation which maps each n-ary relation symbol to a n-ary relation $R \subseteq A^n$ on A, each m-place function symbol F to an m-place function $G : A^m \longrightarrow A$ on A, and each constant symbol c to a constant $x \in A$. Relations are extensional such that $R = R'$ when $x \in R$ if and only if $x \in R'$ for all x (Chang & Keisler, 1990 §1.3).

Indexed structures are independent of particular signatures and determine the types of signature (rather than particular signatures). For instance, a standard example of this is a definition of structures as a pair $<A, \{R_i\}_{i \in I}>$ where A is a non-empty domain and $\{R_i\}_{i \in I}$ is an indexed set of extensional relations. The signature is interpreted by a bijection between the signature and the index set I of relations (Bell & Slomson, 1974, §3.2). The greater independence of indexed structures from particular signatures is valuable when formalising scientific theories. Indexed structures are also preferable to labelled structures when considering the categoricity of theories. A theory T is categorical if it has a unique model, up to isomorphism and T is κ-categorical for a cardinal κ if T has a unique model of cardinality κ. Structures describing scientific theories are themselves only describable up to structural isomorphism (van Fraassen, 2002, 2008). It is frequently the case that different types of structures describe a theory which means that not all these structures are isomorphic and thus the theory is not categorical. Given this it is more natural and useful to describe theories by types of indexed structures rather than by a single structure dependent on a particular signature.

When considering what might shape a suitable formal framework for scientific theories, it is also helpful to examine the criticism that formalisation in semantic approaches does not individuate theories appropriately. For example, Halvorson (2013) claims that semantic approaches do not distinguish between different theories using the idea that two structures $\langle A, R_1, \ldots, R_n \rangle$, $\langle B, S_1, \ldots, S_n \rangle$ are H-isomorphic if there is a bijection $j : A \to B$ and a bijection $k : \{R_i\}_{i \in \{1, \ldots, n\}} \to \{S_i\}_{i \in \{1, \ldots, n\}}$ such that if $\langle a_1, \ldots, a_n \rangle \in R_i$ then $\langle j(a_1), \ldots, j(a_n) \rangle \in k(R_i)$. However, this claim assumes that a theory is described by an equivalence class of classes of structures and two classes of structures are equivalent if and only if there is a bijection F from a class of structures to the other such that $F (\mathfrak{U})$ is H-isomorphic to $\mathfrak{U}$ (Halvorson, 2012). These claims have been objected to for a number of reasons. For instance, Glymour (2013) criticizes Halvorson's objection on the grounds that H-isomorphism is the incorrect relationship between structures since semantic approaches must depend on the usual model theoretic concept of isomorphism for labelled structures. In response to this it has been argued that as labelled structures uniquely determine particular signatures their use ensures that the semantic approach is essentially dependent on particular signatures (Lutz, 2017) and once language is added to the semantic view then it becomes a syntactic view (Halvorson, 2013).

Debate of this kind indicates that the difference between the syntactic and semantic approaches frequently turns on the particular choice of logical formalisms. The problem is that the use of these formalisms is often dependent upon complex considerations about logic itself rather than the nature of scientific theories. This in conjunction with the plausibility of Lutz's (2017) view that there is little real difference between the syntactic and semantic views of scientific theories, suggests that neither approach is generally preferable. It is therefore valuable to develop a framework for formalising scientific theories which is consistent with this arguable lack of real difference between the syntactic and semantic approaches, and with syntactic approaches which are not too dependent on particular logics and languages. As will be seen, the use of the abstract model theoretic approach of the theory of institutions for the formalisation of scientific theories enables the creation of such a framework.

9.2 The Theory of Institutions

The study of logic beyond the realm of classical first order logic has been going on since at least the late 1950s (such as with work on infinitary logics) and resulted in the general growth of abstract model theory. This growth marked a decisive shift away from a focus upon the isolated investigation of specific especially first order logical systems to one upon the relationships between a wide range of logics. Early abstract model theory assigned a central place to the notion of an abstract logic (with major results being Lindström's theorem (Lindström, 1969) and Barwise's axiomatisation (Barwise, 1974)) but made limited use of ideas from category theory. In the 1980s, Goguen and Burstall introduced the theory of institutions as a type of model theoretic framework which combined the distinct mathematical strands of abstract model theory and category theory (MacLane, 1998). Category theory is good at representing mathematical structures on a higher level (such as the category **Grp** where the objects are groups and the arrows group homomorphisms) through a process of gradual abstraction as the emphasis is not upon the internal structure of particular objects but rather on mappings including mappings between objects and mappings between maps. Institutions are category theory structures but their behaviour is that of abstract model theory structures.

The approach of the theory of institutions is a very general model-theoretically oriented study of logical systems which does not involve a commitment to or give priority to any particular logical system. The concept of an institution is that it is a logical system which includes syntax, semantics, and the relationships between them. For example, by contrast classical model theory is concerned with sets of sentences defined in a first order language. The theory of institutions was used to relate various logics (such as fragments of many sorted first order logic and higher order logic with polymorphic types) employed in specification and programming in computer science (Goguen & Burstall, 1984). Subsequently, many more logical systems including first order logic, higher order logic, intuitionistic logic, many valued logics, modal logics, temporal logics, fuzzy logics and equational logics have been defined as institutions. The very high level of abstraction of the theory of institutions ensures that it can both define well established logical systems and very unconventional ones (such as the logic of semantic networks (Dimarogkona & Stefaneas, 2013)), and be used as a framework for defining new logical systems.

The concept of an institution is more general than that of an abstract logic in that it achieves independence from actual logical systems through a fully categorical abstraction of the main logical concepts of signature, sentence, model and of the satisfaction relation between sentences and models (Diaconescu, 2008). It is important to emphasize that signatures, sentences and models are treated as objects and that the use of categories permits the modelling of changes (including possible combinations) between these objects. For example, signatures can be composed. The only assumption is that there is a satisfaction condition between sentences and models indicating whether a sentence holds in a model or not. The satisfaction condition extends Tarski's (1944) semantic definition of truth and generalises Barwise's translation axiom (1974) by formalising the idea that truth is invariant under change of notation (Goguen & Burstall, 1984). This accords with the notion that an important conceptual requirement for any abstract concept of semantics is that truth is independent from the symbolism it is formulated in.

Definition 1 An institution I is classically defined as consisting of:

- a category **Sign** whose objects are signatures and whose arrows are signature morphisms
- a functor Sen : **Sign** $\rightarrow$ **Set** mapping each signature Σ in **Sign** to a set of Σ-sentences over that signature
- a functor Mod : **Sign** $\rightarrow$ **Cat**^{op} assigning to each signature Σ in **Sign** a category whose objects are Σ-models and whose morphisms are Σ-model morphisms
- and a relation $\models_\Sigma \subseteq |Mod(\Sigma)| \times Sen(\Sigma)$ for each $\Sigma \in$ |**Sign**| called Σ-satisfaction such that for each signature morphism $\phi : \Sigma \rightarrow \Sigma'$ the satisfaction condition $m' \models_{\Sigma'} Sen(\phi)(e)$ iff $Mod(\phi)(m') \models_\Sigma e$ holds for each $m' \in |Mod(\Sigma')|$ and each $e \in Sen(\Sigma)$

This classical definition of an institution applies to any logic which has a model (for a detailed argument for this claim, see Mossakowski et al. (2005)). It is possible to generalise institutions in a variety of ways such as by letting the satisfaction condition take values other than true and false (Goguen, 1986) or giving classes of sentences and models more structure (Goguen & Rosu, 2002).

Although the classical definition and most of the literature on the theory of institutions uses the concept of a signature, the growing range of applications of institutional theory are better characterised by the use of the concept of a context. It is therefore useful to define an institution without the explicit use of the concept of a category to show how category theory formalises the concept of a context (Goguen, 2004, appendix A). However, the definition still involves category theory in the form of the assumptions that there is a given category of contexts and that there are functors on this category. Unlike the classical definition of an institution, in this definition axioms may-but do not need to-be sentences.

Definition 2 An institution I consists of contexts C and context morphisms $\phi : C \to C'$ such that:

- there is a partially or fully defined composition operation; for a context C and context morphisms $\varphi : C \to C'$ and $\psi : C' \to C''$ $\varphi; \psi : C \to C''$ denotes their composition. This composition operation is associative $((\varphi; \psi); \xi = \phi;(\psi; \xi)$ whenever these compositions are defined) and has identities (given a context C an identity operation is a context morphism 1_C such that $1_C; \varphi = \varphi$ and $\varphi; 1_C = \varphi$)
- a context C has a given set of axioms, or sentences, Sen (S). The translation of an axiom a from context C to context C' is $Sen(\varphi)(a)$, or $\varphi(a)$, assuming that φ; $\psi (a) = \psi(\phi(a))$ and $1_C(a) = a$
- a context C has a given set of models Mod (S) (strictly speaking this is a class, in the sense of Gödel-Bernays set theory). The contravariant translation of a model M' from context C' to context C is $Mod(\varphi)(M')$ assuming that ψ; $\varphi (M') = \psi(\phi(M'))$ and $1_C(M') = M'$
- *a satisfaction condition* $M' \models_{C'} \phi(x)$ iff $\phi(M') \models_C x$ for all models M' in contexts C' and all axioms x in contexts C.

As can be seen by comparing Definitions 1 and 2, the theory of institutions uses category theory to formalise the concepts of signature or contexts, translations amongst signatures or contexts, and the effects of such translations on sentences and models. Each translation is parameterised by signatures or contexts and by mappings termed signature or context morphisms which together form the category denoted by **Sign**. The description of contexts and their morphisms given in Definition 2 actually constitutes a precise definition of the category **Sign**. Institutions form the important category **Ins**, whose objects are institutions and whose morphisms are institution morphisms. The institution morphisms enable the translation of sentences from one logical system to another. Within the category **Ins**, there are categorical constructions which produce a general systems theory (such as the use of colimits to combine two institutions and so on).

Syntactic theories over institutions are used to define parts of a system of theories and to describe the behaviour of the system in terms of sets of sentences describing that behaviour. In Definitions 3 and 4 below, the definition of closure depends upon the idea that a closed theory already contains all the consequences of its sentences. For reasons of generality the definition of closure is taken to be model-theoretic closure. However, it should be remarked that for institutions (such as equational logics) with a complete set of inference rules a corresponding proof theoretic definition of closure can be given (Goguen & Burstall, 1992). Theory morphisms can be used to define various views of and modifications to a system of theories (Diaconescu, 2008).

Definition 3 A syntactic theory T over an institution I is defined by:

- A Σ-theory presentation is a pair $\langle \Sigma, E \rangle$, where Σ is a signature and E is a set of Σ-sentences.
- A Σ-model A satisfies $\langle \Sigma, E \rangle$ if A satisfies each sentence in E in which case $A \vDash E$.
- The closure of E is the set $E^{\bullet}$. E is closed if and only if $E = E^{\bullet}$. A syntactic Σ-theory is a syntactic presentation $\langle \Sigma, E \rangle$ such that E is closed.
- The syntactic Σ-theory corresponding to the syntactic presentation $\langle \Sigma, E \rangle$ is $\langle \Sigma, E^{\bullet} \rangle$.

In **Th** a morphism $G: T \rightarrow T'$ between two syntactic theories $\langle \Sigma, E^{\bullet} \rangle$ and $\langle \Sigma', E'^{\bullet} \rangle$ is a signature morphism $\varphi: \Sigma \rightarrow \Sigma'$ such that $\varphi(e) \in E'$ holds for any sentence $e \in E$.

Syntactic theories T over an institution I form the category **Th** whose objects are syntactic theories and whose morphisms are syntactic theory morphisms. The dual of the definition of a syntactic theory over an institution I is the definition of a semantic theory over I. Semantic theories are language independent. A set of models is called closed when its elements are all the models of some set of sentences.

Definition 4 A semantic theory V over an institution I is defined by:

- A Σ-theory presentation is a pair $\langle \Sigma, M \rangle$ where Σ is a signature and M is a set of Σ-models.
- A Σ-model A satisfies a set of Σ-sentences E if A satisfies each sentence in E in which case $A \vDash E$.
- The closure of M is the set $M^{\bullet}$. M is closed if and only if $M = M^{\bullet}$. A semantic Σ-theory is a semantic presentation $\langle \Sigma, M \rangle$ such that M is closed.
- The semantic Σ-theory corresponding to the semantic presentation $\langle \Sigma, M \rangle$ is $\langle \Sigma, M^{\bullet} \rangle$.

In **Vth** a morphism $G: V \rightarrow V'$ between two semantic theories $\langle \Sigma, M^{\bullet} \rangle$ and $\langle \Sigma', M'^{\bullet} \rangle$ is a signature morphism $\varphi: \Sigma \rightarrow \Sigma'$ such that $\varphi(m) \in M'$ holds for any model in M.

Semantic theories V over an institution I form the category **Vth** whose objects are semantic theories and whose morphisms are semantic theory morphisms. The concept of syntactic and semantic morphisms of theories over an institution is generalised by the concept of morphisms between theories belonging to different institutions (where mappings between theories take the form of embeddings) through a satisfaction condition for morphisms between theories belonging to different institutions (Diaconescu, 1998).

In category theory, syntax and semantics are adjoint with a Galois connection between sets of axioms and classes of models for a fixed signature, being a particular case of this connection (Lawvere, 1969). The duality of the definitions of a syntactic theory and a semantic theory over an institution between a set of Σ-sentences and the closed set of Σ-models satisfying those sentences, and between a set of Σ-models and the closed set of Σ-sentences satisfying those models is a Galois connection. Using this Galois connection, it is straightforward to show the logical equivalence of the definitions of a syntactic theory and a semantic theory over an institution.

9.3 Formalising Computer Science Theories

Before considering the methodological benefits of the use of the theory of institutions for the formalisation of scientific theories, it is useful to briefly review some illustrative examples of the application of institutions in the formalisation of computer science theories. These examples provide insight into the capacities of institutions to describe and analyse relationships in complex systems, and indicate that the institutions approach can be applied beyond the field of computer science. A wide variety of logics are employed in theoretical computer science, with the theory of institutions being successfully applied in a range of areas such as algebraic specifications (Diaconescu, 2008). An important development was the utilisation of institutions to construct larger specifications from smaller ones. Given institutions I and I' whose signatures can be combined or integrated, syntactic theories over I can be combined and integrated with syntactic theories over I' using colimits to construct larger specifications from smaller ones (Goguen & Burstall, 1992).

Constructing larger software specifications from smaller ones is useful when developing modular software systems (such as those involving object-orientated programs) with system specifications being constructed from combinations and integrations of module specifications (Diaconescu et al., 1993). This ability to construct larger specifications from smaller ones has been used to study the logical structure of modular software systems through the modelling of the semantics of these systems. A modular semantic theory is defined by a semantic theory for each module of a system and relationships connecting the various semantic theories. The logical equivalence of the definitions of a syntactic theory and a semantic theory over an institution is useful when formulating a modular semantic theory. Interactions take place between individual modules and groups of modules. For example, program operations arising from the interactions of two modules may subsequently interact with other operations. A semantic theory for each module of a system can be constructed by defining morphisms in the category **Th** of theories over an institution to generate program specifications based on sets of sentences which describe allowable program behaviour for that module. Interactions between individual modules and groups of modules can be constructed by defining morphisms in the category **Ins** of module institutions, thereby allowing the construction of larger institutions from smaller ones. In principle, this process can be iterated to construct an institution which describes the whole of a modular software system (Angius & Stefaneas, 2016). Institutions facilitate the extensive use of model checking in software verification, as many program specifications are semantically defined as state transition systems (such as Büchi automata) particularly where model checking evaluates program correctness (Baier & Katoen, 2008). A semantic theory of program behaviour defined over an institution is a method of constructing combined and extended state transition systems from elementary specifications (Angius & Stefaneas, 2016). These examples of the application of institutions in the formalisation of computer science theories provide a useful background against which to examine the general methodological benefits of this approach.

9.4   Methodological Benefits of Institution Theory

The use of the theory of institutions for the formalisation of scientific theories has a number of methodological benefits. On this approach, a scientific theory can be defined as a theory over an institution I where the institution represents the underlying logical form of that theory. Since institutions go far beyond first order logic to encompass any possible logical system, scientific theories can have a variety of formalisations. The Galois connection between closed sets of sentences and closed sets of models in syntactic and semantic theories over an institution can be applied to the formalisation of scientific theories to relate sentences of and classes of models of a scientific theory over an institution without there being any direct identification between them. Two syntactic scientific theories $T=\langle\Sigma,E^{\bullet}\rangle$ and $T'=\langle\Sigma',E'^{\bullet}\rangle$ are equivalent over an institution I if and only if $F{:}T{\rightarrow}T'$ is an isomorphism. Two semantic scientific theories $V=\langle\Sigma,M^{\bullet}\rangle$ and $V'=\langle\Sigma',M'^{\bullet}\rangle$ are equivalent over an institution I if and only if $H{:}V \rightarrow V'$ is an isomorphism. Applying these definitions in conjunction with the Galois connection it is straightforward to prove the logical equivalence of the definitions of a syntactic scientific theory and a semantic scientific theory over an institution. Two syntactic scientific theories $T=\langle\Sigma,E^{\bullet}\rangle$ and $T'=\langle\Sigma',E'^{\bullet}\rangle$ over an institution I are equivalent if and only if the semantic scientific theories $V=\langle\Sigma,M^{\bullet}\rangle$ and $V'=\langle\Sigma',M'^{\bullet}\rangle$ that they define are equivalent. This equivalence demonstrates the logical equivalence of the syntactic and the semantic formalisations of scientific theories. Institutions can provide a flexible framework for the study of scientific theories from both the syntactic and semantic approaches and it is clearly valuable to be able to formalise them in a way that permits their interchangeability according to the requirements of particular situations. Given this basis, an algebraic theory calculus for formalised scientific theories which resembles interpolation theory with main operators such as sum, extension, transformation, and inclusion can be developed.

The logical equivalence of the syntactic and semantic formalisations of scientific theories has the consequence that there are no good logical grounds for rejecting either the syntactic or semantic approach to the formalisation of scientific theories, although there might be other philosophical grounds for preferring one approach to the other. This has significant consequences for the current philosophical debate about these approaches discussed earlier. For example, the logical equivalence of the definitions of a syntactic scientific theory and a semantic scientific theory over an institution indicates that the debate between Glymour (2013) and Halvorson (2013) over whether semantic approaches can distinguish between different theories could be reframed in such way that their views are less distinct than they initially appear to be. More generally, much of the discussion of whether the syntactic or semantic approach to the formalisation of scientific theories can usefully be reframed using the logical equivalence of these formalisations also shows what is really a significant philosophical issue and what is a matter of particular logical formulation.

The possibility of various formalisations effectively addresses the criticism that formalisation in the syntactic approach is too dependent on particular logics and languages. Due to the Galois connection between closed sets of sentences and closed sets of models in syntactic and semantic theories over an institution, syntactic similarity between signatures ceases to be important. Institutions enable syntactic approaches to the formalisation of scientific theories which simultaneously require the use of more than one theoretical vocabulary because different theoretical vocabularies can be modelled as theories for various signatures over an institution with theory morphisms enabling transitions between them. In so doing, institutions considerably strengthen the view that the syntactic approach to scientific theories is viable. The theory of institutions allows transitions between different levels of abstraction when formalising scientific theories. Syntactic and semantic theories in the category **Th** of theories over an institution are part of the category **Ins** of institutions and this enables the construction of larger scientific theories from smaller ones through the use of categorical constructions (Angius, Dimarogkona & Stefaneas, 2017). Finally, it should also me mentioned that institutional theory supports automated theorem proving so that institutions can be employed in automating the generation and refinement of scientific theories.

9.5   Formalising Social Science Theories

Formal theories have become increasingly prevalent across the whole range of social science disciplines due to their increasing mathematisation and use of computational methods coupled with growth in the amount of accessible data. Such theories trade off levels of analytical detail in return for general explanatory power and greater ease in empirical testing. A whole range of mathematical fields are used in the formalisation of social science theories, with logic being most appropriate for some of these. Within the area of logic, the theory of institutions has significant potential as a useful formalisation tool. Here it might be objected that the formalisation of social science theories does not require the highly abstract mathematical approach of the theory of institutions and that first-order logic would suffice. However, as has been observed earlier, a range of theories use the kind of mathematics whose formulation in first order logic is completely impractical and so favouring this logic over the theory of institutions would be unnecessarily restrictive. The benefits of using institutions include the logical equivalence of the syntactic and semantic formalisations of social science theories and transitions between different levels of abstraction. These general points will be illustrated by considering the example of formal learning theory.

Following Kelly (2004), the background to formal learning theory is the idea that learning can be very broadly characterised as adaptive change in either beliefs or actions in response to alterations in the environment. This change can occur through the acquisition of new information and through learning processes which are guaranteed to arrive at correct conclusions prior to the actual acquisition of any new knowledge, with such processes being deemed strategically reliable. Formal learning theory is a logical investigation of the concept of strategic reliability where the concern is how reliable any learning system could possibly be. This approach to learning examines a situation and a set of cognitive objectives with the aim of identifying the best method of achieving those objectives. Although formal learning theory is pure normative a priori epistemology in that it is concerned with norms for learning processes, it does not seek universal context-free methodological strategies for reliable learning. Methodological strategies depend on various factors including norms in a given situation, subjects of inquiry, background assumptions, information acquisition abilities, and the cognitive capacities and goals of the leaner. Formal learning theory addresses the vagueness of the concept of reliability-which can very broadly be identified with a disposition to acquire new skill over a wide range of environments-by investigating a variety of possible explanations of what reliability could consist of, without privileging any particular one as correct. In doing so the emphasis is no longer upon problematic analysis about what the correct definition of the concept of reliability is and instead is upon the far more sharply defined investigation of exactly which kinds of reliability are realisable for given precisely specified learning problems. A formal learning problem specifies what is to be learned, a range of relevantly possible environments in which the learner may succeed, the kinds of inputs these environments provide to the learner, what it means to learn over a range of relevant possible environments, and the sorts of learning strategies that will be considered as a solution. A learning problem is solved by a learning strategy if that problem accepts it as a potential solution and that strategy succeeds in a relevant way over the possibilities. If some admissible strategy solves a problem, that problem is solvable. The construction of an admissible learning strategy coupled with proof of success in a relevant way establishes a positive solvability result. A general proof that every permissible learning strategy fails establishes a negative solvability result. Positive and negative solvability results combine to produce permissible learning strategies which are more complex and interesting than the sum of the individual solvability results (Kelly, 2004).

The context dependence of learning strategies in formal learning theory can be represented by modelling a formal learning theory as both a syntactic and semantic theory over an institution with objects syntactic formal learning theories and morphisms syntactic formal learning theory morphisms, and objects semantic formal learning theories and morphisms semantic formal learning theory morphisms, respectively. The Galois connection guarantees the logical equivalence of the definitions of a syntactic formal learning theory and a semantic formal learning theory over an institution. Morphisms between syntactic theories over this institution generate learning strategies based on sets of sentences which describe allowable learning behaviour for that institution. Interactions between individual and groups of formal learning theories can be represented by defining the category of formal learning theory institutions, and defining morphisms between formal learning theories belonging to different formal learning theory institutions which are mappings of how these theories are embedded. Such mappings allow the comparison of different learning strategies in formal learning theory. What this example shows is that the theory of institutions has clear applicability to modelling complex social science theories due to its flexibility and capacity to handle different levels of abstraction. Due to these benefits, there should be increased use of institutions in the formalisation of social science theories.

9.6   Conclusion

The theory of institutions offers a new framework for formalising scientific theories whose value is clearly evident particularly after some familiarity with its use has been gained. This way of formalising scientific theories accommodates both the syntactic and semantic approaches, and is consistent with the philosophical view that there is a lack of real difference between these approaches. Due to the categorically defined logical equivalence of the syntactic and the semantic formalisations of scientific theories, free movement between them is possible and equivalence is across abstract logical systems (rather than being restricted to first order logic). Importantly, this logical equivalence means that there are no good logical-as opposed to philosophical-grounds for rejecting either the syntactic or the semantic approach. The theory of institutions considerably strengthens the view that the syntactic approach to scientific theories is viable as it enables syntactic approaches which are not too dependent on particular logics and languages. It follows that a considerable part of the reassessment of syntactic approaches to scientific theories should be framed in terms of logical issues raised by the institutional approach. More generally, the value of the theory of institutions accords with the increasing general recognition of the significance of category-theoretic methods in the philosophy of science. The well-established effectiveness of the theory of institutions for computer science indicates their potential for social science. There are a number of benefits to formalising social science theories using institutions, such as enabling approaches which simultaneously require the use of more than one theoretical vocabulary and permitting transitions between different levels of abstraction. The increasing prevalence of formal theories across the whole range of social science disciplines shows the scope for significant gains from the application of the theory of institutions.

Acknowledgements   The first author was supported by a PhD grant from the National Technical University of Athens.

References

Angius, N., Dimarogkona, M., & Stefaneas, P. (2017). Building and integrating semantic theories over institutions. In S. Lambropoulou, P. Stefaneas, D. Theodorou, & L. Kauffman (Eds.), *Algebraic modeling of topological and computational structures and applications* (pp. 363–374). Berlin, Germany: Springer.

Angius, N., & Stefaneas, P. (2016). Discovering empirical theories of modular software systems: An algebraic approach. In V. Müller (Ed.), *Computing and philosophy: Selected papers from IACAP 2014* (pp. 99–115). Berlin, Germany: Springer.

Baier, C., & Katoen, J.-P. (2008). *Principles of model checking*. Cambridge, UK: MIT Press.

Barwise, J. (1974). Axioms for abstract model theory. *Annals of Mathematical Logic, 7*, 221–265.

Bell, J., & Slomson, A. (1974). *Models and ultraproducts: An introduction* (3rd ed.). Amsterdam: North Holland.

Carnap, R. (1939). Foundations of logic and mathematics. *International Encyclopedia*, I, no. 3. Chicago: University of Chicago Press.

Chang, C., & Keisler, J. (1990). *Model theory*. Amsterdam: North Holland.

Diaconescu, R. (1998). Extra theory morphisms for institutions: Logical semantics for multi-paradigm languages. *Applied Categorical Structures, 6*, 427–453.

Diaconescu, R. (2008). *Institution-independent model theory*. Basel, Switzerland: Birkhäuser.

Diaconescu, R., Goguen, J., & Stefaneas, P. (1993). Logical support for modularization. In G. Huet & G. Plotkin (Eds.), *Logical environments* (pp. 83–100). Cambridge, UK: Cambridge University Press.

Dimarogkona, M., & Stefaneas, P. (2013). Semantic networks and institutions. In A. Pinus, K. Ponomarev, S. Sudoplatov, & E. Timoshenko (Eds.), *Algebra and model theory 9* (pp. 8–18). Novosibirsk, Russia: Novosibirsk State Technical University.

Glymour, C. (2013). Theoretical equivalence and the semantic view of theories. *Philosophy of Science, 80*, 286–297.

Goguen, J. (1986). A study in the functions of programming methodology: Specifications, institutions, charters and parchments. In C. Pitt, S. Abramsky, A. Poigne & D. Rydeheard (Eds.). *Category theory and computer programming* (Lecture notes in computer science 240, pp. 313–333). Heidelberg, Germany: Springer.

Goguen, J. (2004). *Information integration in institutions*. https://cseweb.ucsd.edu/~goguen/pps/ifi04.pdf

Goguen, J., & Burstall, R. (1984). Introducing institutions. In E. Clarke & D. Kozen (Eds.), *Proceedings of logics of programming workshop* (Lecture notes in computer science 164, pp. 221–256). Heidelberg, Germany: Springer.

Goguen, J., & Burstall, R. (1992). Institutions: Abstract model theory for specification and programming. *Journal of the Association for Computing Machinery, 39*, 95–146.

Goguen, J., & Rosu, G. (2002). Institution morphisms. *Formal Aspects of Computing, 13*, 274–307.

Halvorson, H. (2012). What scientific theories could not be. *Philosophy of Science, 79*, 183–206.

Halvorson, H. (2013). The semantic view, if plausible, is syntactic. *Philosophy of Science, 80*, 475–478.

Hempel, C. (1970). On the "standard conception" of scientific theories. In M. Radner & S. Winokur (Eds.), *Theories and methods of physics and psychology, Minnesota studies in philosophy of science volume iv* (pp. 142–163). Minneapolis, MN: University of Minnesota Press.

Kelly, K. (2004). Learning theory and epistemology. In I. Niiniluoto, M. Sintonen, & J. Wolenski (Eds.), *Handbook of epistemology* (pp. 183–203). Dordrecht, the Netherlands: Kluwer Academic Publishers.

Lawvere, F. (1969). Adjointness in foundations. *Dialectica, 23*, 281–296.

Lindström, P. (1969). On extensions of elementary logic. *Theoria, 35*, 1–11.

Lutz, S. (2012). On a straw man in the philosophy of science: A defense of the received view. *HOPOS: The Journal of the International Society for the History of Philosophy of Science, 2*, 77–120.

Lutz, S. (2014). What's right with a syntactic approach to theories and models? *Erkenntnis, 79*(8 Suppl), 1475–1492.

Lutz, S. (2017). What was the syntax-semantics debate in the philosophy of science about? *Philosophy and Phenomenological Research, 95*, 319–352.

MacLane, S. (1998). *Categories for the working mathematician.* New York: Springer.

Mossakowski, T., Goguen, J., Diaconescu, R., & Tarlecki, A. (2005). What is a logic? In J.-Y. Beziau (Ed.), *Logica universalis: Towards a general theory of logic* (pp. 113–133). Basel, Switzerland: Birkhauser.

Muller, F. (2010). Reflections on the revolution at Stanford. *Synthese, 183*, 87–114.

Nagel, E. (1961). *The structure of science: Problems in the logic of scientific explanation.* New York: Harcourt, Brace and World.

Putnam, H. (1962). What theories are not. In E. Nagel, P. Suppes, & A. Tarski (Eds.), *Logic, methodology, and philosophy of science: Proceedings of the 1960 international congress* (pp. 240–251). Stanford, CA: Stanford University Press.

Suppe, F. (1989). *The semantic conception of theories and scientific realism.* Urbana, IL: University of Illinois Press.

Suppe, F. (2000). Understanding scientific theories: An assessment of developments, 1969–1998. *Philosophy of Science, 67*, S102–S115.

Suppes, P. (2002). *Representation and invariance of scientific structures.* Stanford, CA: CSLI Publications.

Tarski, A. (1944). The semantic conception of truth and the foundations of semantics. *Philosophy and Phenomenological Research, 4*, 341–376.

van Fraassen, B. (1989). *Laws and symmetry.* Oxford, UK: Clarendon Press.

van Fraassen, B. (1980). *The scientific image.* Oxford, UK: Clarendon Press.

van Fraassen, B. (2002). *The empirical stance.* New Haven, CT: Yale University Press.

van Fraassen, B. (2008). *Scientific representation: Paradoxes of perspective.* Oxford, UK: Clarendon Press.

van Fraassen, B. (2014). One or two gentle remarks about Hans Halvorson's critique of the semantic view. *Philosophy of Science, 81*, 276–283.

Chapter 10
Semi-Automatic Generation of Cognitive Science Theories

Mark Addis, Fernand Gobet, Peter C. R. Lane, and Peter D. Sozou

Abstract Developing computational models constitutes an important aspect of research in science in general and cognitive science in particular. It is a notoriously difficult enterprise and methods for (semi-)automatically developing models are desirable, possibly using evolutionary mechanisms. Although the evolutionary properties of scientific knowledge have received some attention in the philosophy of science, the actual use of computationally based Darwinian selection processes to develop theories has been limited to research by the present authors. The optimisation capacities of genetic programming are employed as a basis for the semi-automatic generation and testing of cognitive science models. A population of models is subjected to Darwinian selection processes and evolved using a genetic programming algorithm. Good models make predictions that are consistent with the data. A number of philosophical issues raised by this approach are explored, including the role of Lakatos research programmes in the development of cognitive science theories, simulation as a kind of fictional modelling, the nature of explanations produced by models generated by genetic programming, problems of theory confirmation, and the extent to which theory development can be regarded as an exclusively human activity.

Keywords Computational modelling · Fictional model · Formal modelling · Informal theory · Genetic programming · Lakatos programme · Machine discovery · Robust testing · Theory generation

M. Addis (✉) · P. D. Sozou
Centre for Philosophy of Natural and Social Science, London School of Economics and Political Science, London, UK
e-mail: m.addis@lse.ac.uk; p.sozou@lse.ac.uk

F. Gobet
Department of Psychological Sciences, University of Liverpool, Liverpool, UK
e-mail: fernand.gobet@liverpool.ac.uk

P. C. R. Lane
Department of Computer Science, University of Hertfordshire, Hatfield, UK
e-mail: p.c.lane@herts.ac.uk

© Springer Nature Switzerland AG 2019   155
M. Addis et al. (eds.), *Scientific Discovery in the Social Sciences*,
Synthese Library 413, https://doi.org/10.1007/978-3-030-23769-1_10

10.1 Introduction

In the philosophy of science, substantial attention has been paid to the evaluation, testing, and interpretation of scientific theories with rather less examination of questions around how new scientific theories are constructed. In contrast, in the history of science, science and technology studies and psychology, there is considerable interest in the particularities of the process of theory construction. Traditionally, scientists have engaged in theory construction using a number of methods, including systematic and random search strategies. In the last few decades, improvements in computational methods have enabled automatic or semi-automatic scientific discovery, resulting in a significant change in the heuristics of scientific theory construction. These developments are part of the rising importance of big data in the processes of scientific discovery, especially with respect to hypothesis formulation and the role of theories in the explanation of data. Due to these developments, progress in better characterising the processes of theory construction, confirmation and evaluation can contribute to understanding computational scientific discovery (Simon, 1977; Thagard, 1988). Analysis of particular philosophical aspects of the semi-automatic generation of cognitive science theories should be located within a more general assessment of the benefits and drawbacks of computationally-based theory development in cognitive science.

Most social science theories have informal (usually verbal) formulations, which may lack precision in varying degrees; a number of potential difficulties may result from this. A lack of precision about concepts allows the possibility that an informal theory is a redescription rather than an explanation of the data it is intended to account for. Discussion of these theories frequently focuses upon clarification of the concepts which they use. As a consequence of this, it may be difficult to precisely determine the implications of a disagreement about specific parts of a theory. This is a particular problem when attempting to compare models produced by informal theories as it may be unclear exactly what is being compared. Due to this lack of precision, informal theories may be of limited use in predicting how mechanisms (especially complex ones) interact. As the level of interactive complexity increases, the predictive power of informal theories gradually declines and it is not possible for these theories to explain empirical phenomena because the limits of human cognition prevent a theorist from keeping track of all the constraints involved. As well as problems with predictability, informal theories may have difficulties with confirmation such as being non-falsifiable in Popper's (1959) sense, where falsifiability is deemed a crucial indicator of being a worthwhile scientific theory. These potential difficulties are significant grounds for the increasing use of mathematical and computational modelling in social science. Despite this, relatively few social science theories are expressed as formal models such as mathematical and computational models because in many instances there is a tradition of collecting and analysing data, but no tradition of constructing formal models; this is especially the case in cognitive science, including psychology.

The contribution of formal modelling to scientific discovery is manifold. In addition to the obvious fact that formal models contribute to the theoretical development of a field, and thus to understanding, they also in some cases enable unification of several explanations that were previously disconnected. For example, in research on children's acquisition of vocabulary, a model combining mechanisms from the fields of language acquisition, memory and learning accounts for some key empirical data in great detail (Jones, Gobet, & Pine, 2007; Tamburelli, Jones, Gobet, & Pine, 2012). Another important contribution of formal models is that they can predict new phenomena. For example, the received wisdom in psychology was that experts memorise material from their domain of expertise better than non-experts when this material is meaningful, but not when it is randomised. However, the CHREST computational model (Gobet, 1993; Gobet & Lane, 2010) predicted that, in the domain of chess, the skill effect in memory should remain even with randomised material, because chess experts can recognize small patterns even in board positions apparently lacking any structure. CHREST's predictions were supported by a re-analysis of previous experiments in the literature (Gobet & Simon, 1996) and by the collection of new data (e.g. Gobet & Waters, 2003). Even more strikingly, the predictions of the model turn out to be accurate beyond chess, as experts maintain an advantage with randomised material in nearly all the domains of expertise where such experiments have been carried out (Sala & Gobet, 2017). Thus, in this case, a computational model led to a re-evaluation of the empirical evidence, with considerable theoretical consequences, as many theories of expertise cannot explain the small but robust skill effect with random material.

10.2   Mathematical Modelling in Cognitive Science

Mathematical models permit the precise expression, derivation and proof of theories, and may display elegance and sophistication in doing so. However, a number of specific aspects of data and theories in cognitive science pose difficulties for mathematical modelling (Simon, 1967). A first drawback is that theories which are founded on unrealistic assumptions (which may be at variance with known empirical data) about cognitive structures and processes may be generated. For example, there may be assumptions about the rationality of agents in Bayesian mathematical decision models which are not commensurate with known empirical data about human choice in situations of incomplete information. In a similar manner, a mathematical model may impose unrealistic constraints about the mathematical forms cognitive structures and processes can take. For instance, a mathematical model of cognitive relations formulated as solvable equations will require substantial simplification including the introduction of some strict restrictions (such as ones about linearity).

There are significant limitations to the capacity of mathematical models to predict how mechanisms (especially complex ones) interact. A major reason for these limitations is that relating very detailed predictions (such as verbal protocols and eye movements) to particular stimuli or alterations in experimental design is hard (Gregg & Simon, 1967). In most mathematical models, stimuli have to be coded into numerical data using scaling methods (such as a mathematical model of language coding all linguistic data as numerical data). The problem with this method of coding is that it results in significant information loss (such as that of the respective cognitive demands of various stimuli). In addition, individual heuristics and strategies have a key role in explaining behaviour but these are hard to capture in mathematical models and so these models may have difficulty producing the behaviour they are intended to explain (Newell & Simon, 1972). Mathematical models are insufficiently flexible to produce veridical models of complex cognitive structures and process. For example, in mathematical models it is problematic to capture the recursive and hierarchical organisation aspects of cognitive structures and processes.

10.3   Computational Modelling in Cognitive Science

The difficulties which a number of specific aspects of data and theories in cognitive science pose for mathematical modelling make computational modelling a generally preferable approach (Newell & Simon, 1972). Computational modelling seeks to develop models of cognition which account for behaviour through the computational simulation of cognitive structures and processes. In doing so the mechanisms and parameters which cognitive science theories rely upon are clearly and rigorously stated thereby avoiding potential difficulties resulting from a lack of precision in the informal formulations of these theories. Conceptual clarity in a computational model takes the form of examining how alterations in the value of specific parameters affect model predictions. Since these models represent some or all elements of cognitive science theories in the form of computer programs which can be executed, they strongly emphasize mechanisms. For example, explanations of working memory in informal cognitive science theories (such as Baddeley & Hitch, 1974), where many aspects of these theories are not specified, differ from those in computational models, such as ACT-R (Anderson et al., 2004), where the mechanisms for each cognitive step must be specified. The level of precision required by computational models of cognitive science theories raises issues (which will be considered later on) about what constitutes a good scientific theory in this area going beyond the standard philosophy of science criterion that a good theory must be formulated with an appropriate degree of accuracy.

10.3.1   Strengths of Computational Modelling

A strength of computational models is that they are able to process symbols as well as numerical data, which generally gives them more flexibility than mathematical models (Newell & Simon, 1972). Data inputs can be symbolic (such as linguistic data) and do not have to be coded into numerical data as in most mathematical modelling. The advantage of symbolic data input is that it avoids the significant information loss which would result from recoding into numbers. In particular, symbolic data input allows use of the same stimuli as those used by human participants in experiments and the predictions of the model can be directly compared to participants' responses. These symbol processing capacities also enable computational models to contribute to the understanding of rich and dense datasets.

In computational models it is easy to capture the recursive and hierarchical organisation of cognitive structures and processes. Computational models can use simple building blocks to simulate complex behaviour (such as thinking) in both a qualitative and quantitative manner regardless of the number of variables involved. A computational model can be explored by systematically manipulating some of its parameters to produce a better understanding of the dynamics of the system it is modelling. System dynamics can be complicated due to a large number of variables and the fact that many of these may display complex non-linear behaviour. In general, the behaviour of a computational model is a dynamical system whose trajectory is specified as a function of previous states and inputs.

The capacity to manipulate some variables whilst keeping others constant can assist in systematic study of the environment, which matters as environmental factors often play an important role in determining behaviour. For example, manipulating the data input in models of language acquisition produces information both about model dynamics and environmental properties (Freudenthal, Pine, Aguado-Orea, & Gobet, 2007). The level of precision in computational models of cognitive science theories enables the derivation of testable predictions (such as the number of errors) about how mechanisms interact.

In computational models, there is a strong orientation towards the explanation of data, structures and processes in terms of mechanisms. Computational models explain behaviour by generating the behaviour being studied and explanations are deemed adequate if they can reproduce the behaviour in question (Gobet & Waters, 2003; Newell & Simon, 1972; Pew & Mavor, 1998). Although not all models are capable of fully generating the behaviour being studied, successful ones can reproduce at least some important aspects of the behaviour. For instance, a good model of how people play chess should be able to play chess at the level of the humans being modelled, and models of the effect of using a mobile phone whilst driving which predict that driver performance would be significantly affected by dialling methods should be validated by data collected in a driving simulator (Salvucci & Macuga, 2002). These explanations of behaviour can have important implications for applied research. For example, in the area of clinical psychology, computational models of problem gambling can inform the design of treatments and provide guidance for policy making including prevention measures (Gobet & Schiller, 2011).

10.3.2 Issues with Computational Modelling

Despite its benefits, computational modelling of cognitive science theories has some disadvantages which research in the field has attempted to mitigate. When considering the role of models in developing cognitive science theories, there can be a problem about determining what the theory is and what is there for reasons of implementational convenience (Cooper, 2002; Lane & Gobet, 2003). In some cases, it is obvious that some element is not part of a theory (such as a statement for printing simulation results on the screen) but other cases are less clear. For instance, connectionist models come with a specified number of units and it is not obvious whether these units are part of a theory or just artefacts of the way a theory was implemented. Another potentially difficult case is where cognitive structures and processes can be suitably formalised in an information processing programming language, as the boundary between the language and a theory of the structures and processes in question can be unclear. This blurring of boundaries can occur because some concepts in the language, such as "same", are endowed with assumptions about cognition with the result they become theoretical terms (Simon, 1967).

Most cognitive science theories have a number of parameters, with some having a substantial number. Typically, computational models have both fixed parameters which cannot be altered to account for data sets and free parameters which can be altered for new data sets. Maintaining a suitable balance between explanatory power in accounting for data and parsimony is a significant issue in the computational modelling of cognitive science theories. For instance, it may be unclear whether a model with a large number of free parameters which almost perfectly accounts for a small number of phenomena is preferable to another model with few free parameters which accounts for many phenomena reasonably well. There are a variety of ways of estimating free parameters whose appropriateness depends upon the particular situations in question. For instance, the method of estimating free parameters by searching for values that best fit each individually measured experimental performance can be problematic in the majority of cases. It follows that a preferable approach is to independently estimate the value of the free parameters (such as through performing additional experiments) followed by using these values in a computational model. In modelling, particularly in the estimation of statistical models, a common method is to set the parameters of a model using the data to be simulated and subsequently claim that the model can simulate the data. There has been some discussion in the philosophy of science about whether this common method is potentially problematic but there is no general agreement that this is an unsatisfactory method (Steele & Werndl, 2018). However, estimation of the values of too many free parameters can result in problems of overfitting when developing models (Gobet, Chassy, & Bilalić, 2011; Roberts & Pashler, 2000). For example, a simple linear function might fit the data reasonably well whilst an overfitted polynomial function with a number of variables might fit the data perfectly but the overfitted function is unable to generalise beyond the specific data used to estimate it to account for new data describing the same phenomena.

A general problem is that at best there are few standardised guidelines for how parameters should be adjusted to fit a dataset in order to develop and improve a model (Pew & Mavor, 1998), and for comparing different models especially when they differ in complexity and the number of parameters used (Ritter et al., 2003). For instance, a possible development method (Cooper, 2002) uses a Monte Carlo simulation approach which involves repeatedly running the same model over the same input in order to obtain descriptive statistics about model behaviour. This approach regards the repeated runs of the model as generating the behaviour of a group of individuals, with these runs being compared to individually measured experimental performances. However, the approach does not provide any detailed techniques to ensure the development and comparison of good models. Many other possible approaches to the development and comparison of computational models are given in the literature but there are no simple ways to determine which ones are most appropriate for particular situations.

A further problem for comparing models is that most models do not optimise parameters using formal automated techniques and it is unclear what comparisons between models mean if parameters are not optimised (Ritter, 1991). A related difficulty is that, at most, there are few standardised guidelines for comparing models against empirical data (Roberts & Pashler, 2000). For example, disagreement about some frequently used methods to validate models is widespread. A case of this is criticism of the use of standard statistical tests (such as t-tests) for comparison of the results of computational simulations with experimental data because noisy data may significantly reduce or even eliminate any difference between the simulations and experimental data. Instead, in such situations, the use of statistical tests can be replaced by analysis of data patterns thus bringing cognitive science more into line with common practice in many areas of natural science (Newell & Simon, 1972). As with the development and comparison of computational models there are no simple ways to determine which methods of comparing models against empirical data are most appropriate for particular situations.

10.4   Unified Theories of Cognition

Computational models of cognitive science theories need to account for data reasonably well whilst remaining parsimonious and avoiding overfitting, but there is no general method for developing these. As noted above, there are substantial issues with focusing on goodness of fit for developing models and a number of methods have been proposed which decrease the importance of fitting data closely. These include accepting relatively poor data fits provided the computational models are informative and evaluating the success of a model by considering the ratio of the number of different data points simulated to the number of free parameters in a model (Simon, 1992). A slightly more controversial method, which follows standard modelling practice in physics, is that the value of parameters should be incrementally set during the lifetime of a theory and remain unchanged unless new data necessitates alteration with the validity of previous models being checked against altered parameter values (Simon, 1990).

A significantly more controversial method is to develop unified theories of cognition: computational models which summarise findings from a large number of distinct experimental paradigms into a coherent and comprehensive architecture providing a process-based description of the implemented theories. For instance, Newell (1990) claimed that different models of various experimental phenomena should be brought together and unified into a single cognitive architecture applied to many phenomena, with a unified theory of human cognition containing an estimated 1000–10,000 immediate behaviour regularities. This methodology of developing unified cognitive science theories as computational models has a number of benefits. These include the fact that models of this kind address the potential problem of keeping the number of parameters small, as the quantity of data will force implemented cognitive science theories to settle on fixed rather than free parameters, and allow quantitative predictions to be made. Cognitive science theories are stated in their most general form, with cognitive architectures typically clustering around certain core properties thereby providing a framework which permits the development of different kinds of models.

However, computational models of unified cognitive science theories also face a number of significant difficulties. These problems include understanding the nature of the theories being implemented and what would constitute falsification of these theories, issues around how theories should be interpreted, reliable evaluation of the role of task knowledge in these theories, difficulties in reliably reproducing quantitative predictions, and control of multiple versions of models. Taken together these problems ensure that computational models of unified cognitive science theories remain a controversial approach.

10.5   Reproducibility of Cognitive Models: The Robust Testing Methodology

A central part of good scientific practice is that findings should be verifiable by researchers, which means that computational models of cognitive science theories should be reproducible. Experimental results are verified by running the same experiments again and models are verified by reproducing the process by which theoretical predictions are derived. Reproducing predictions in areas where theories are expressed mathematically (such as physics) requires reproduction of the mathematical processes which produced the predictions. Such reproduction is in principle straightforward, as it involves reproducing given mathematics processes where all the required information is supplied in the description of the processes and problems of reproduction tends to be ones of practice rather than principle. Reproducing predictions in cognitive science where these are derived from computational models requires reproduction of the computational processes which produced behavioural predictions. In principle, reproducing these predictions is less straightforward than reproducing predictions produced by mathematically expressed theories. A major reason for the failure to fully reproduce the computational processes which produced behavioural predictions is that the complexities of implementing computational models (such as ACT-R) force high level published descriptions and this level is inappropriate for a programmer seeking to reproduce the original model. An additional reason is that reproducing computational models involves attempts to reproduce the effects of executable code in situations with potentially different software and hardware environments. These environmental factors may have no direct connection at all with the computational models but they may well affect how the models run. Difficulties around reliable reproduction are not unique to computational modelling as they are prevalent in any reasonably large software project. In practice in virtually all cases it is impossible to fully reproduce the computational processes which produced behavioural predictions. One significant consequence of this is that processes in the model which led to particular predictions being made may be inaccessible to other researchers.

Lane and Gobet (2003, 2012) propose the Robust Testing Methodology (RTM) as a methodology for implementing computational models which are more informative, and facilitate other researchers in understanding and reproducing the main findings of an original model. Requirements involve better documentation and testing processes to enhance the comprehensibility and reproducibility of models. It is proposed that computational models should have three components: a well-documented implementation; a set of tests to verify that the code is implemented correctly, and illustrate and confirm each key process in the model; and a set of canonical results for reproducing model predictions for important experiments. The set of tests serves as a standard for testing new implementations, variants and versions of models thereby promoting extensions, and partial or full reproductions of models. The set of canonical results facilitates understanding of basic processes in complex models and the development of new sets of predictions. In conjunction, the sets of tests and canonical results give a descriptive definition of model behaviour, with such a description being more readily accessible than specification based descriptions.

The presence of canonical results makes it possible to compare architectures across all the provided sets of data simultaneously, using specially adapted optimisation techniques, selecting for each architecture parameters that yield the best models possible across the multiple data sets. This multiple modelling problem can be formulated as one of multi-objective optimisation where a non-dominated sorting genetic algorithm is used to locate models which are not outperformed by any other model (Goldberg, 1989). Lane and Gobet (2014) describe a method producing a set of candidate models where the models are evaluated against multiple datasets and with an arbitrary number of measures. A unique characteristic of this method is that models issued from different theories compete directly in the evolutionary process. Generation of a truly optimal model cannot be guaranteed by this method but it does develop a set of models that are superior to a significant number of competing optimisation methods.

RTM can be generalised from computational models in cognitive science to all fields where computer modelling is used to produce quantitative predictions from theories (Lane & Gobet, 2003, 2012). This methodology ensures the validity of models through systematic testing at three levels: system testing to locate any errors in the program, unit testing to demonstrate correct program behaviour both before and after refactoring (Fowler, 1999) and behaviour testing to demonstrate correct global system behaviour. A computational model can be verified as a reproduction of the original model if the program code has been developed to match the prescribed specification of the original model and tests show that the behaviour of the modelling software is the same as that described by the test suite (Beck, 2003). The three testing levels allow the significance of different tests to be clearly identified. This matters because not all tests and all software components are equally important in terms of their contribution to the implemented theories (Cooper & Shallice, 1995). Due to the changing nature of cognitive science theories and the need to construct models in new domains, the development of implemented theories must support constant change at the theoretical level. Models derived from theories must support automated behavioural tests where these tests are comparisons of models with experimental data. The three-layer testing methodology supports this requirement to accommodate possible theories as it can be used to identify any theoretical challenges to the implemented theory. These improvements in informative implementation methodologies do not solve all the problems of reproducing computational models of cognitive science theories but they go some way towards addressing the difficulties.

10.6 Semi-Automatically Evolving Models

Developing computational models in cognitive science is hard work, requiring expertise in a number of domains. For example, in the case of psychology, skills include software engineering, experimental design, statistical data analysis and theoretical psychology. In addition, modellers just like humans in general suffer from a number of potential mind sets such as previous knowledge biases that limit the development of new models (Bilalić, McLeod, & Gobet, 2010; Gobet, Snyder, Bossomaier, & Harre, 2014). This makes it difficult to connect ideas from distinct theories and thus to fruitfully explore the space of possible models. It is to address these issues that the Genetically Evolving Models in Science (GEMS) approach, which automatizes, in part or entirely, the writing of such models has been developed (Addis, Sozou, Lane, & Gobet, 2016; Frias-Martinez & Gobet, 2007).

GEMS uses an evolutionary computational method known as genetic programming (Koza, 1992; Poli, Langdon, & McPhee, 2008) in which a population of computer programs is subject to an evolutionary process. The idea is that each program represents a model, the fitness of which is evaluated by running it on a specific experimental protocol similar to that used with human participants. The model's predictions are then compared with the actual human data. A set of primitive cognitive functions (such as *match two objects* and *inhibit a memory trace*) is provided to GEMS. When put together, these primitives form a model. The search for a theory starts with an initial population of random or pseudo-random models. (It is possible that the primitive cognitive functions could be incorrectly selected which could result in a subsequent failure to evolve viable theory structures.) The genetic program optimally searches the space of possible models using mutation, crossover and selection to create succeeding generations. The search process is repeated with succeeding generations until a stopping criterion is reached (such as the best theory fitting data within some particular threshold). A program which meets a required objective specified as a fitness function to the greatest degree possible is evolved and is a viable theory structure. Pilot studies have shown that the methodology is valid, at least with fairly simple experimental protocols.

The structure of programs evolved with genetic programming is convenient for representing cognitive processes and structures because some sub-programs can evolve as particular modules. A systematic, exhaustive search of all possible computational models accounting for a set of empirical data is generally not feasible due to the size of the search space required and this is where the optimisation capabilities of genetic programs are valuable. A good theory structure makes predictions consistent with experimental data (such as reaction times) and is parsimonious. Parsimony can be included in the evolutionary process by adding penalties for excessively complex programs in the fitness function (which enables a trade-off between data fitting and parsimony). Viable theory structures involve a series of processes (such as comparing between two memory traces or adding items to short-term memory). Evaluation of theory structures should include the level and type of evidential support required for these structures and the potential applicability of these structures to more complex, diverse and extensive data.

10.7   Philosophical Aspects of the Semi-Automatic Generation of Models in Cognitive Science

Despite the growing importance of genetic programming in modelling generally there is very little specific discussion of it in the philosophy of science literature. In what follows some important philosophical issues raised by the methodology for the semi-automatic generation of models in cognitive science are considered. A useful general framework for evaluating the progress and potential of the methodology is the Lakatos (1970) research programme approach. The research programme approach is the idea that a research programme is a sequence of theories within a particular area of science. Succeeding theories are advances over their predecessors and transition from a theory to its successor is a problem shift. Problem shifts are empirically progressive if new data is predicted and then these predictions are confirmed and theoretically progressive if a new theory enables more predictions than a predecessor. Research programmes which are not progressive are degenerating and should no longer be pursued. The evidence to date (Addis et al., 2016) clearly suggests that the methodology for the semi-automatic generation of cognitive science theories is a progressive research programme as a number of cognitive science experiments have been modelled successfully.

An important issue is whether the methodology for the semi-automatic generation of cognitive science theories raises any new philosophical questions about the character of experiments and theories. One view is that since there is nothing philosophically new about computational simulations (Frigg & Reiss, 2009), this methodology does not open up new lines of philosophical inquiry. However, taking the plausible general position (Winsberg, 2010) that computational simulations lie somewhere between experiments and theories, the methodology for the semi-automatic generation of theories is philosophically important as it grounds a class of explanations which reside in the area between experiments and theories. A satisfactory account of how these explanations might operate should include a suitable philosophical perspective on the central role that probabilistic inference has in genetic programming. In Bayesian approaches to probabilistic inference, the formulation of theories can vary according to the favoured interpretation of probability. Such potential variation in theory formulation is problematic in the context of genetic programming. A better methodological approach is to frame probabilistic inference in genetic programming in the most philosophically neutral and mathematically general terms. A measure theory (Halmos, 1950) approach to probability which defines probability on a sample space in conjunction with a σ-algebra of sets which represents the collection of all events satisfies these neutrality and generality requirements as it effectively handles continuous and discrete probability distributions. The methodology for the semi-automatic generation of theories can give indications of when there are potentially errors in the structure of models. Repeated failure to find suitable fitness functions with appropriate data sets and suitably selected control parameters might suggest the occurrence of this kind of error. This sort of error provides clear grounds for the falsification of potential cognitive science theories and thus contributes to the eventual formation of robust theories.

The ontological status of the computational models produced by the methodology for the semi-automatic generation of cognitive science theories is important as there is substantial debate around whether models of scientific theories are best seen as fictional or realist models. The view that models are fictional has become increasingly prominent in recent years with a range of views regarding models as fictions of some kind with most versions being developed in the philosophy of natural science. One instance of this is the claim that many theories in physics should be regarded as fictional models (Cartwright, 1983). Since computational simulations are exemplary cases of fictional models, it follows that the computational models produced by the methodology for the semi-automatic generation of theories clearly belong within the category of fictional modelling approaches. Treating these models as fictional permits straightforward explanations of reasoning based on the models since what matters is not the realism of the models but their ability to account for data and to produce correct predictions. However, this still leaves a number of difficult philosophical issues. A problem is what status entities within computational models of cognitive science have and how claims about truth in models should be regarded. Work in the philosophy of fiction offers a variety of possibilities about the nature of and ascriptions of truth to fictional entities (Walton, 1990) but there is no general agreement about what the correct account of these entities is. For practical modelling purposes, any reasonable account of fictional entities is acceptable as it will suffice to ground explanations based on models.

Explanation in the computational models produced by the methodology for the semi-automatic generation of theories aligns with that in other computational modelling by aiming to produce theories which explain how mechanisms (especially complex ones) interact. Within this general framework a philosophically pluralist stance on explanation (with a possible emphasis on inference to the best explanation) is desirable as it helps to accommodate the wide range of potential cognitive science theories and data. This stance allows for mechanism-based explanations with a role for additional causal, intentional or teleological explanations as appropriate and such flexibility enhances explanatory power. Allowing a role for explanations which are not necessarily causal is useful because many mathematical explanations of cognitive science experiments produce formulae which may indicate regularities in data rather than causally explaining it. For example, reaction time experiments are often modelled using a log formula (Brown, Steyvers, & Wagenmakers, 2009; Usher, Olami, & McClelland, 2002) but it is not clear that the formula causally explains the reaction time data rather than indicating regularities in it. This reflects a difference with natural science, particularly physics, where such indication of regularities is much more likely to constitute the basis of a satisfactory causal explanation.

The methodology for the semi-automatic generation of cognitive science theories raises a question about the extent to which the development of these theories is considered an exclusively human activity. A possibility this opens up is that cognitive science theories could change from being viewed as abstract conceptualisations to being seen as computationally tractable concrete objects. The extent to which cognitive science theories can be reasonably viewed as computationally tractable concrete objects relates to the extent to which computational models produced by genetic programming represent cognitive systems. Genetic programs are used to efficiently search the space of possible cognitive models but the generated models are not complete cognitive science theories in themselves since they lack the context and appropriate qualifications which such theories possess. This relationship between models and theories accords with most computational modelling which claims that programs only implement aspects of a cognitive science theory and that additional information is provided outside of the program itself (such as mappings between variables in the computer code and particular theoretical terms).

Despite only implementing aspects of a cognitive science theory, computational models produced by genetic programming allow confirmation theory (broadly construed to include evidential support and inductive strength) to move significantly beyond traditional inductive logic and utilise algorithms in the process of structuring and evaluating theories (Glymour, 1980). Although the inclusion of algorithms is a significant gain in the scope of confirmation theory, an important problem about confirmation remains, namely, how it is possible to be certain that computational models produced by genetic programming have identified the correct theory structure. As has been seen there may be indications of when there are potentially errors in the structure of models but this is sufficient for falsification and not confirmation. The reason for the confirmation problem is that the method of genetic programming allows the evolution of viable theory structures but precursors to potentially good theory structures can be eliminated due to the role of mutation and crossover in the process of theory generation, and diverse incompatible theories with empirically testable direct predictions which account for the data approximately equally well can be evolved.

Part of the reason that confirmation is a significant problem is that current knowledge levels in cognitive science may be insufficient for the development of precise computer models. This general point can usefully be illustrated by a case from the area of categorisation which is the process of placing instances of stimuli into classes. A classic categorisation experiment requires participants to place stylised faces into one of two categories (Smith & Medin, 1981) with the experiment being subjected to intense study resulting in a large number of competing models and theories of how categorisation occurs (Smith & Minda, 2000). In itself the use of genetic program computational models will not resolve these kinds of difficulties about correct theory identification (such as those about categorisation), particularly since representing cognitive science theories of any complexity in computational models produced by genetic programming inevitably involves postulating psychologically implausible entities.

A significant line of response to the potential problem that current knowledge levels in cognitive science may not suffice for the development of precise computer models is to take an information processing approach to cognitive science which disregards the issues arising from the details of neural implementation (although working with the assumption that structures and mechanisms implemented by cognitive science theories are implemented by neurons in the brain). On this view behavioural complexity is a reflection of the environmental complexity which humans encounter. Complex phenomena should be studied by considering different levels of analysis separately with it being preferable to postpone examination of links between levels until there is better independent understanding of each level (Simon, 1969). The underlying assumption for this view is that nature has a hierarchy of complexity and explanation levels with different scientific laws holding at each level so individual levels of complexity can be focused upon without the need to consider them all. When this assumption is applied to cognitive science theories it has the consequence that cognition in general is decomposed into various elementary processes, and cognitive invariants with parameters (such as time taken to learn a chunk) and heuristics are sought (Simon, 1990). This view provides the grounds for an information processing approach to cognitive science theories. The extent to which general cognition can be decomposed in this way remains the subject of considerable disagreement but taking this perspective has resulted in considerable progress in cognitive science to date.

10.8 Conclusion

Computational models in cognitive science have usefully advanced the field through demonstrating that understanding of cognition has reached the stage of developing models which can simulate experimental data. Some difficult technical questions remain around what constitutes a theory in a computational model including ones of comprehension and reproducibility, and on how theories should be compared with data, particularly in cases where theories do not have optimised parameters. Improvements in the area of informative implementation methodologies involving better documentation and testing processes to enhance the comprehensibility and reproducibility of models are promising advances. The methodology for the semi-automatic generation of cognitive science theories using genetic programming is an effective modelling technique particularly for the simulation of multiple data sets arising from the same experimental paradigm. Philosophically the Lakatos research programme approach coupled with a fictional modelling stance offers a secure and flexible framework for current and future work in this area.

Acknowledgments This research was supported by Economic and Social Research Council grant ES/L003090/1.

References

Addis, M., Sozou, P. D., Lane, P. C. R., & Gobet, F. (2016). Computational scientific discovery and cognitive science theories. In V. Müller (Ed.), *Computing and philosophy: Proceedings of IACAP 2014* (pp. 83–97). Heidelberg, Germany: Springer.

Anderson, J., Bothell, D., Byrne, M., Douglass, S., Lebiere, C., & Qin, Y. (2004). An integrated theory of the mind. *Psychological Review, 111*, 1036–1060.

Baddeley, A., & Hitch, G. (1974). Working memory. In G. Bower (Ed.), *The psychology of learning and motivation: Advances in research and theory* (Vol. 8, pp. 47–90). New York: Academic.

Beck, K. (2003). *Test-driven development: By example*. Boston: Pearson Education.

Bilalić, M., McLeod, P., & Gobet, F. (2010). The mechanism of the Einstellung (set) effect: A pervasive source of cognitive bias. *Current Directions in Psychological Science, 19*, 111–115.

Brown, S., Steyvers, M., & Wagenmakers, E. (2009). Observing evidence accumulation during multi-alternative decisions. *Journal of Mathematical Psychology, 53*, 453–462.

Cartwright, N. (1983). *How the laws of physics lie*. Oxford, UK: Oxford University Press.

Cooper, R. (2002). *Modelling high-level cognitive processes*. Mahwah, NJ: Erlbaum.

Cooper, R., & Shallice, T. (1995). Soar and the case for unified theories of cognition. *Cognition, 55*, 115–149.

Fowler, M. (1999). *Refactoring: Improving the design of existing code*. Reading, MA: Addison-Wesley.

Freudenthal, D., Pine, J. M., Aguado-Orea, J., & Gobet, F. (2007). Modelling the developmental patterning of finiteness marking in English, Dutch, German and Spanish using MOSAIC. *Cognitive Science, 31*, 311–341.

Frias-Martinez, E., & Gobet, F. (2007). Automatic generation of cognitive theories using genetic programming. *Minds and Machines, 17*, 287–309.

Frigg, R., & Reiss, J. (2009). The philosophy of simulation: Hot new issues or same old stew? *Synthese, 169*, 593–613.

Glymour, C. (1980). *Theory and evidence*. Princeton, NJ: Princeton University Press.

Gobet, F. (1993). A computer model of chess memory. In W. Kintsch (Ed.), *Fifteenth annual meeting of the cognitive science society* (pp. 463–468). Hillsdale, NJ: Erlbaum.

Gobet, F., Chassy, P., & Bilalić, M. (2011). *Foundations of cognitive psychology*. London: McGraw Hill.

Gobet, F., & Lane, P. C. R. (2010). The CHREST architecture of cognition: The role of perception in general intelligence. In E. Baum, M. Hutter, & E. Kitzelmann (Eds.), *Proceedings of the third conference on artificial general intelligence* (pp. 7–12). Amsterdam: Atlantis Press.

Gobet, F., & Schiller, M. (2011). A manifesto for cognitive models of problem gambling. In *European perspectives on cognitive sciences—Proceedings of the European conference on cognitive science*. Sofia, Bulgaria: New Bulgarian University Press.

Gobet, F., & Simon, H. A. (1996). Recall of rapidly presented random chess positions is a function of skill. *Psychonomic Bulletin & Review, 3*, 159–163.

Gobet, F., Snyder, A., Bossomaier, T., & Harre, M. (2014). Designing a "better" brain: Insights from experts and savants. *Frontiers in Psychology, 5*, 470.

Gobet, F., & Waters, A. (2003). The role of constraints in expert memory. *Journal of Experimental Psychology. Learning, Memory, and Cognition, 29*, 1082–1094.

Goldberg, D. (1989). *Genetic algorithms in search optimization and machine learning*. Reading, MA: Addison-Wesley.

Gregg, L., & Simon, H. (1967). Process models and stochastic theories of simple concept formation. *Journal of Mathematical Psychology, 4*, 246–276.

Halmos, P. (1950). *Measure theory*. Princeton, NJ: Van Nostrand.

Jones, G., Gobet, F., & Pine, J. M. (2007). Linking working memory and long-term memory: A computational model of the learning of new words. *Developmental Science, 10*, 853–873.

Koza, J. (1992). *Genetic programming: On the programming of computers by means of natural selection* (Vol. 1). Cambridge, MA: MIT Press.

Lakatos, I. (1970). Falsification and the methodology of scientific research programs. In I. Lakatos & A. Musgrave (Eds.), *Criticism and the growth of knowledge* (pp. 91–196). Cambridge, UK: Cambridge University Press.

Lane, P. C. R., & Gobet, F. (2003). Developing reproducible and comprehensible computational models. *Artificial Intelligence, 144*, 251–263.

Lane, P. C. R., & Gobet, F. (2012). A theory-driven testing methodology for developing scientific software. *Journal of Experimental & Theoretical Artificial Intelligence, 24*, 421–456.

Lane, P. C. R., & Gobet, F. (2014). Evolving non-dominated parameter sets for computational models from multiple experiments. *Journal of Artificial General Intelligence, 4*, 1–30.

Newell, A. (1990). *Unified theories of cognition*. Cambridge, MA: Harvard University Press.

Newell, A., & Simon, H. A. (1972). *Human problem solving*. Englewood Cliffs, NJ: Prentice-Hall.

Pew, R., & Mavor, A. (Eds.). (1998). *Modeling human and organizational behavior: Application to military simulations*. Washington, DC: National Academy Press.

Poli, R., Langdon, W., & McPhee, N. (2008). *A field guide to genetic programming*. http://www.gp-field-guide.org.uk

Popper, K. (1959). *The logic of scientific discovery*. New York: Basic Books.

Ritter, F. (1991). Towards fair comparisons of connectionist algorithms through automatically optimized parameter sets. In K. Hammond & D. Gentner (Eds.), *Proceedings of the thirteenth annual conference of the cognitive science society* (pp. 877–881). Hillsdale, MI: Lawrence Erlbaum.

Ritter, F., Shadbolt, N., Elliman, D., Young, R., Gobet, F., & Baxter, G. (2003). *Techniques for modeling human performance in synthetic environments: A supplementary review*. Wright-Patterson Air Force Base, OH: Human Systems Information Analysis Center.

Roberts, S., & Pashler, H. (2000). How persuasive is a good fit? A comment on theory testing. *Psychological Review, 107*, 358–367.

Sala, G., & Gobet, F. (2017). Experts' memory superiority for domain-specific random material generalizes across fields of expertise: A meta-analysis. *Memory & Cognition, 45*, 183–193.

Salvucci, D., & Macuga, K. (2002). Predicting the effects of cellular-phone dialing on driver performance. *Cognitive Systems Research, 3*, 95–102.

Simon, H. (1969). *The sciences of the artificial*. Cambridge, MA: MIT Press.

Simon, H. (1990). Invariants of human behavior. *Annual Review of Psychology, 41*, 1–20.

Simon, H. A. (1967). The use of information processing languages in psychology. In P. Fraisse (Ed.), *Les modèles de la formalisation du comportement* (pp. 303–326). Paris: CNRS-Editions.

Simon, H. A. (1977). *Models of discovery and other topics in the methods of science*. Dordrecht, the Netherlands: Reidel.

Simon, H. A. (1992). What is an "explanation" of behavior? *Psychological Science, 3*, 150–161.

Smith, D., & Minda, J. (2000). Thirty categorization results in search of a model. *Journal of Experimental Psychology: Learning, Memory, and Cognition, 26*, 3–27.

Smith, E., & Medin, D. (1981). *Categories and concepts*. Cambridge, MA: Harvard University Press.

Steele, K., & Werndl, C. (2018). Model-selection theory: The need for a more nuanced picture of use-novelty and double-counting. *British Journal for the Philosophy of Science, 69*, 351–375.

Tamburelli, M., Jones, G., Gobet, F., & Pine, J. M. (2012). Computational modelling of phonological acquisition: Simulating error patterns in nonword repetition tasks. *Language & Cognitive Processes, 27*, 901–946.

Thagard, P. (1988). *Computational philosophy of science*. Cambridge, MA: MIT Press.

Usher, M., Olami, Z., & McClelland, J. (2002). Hick's law in a stochastic race model with speed–accuracy. *Journal of Mathematical Psychology, 46*, 704–715.

Walton, K. (1990). *Mimesis as make-believe: On the foundations of the representational arts*. Cambridge, UK: Harvard University Press.

Winsberg, E. (2010). *Science in the age of computer simulation*. Chicago: University of Chicago Press.

Chapter 11
Scientific Discovery, Process Models, and the Social Sciences

Pat Langley and Adam Arvay

Abstract In this chapter, we review research on computational approaches to scientific discovery, starting with early work on the induction of numeric laws before turning to the construction of models that explain observations in terms of domain knowledge. We focus especially on inductive process modeling, which involves finding a set of linked differential equations, organized into processes, that reproduce, predict, and explain multivariate time series. We review the notion of quantitative process models, present two approaches to their construction that search through a space of model structures and associated parameters, and report their successful application to the explanation of ecological data. After this, we explore the relevance of process models to the social sciences, including the reasons they seem appropriate and some challenges to discovering them. In closing, we discuss other causal frameworks, including structural equation models and agent-based accounts, that researchers have developed to construct models of social phenomena.

11.1 Introduction

The scientific enterprise is a diverse collection of activities that is distinguished from other areas of human endeavor by a number of important characteristics. These include the systematic collection and analysis of observations, the formal statement of theories, laws, and models, invoking those theories and models to explain and predict observations, and using those observations in turn to evaluate theories and models. Within this broad endeavor, a central element – *scientific discovery* – is widely viewed as one of the highest forms of human achievement. Clearly,

P. Langley (✉)
Institute for the Study of Learning and Expertise, Palo Alto, CA, USA
e-mail: langley@cs.auckland.ac.nz

A. Arvay
Department of Computer Science, University of Auckland, Auckland, New Zealand
e-mail: aarv914@aucklanduni.ac.nz

© Springer Nature Switzerland AG 2019
M. Addis et al. (eds.), *Scientific Discovery in the Social Sciences*,
Synthese Library 413, https://doi.org/10.1007/978-3-030-23769-1_11

computational insights into discovery processes would have important implications, both theoretical and practical.

This holds especially in the *system sciences*, like ecology, that examine many interacting variables, develop complex models with feedback loops, and typically lack experimental control. Such fields are arguably less advanced that disciplines like biology, chemistry, and physics because they are more complicated and present so many difficulties. The latter have developed more precise and complete accounts not because they are 'hard' sciences, but rather because they are 'easy' disciplines that involve relatively simple phenomena and lend themselves to experimental study. In contrast, the system sciences – including those focused on social phenomena – stand to benefit more from a deeper understanding of scientific discovery and tools that might aid them.

In this chapter, we examine the problem of model construction in such disciplines, with special emphasis on the social sciences. We review efforts to understand the discovery process in computational terms, recounting its progress and successes over the past 35 years. Most research in the area has focused on induction of empirical laws, but some work has addressed construction of explanatory models that are more relevant to the social sciences. We examine one paradigm – *inductive process modeling* – in some detail, as it deals with discovery of explanatory models from multivariate time series in the absence of experimental control. Research in this framework has concentrated on ecological phenomena, but we argue that it also lends itself nicely to social science problems, presenting examples to support this claim. In closing, we discuss challenges to the use of inductive process modeling in this area, along with other approaches to constructing explanatory accounts in the social sciences.

11.2 Computational Scientific Discovery

There is no question that discovery plays a central role in the scientific enterprise. Science could not proceed without using laws and models to generate testable predictions. Neither could it make progress without collecting observations that let it evaluate those laws and models. But discovery brings these two activities together by generating new laws and models, or revising existing ones, in response to anomalies and surprising results. Prizes in science are typically awarded for researchers' role in discovering new laws or mechanisms, not for making predictions or collecting data, even when the latter lead to the former.

However, the philosophy of science, which attempts to understand and formalize scientific structures and processes, has generally avoided addressing issues related to discovery. The standard argument has been that this important activity is immune to logical analysis. For example, Popper (1961) wrote:

> The initial stage, the act of conceiving or inventing a theory, seems to me neither to call for logical analysis nor to be susceptible of it ... My view may be expressed by saying that every discovery contains an 'irrational element', or 'a creative intuition' ...

Many others adopted Popper's position in the decades that followed. Hempel (1966) and other scholars also maintained that discovery was inherently irrational and thus beyond understanding, at least in terms that philosophers accepted. This mystical attitude toward discovery hindered progress on the topic for many years.

Yet advances made by two fields – cognitive psychology and artificial intelligence – in the 1950s suggested a path forward. In particular, (Simon 1966) proposed that scientific discovery is a variety of problem solving that involves search through a space of problem states – in this case laws, models, or theories. These structures are generated by applying mental operators to previous ones, with search through the space of candidates guided by heuristics to make it tractable. Heuristic search had been implicated in many cases of human cognition, from proving theorems to playing chess. This framework offered not only an approach to understanding scientific discovery, but also ways to automate this mysterious process.

Early research in this area focused on discovery of empirical laws. For instance, BACON (Langley 1981; Langley, Simon, Bradshaw, & Żytkow 1987) carried out search through a problem space of algebraic terms, using operators like multiplication and division to generate new terms from old ones. The system was guided by heuristics that noted regularities in data, one of which was defining a new product term, $x \cdot y$, when it found that x increased as y decreased. In many cases, this led BACON toward higher-level terms with constant values, as in its rediscovery of Kepler's third law of planetary motion. The system also applied this idea recursively, treating parameters at lower levels as variables at higher ones, to formulate complex relations, as in its rediscovery of the ideal gas law. BACON reconstructed a variety of numeric relations from the history of physics and chemistry, lending evidence to Simon's claim that heuristic search underlies scientific discovery.

Responses to the BACON work were mixed, with some critics viewing it as clarifying important aspects of the discovery process. But others claimed that the 'real' key to discovery instead lay in other activities the system did not address, such as deciding which variables to measure and relate, determining which problem space to search, or selecting which scientific problem to pursue. Others held that BACON 'only did what it was programmed to do', and thus did not really 'discover' anything. The system's developers only claimed that it offered insights into the operation of scientific discovery and removed much of its mystery, but they acknowledged that it offered only a partial account and that much work remained to be done.

Later research took inspiration from the initial BACON results and developed more powerful approaches to discovering numeric laws. Papers by Falkenhainer and Michalski (1986), Moulet (1992), Żytkow, Zhu, and Hussam (1990), Kokar (1986), Schaffer (1990), Nordhausen and Langley (1990), Gordon, Edwards, Sleeman, and Kodratoff (1994), Murata, Mizutani, and Shimura (1994), Washio and Motoda (1997), and Saito and Nakano (1997) all reported systems that induced algebraic laws describing relations among quantitative variables, many of them reproducing results from the history of science. Other work – by Džeroski and Todorovski (1995), Bradley, Easley, and Stolle (2001), Koza, Mydlowec, Lanza, Yu, and Keane (2001), Džeroski and Todorovski (2008), and Schmidt and Lipson (2009) – extended this idea to differential equations for dynamic systems, often focusing on novel scientific data. These relied on different methods but also searched for explicit mathematical laws that matched data. Interest in computational discovery spread to other aspects of science, including induction of qualitative laws and construction of explanatory models (Džeroski & Todorovski 2007; Shrager & Langley 1990).

Although early work in this area emphasized reconstructions of discoveries from the history of science, later efforts went on to help generate new knowledge in many scientific fields. These success stories have included discovery of:

- reaction pathways in catalytic chemistry (Bruk, Gorodskii, Zeigarnik, Valdés-Pérez, and Temkin 1998; Valdés-Pérez 1994);
- qualitative chemical factors in mutagenesis (King & Srinivasan 1996);
- quantitative laws of metallic behavior (Mitchell, Sleeman, Duffy, Ingram, and Young 1997);
- quantitative conjectures in graph theory (Fajtlowicz 1988);
- qualitative conjectures in number theory (Colton, Bundy, & Walsh 2000);
- temporal laws of ecological behavior (Todorovski, Džeroski, & Kompare 1998);
- models of gene-influenced metabolism in yeast (King et al. 2004).

In each case, the authors published their findings in the refereed literature of the relevant scientific field, showing that experts in the discipline viewed them as relevant and interesting. (Langley 2000) has analyzed a number of these successes, identifying elements in each case that were handled by computer and others that were done manually. Together, these results demonstrate convincingly that we can automate important aspects of the scientific process.

Before continuing, we should distinguish between research on computational scientific discovery and another research paradigm – *data mining* – that emerged in the 1990s, which also aims to find regularities in observations and uses heuristic search through a space of hypotheses to this end. Work in this area typically focuses on commercial applications and emphasizes the availability of large data sets. Most data-mining research has adopted notations invented by computer scientists, such as decision trees and Bayesian networks, in marked contrast to computational scientific discovery, which focuses on formalisms used by domain scientists. Data-mining methods have been applied to scientific data (e.g., Fayyad, Haussler, & Stolorz 1996), but the results seldom bear a resemblance to scientific knowledge.

11.3   Discovery of Explanatory Process Models

The early stages of science typically focus on finding descriptive laws that summarize empirical regularities. This is understandable, as paucity of knowledge about the area encourages inductive inquiry. For similar reasons, it was natural for most initial research on computational discovery to focus on these early stages. In contrast, more mature sciences emphasize the creation of models that explain phenomena (Hempel 1965) in terms of hypothesized components, structures that relate them, and interactions among these elements. Such explanatory models move beyond description to provide deeper accounts that are linked to theoretical constructs. Can we also develop computational systems that address this more sophisticated side of scientific discovery?

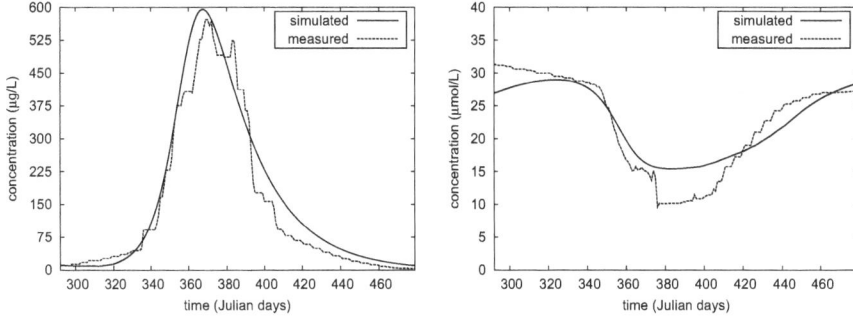

Fig. 11.1 Observed concentrations for phytoplankton (left) and nitrogen (right) from the Ross Sea, along with simulated values (smooth curves) produced by a quantitative process model, from Bridewell, Langley, Todorovski, and Džeroski (2008)

11.3.1   Quantitative Process Models

Consider an example from aquatic ecosystems. Figure 11.1 displays observations for the concentration of phytoplankton and nitrogen, taken at daily intervals, from the Ross Sea in Antarctica. Formal models of ecosystem dynamics are often cast as sets of differential equations, such as those shown in Table 11.1 (a). This model includes four equations, two for observed variables, *phyto.conc* (phytoplankton concentration) and *nitro.conc* (nitrogen concentration), and two for unobserved but hypothesized variables, *zoo.conc* (zooplantkton) and *detritus.conc* (detritus concentration). When simulated, such equations can match observed trajectories with considerable accuracy, as illustrated in the figure.

However, the equations by themselves merely describe the ecosystem's behavior. The text in articles suggests that scientists have a richer story, which might go something like:

> As phytoplankton uptakes nitrogen, its concentration increases and the nitrogen decreases. This continues until the nitrogen is exhausted, which leads to a phytoplankton die off. This produces detritus, which gradually remineralizes to replenish nitrogen. Zooplankton grazes on phytoplankton, which slows the latter's increase and also produces detritus.

Each sentence here refers to some *process* that contributes to the model's equations. The first one focuses on the process of nitrogen absorption; this is associated with the *phyto.conc* term in the first equation, which increases the phytoplankton concentration, and with the *phyto.conc* term in the second equation, which decreases the nitrogen concentration. Similarly, the final sentence describes a grazing process; this contributes to *zoo.conc* in the first equation, to the *zoo.conc* term in the third equation, and to *zoo.conc* in the fourth equation.

We can reformulate such an account by restating it as a quantitative process model, like that shown in Table 11.1 (b). This includes five distinct processes for phytoplankton loss, zooplankton loss, zooplankton grazing on phytoplankton,

Table 11.1 (a) A set of linked differential equations for an aquatic ecosystem that relates concentrations of phytoplankton, nitrogen, zooplankton, and detritus to reproduce trajectories like those in Fig. 11.1 and (b) a process model that compiles into the same set of equations

---

(a) d[phyto.conc,t] = 0.104 · phyto.conc − 0.495 · zoo.conc
    d[nitro.conc,t] = 0.005 · detritus.conc − 0.040 · phyto.conc
    d[zoo.conc,t] = 0.053 · zoo.conc
    d[detritus.conc,t] = 0.307 · phyto.conc + 0.060 · zoo.conc − 0.005 · detritus.conc

---

(b) process phyto_loss(phyto, detritus)
        equations: d[phyto.conc,t] = −0.307 · phyto.conc
                   d[detritus.conc,t] = 0.307 · phyto.conc
    process zoo_loss(zoo, detritus)
        equations: d[zoo.conc,t] = −0.251 · zoo.conc
                   d[detritus.conc,t] = 0.251 · zoo.conc
    process zoo_phyto_grazing(zoo, phyto, detritus)
        equations: d[zoo.conc,t] = 0.615 · 0.495 · zoo.conc
                   d[detritus.conc,t] = 0.385 · 0.495 · zoo.conc
                   d[phyto.conc,t] = −0.495 · zoo.conc
    process nitro_uptake(phyto, nitro)
        equations: d[phyto.conc,t] = 0.411 · phyto.conc
                   d[nitro.conc,t] = −0.098 · 0.411 · phyto.conc
    process nitro_remineralization(nitro, detritus)
        equations: d[nitro.conc,t] = 0.005 · detritus.conc
                   d[detritus.conc,t] = −0.005 · detritus.conc

---

phytoplankton uptake of nitrogen, and remineralization of nitrogen from detritus. Each process describes how one or more variables change as a function of current variables' values. For instance, the equation *d[detritus.conc, t] = 0.05 · phyto.conc* states that the derivative of detritus concentration is five percent of the phytoplankton concentration. After combining terms, this model is equivalent to the differential equations shown earlier if we assume that, when two or more processes influence the same derivative, their effects are additive. For example, summing the effects of processes for *d[phyto.conc, t]* from Table 11.1 (b) produces the expression *−0.307 · phyto.conc + −0.495 · zoo.conc + 0.411 · phyto.conc*, and combining the two *phyto.conc* terms gives the right-hand side of the first equation in Table 11.1 (a). Yet the elaborated version in Table 11.1 (b) also states explicit assumptions about the underlying processes, each of which indicates terms in the differential equations that must stand or fall together.

11.3.2 Inductive Process Modeling

These observations suggest a class of discovery tasks that involve construction of such process accounts. We can state this problem, which we will refer to as *inductive*

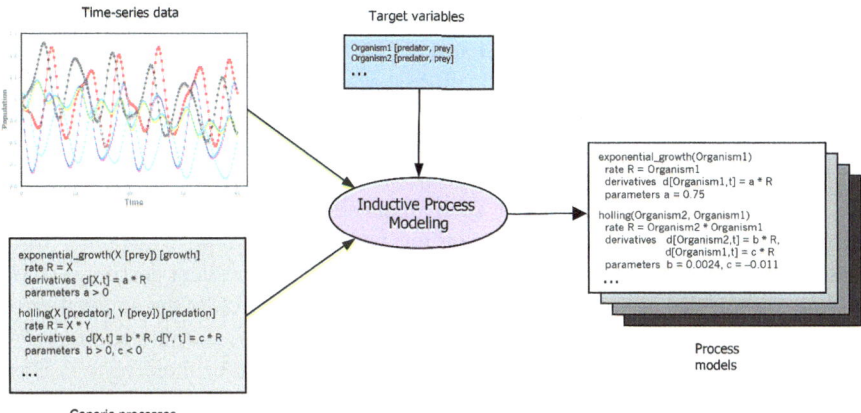

Fig. 11.2   The task of inductive process modeling, which is given a set of variables, time series for their values, and generic knowledge about possible processes. The result is a set of parameterized models that fit the time series and explain its variations in terms of inferred processes

process modeling (Langley, Sanchez, Todorovski, & Džeroski 2002), in terms of its inputs and outputs:

- *Given:* A set of typed entities and observed trajectories for their variables over time;
- *Given:* A subset of these variables whose values one wants to explain;
- *Given:* Background knowledge about process types that might appear in these explanations;
- *Find:* A quantitative process model that reproduces the observed trajectories, explains them in terms of known processes, and predicts future values.

For instance, given a multivariate time series, like that shown in Fig. 11.1, and background knowledge about candidate processes, inductive process modeling constructs one or more models like the one in Table 11.1 (b). Besides reproducing the observed values, this structure explains the trajectories in terms of unobserved but plausible processes. Figure 11.2 depicts the overall task graphically.

Background knowledge takes the form of *generic* processes that specify possible interactions among entities. These have roughly the same syntax as concrete processes, except that they refer to types of entities (e.g., organisms or nutrients) rather than specific ones (e.g., *phyto*) and they contain functional forms that relate attributes of these generic entities rather than specific equations. Functions do not include particular coefficients but instead refer to parameters with bounds on their possible values (e.g., between zero and one). The same parameter may occur in more than one of a process's equations, thus reducing dimensionality of the parameter space. Generic processes serve as the building blocks for constructing quantitative process models.

Traditional methods for inductive process modeling (e.g., Bridewell et al. 2008) carry out search through a two-level space. The first works in the space of model structures, carrying out exhaustive depth-first search to find all ways to instantiate the known generic processes with specific entities; these become the elements for candidate models. The procedure starts with an empty model and, on each step, adds a new instantiated process if the new structure would not exceed user-specified size limitations.[1] For each such model structure, it then carries out search through a second parameter space. Starting with values sampled randomly from within each parameter's boundaries, this uses a conjugate gradient descent method to find parameters. The objective function that directs search is the squared error of a model's simulated trajectory compared to observations. Because this can halt at local optima, parameter estimation typically includes ten or more restarts from different initial values. This two-level strategy produces a list of parameterized model structures ranked by their error on the training data.

Table 11.2 presents pseudocode for this two-level approach to process model induction, which has been implemented and applied successfully to a variety of modeling tasks (Bridewell et al. 2008, Todorovski, Bridewell, Shiran, and Langley 2005). These comprise fields as diverse as ecology, hydrology, and biochemistry (Asgharbeygi, Bay, Langley, and Arrigo 2006, Bridewell et al. 2008, Langley, Shiran, Shrager, Todorovski, and Pohorille 2006). Papers on the topic have also reported a number of extensions that increase the robustness and coverage of the modeling framework. These include revision of existing quantitative process models (Asgharbeygi et al. 2006), hierarchical generic processes to constrain search (Todorovski, Bridewell, Shiran, and Langley 2005), an ensemble-like method that mitigates overfitting effects (Bridewell, Bani Asadi, Langley, and Todorovski 2005), and an EM-like method that estimates missing observations (Bridewell, Langley, Racunas, and Borrett 2006). Another extension has expanded the framework to models that involve partial differential equations (Park, Bridewell, & Langley 2010), which take into account changes over both time and space. These results suggest that the basic framework is sound, and many encouraging empirical studies have buttressed this impression.

11.3.3   Discovering Rate-Based Process Models

Despite these successes, the initial methods for inductive process modeling have suffered from four drawbacks. They generate and evaluate full model structures exhaustively, which means the number of candidate structures grows exponentially with both the number of variables and the number of generic processes. Moreover,

---

[1] Some variants (e.g., Bridewell & Langley 2010) ensure that candidate structures are consistent with constraints on relations among processes, say that an organism cannot take part in two distinct growth elements. These offer another form of theoretical knowledge about the domain.

Table 11.2 Pseudocode for IPM (Inductive Process Modeler), a system for inducing quantitative process models (Bridewell et al. 2008), which combines exhaustive search through the space of model structures with gradient descent search during parameter estimation

Generate all process instances consistent with type constraints.
Combine these processes into candidate model structures up to a maximum size.
For each structure S,
    Select random parameters values for S within ranges of generic processes.
    Simulate parameterized S to produce a multivariate trajectory.
    Calculate simulation error E by comparing to observations.
    Use conjugate gradient descent to determine new parameter values.
    Repeat until there is no reduction in error E.
    Fix the parameters for S to this values and store E with S.
Return a list of parameterized model structures ranked by error scores.

parameter estimation requires repeated simulation of models to calculate an error score for gradient descent through the parameter space. Even so, this technique often halts at local optima, which can require many random restarts to find acceptable parameter values. Finally, despite these steps, the approach can still find models that fit the observations poorly. In summary, it does not scale well to complex modeling tasks, incurs high computational costs even for moderate tasks, and it is not reliable.

In recent research, Langley and Arvay (2015) have reported a new approach that addresses these problems. In their modeling formalism, each process P must include a *rate* that denotes P's speed or activation on a given time step. This rate is determined by an algebraic equation that is a parameter-free function of known variables. The process also specifies one or more *derivatives* that are proportional to P's rate, with negative coefficients for inputs and positive ones for outputs. Table 11.3 presents an example in this formalism that is equivalent to the one seen earlier in Table 11.1 (a). The notation has an important property that assists discovery substantially: a process model compiles into a set of differential equations that are linear combinations of rate terms. It also comes closer to Forbus' (1984) notion of qualitative processes, which inspired early work in the area.

Langley and Arvay also described RPM (Rate-based Process Modeler), a system that takes advantage of this more constrained formalism. Like its predecessors, the program estimates the derivative for each variable on each time step by calculating successive differences of observed values. It also generates a set of process instances by binding generic processes with variables in all possible ways consistent with their type constraints, but at this point it diverges. Because RPM assumes that each variable is observed, it can calculate the rate of each candidate process instance on each time step. As described in Table 11.4, it uses these derived values to carry out greedy search through the space of process models. For each target derivative, the system invokes multiple linear regression to find an equation that predicts it as a linear combination of process rates. Later differential equations must include processes that are consistent with those in earlier ones and vice versa. For instance, if an equation RPM selected for $d[x]$ includes a process P that influences not only $d[x]$ but also $d[y]$, any equation it considers for $d[y]$ must also include P's rate in its

Table 11.3 A process model that is equivalent to the one in Table 11.1 (b) but that separates algebraic rate expressions from equation fragments. Such a model always compiles into a set of differential equations that are linear combinations of rate expressions

process phyto_loss(phyto, detritus)
rate: r = phyto.conc
equations: d[phyto.conc,t] = $-0.307 \cdot$ r
d[detritus.conc,t] = $0.307 \cdot$ r
process zoo_loss(zoo, detritus)
rate: r = zoo.conc
equations: d[zoo.conc,t] = $-0.251 \cdot$ r
d[detritus.conc,t] = $0.251 \cdot$ r
process zoo_phyto_grazing(zoo, phyto, detritus)
rate: r = $0.495 \cdot$ zoo.conc
equations: d[zoo.conc,t] = $0.615 \cdot$ r
d[detritus.conc,t] = $0.385 \cdot$ r
d[phyto.conc,t] = $-1.0 \cdot$ r
process nitro_uptake(phyto, nitro)
rate: r = $0.411 \cdot$ phyto.conc
equations: d[phyto.conc,t] = $1.0 \cdot$ r
d[nitro.conc,t] = $-0.098 \cdot$ r
process nitro_remineralization(nitro, detritus)
rate: r = detritus.conc
equations: d[nitro.conc,t] = $0.005 \cdot$ r
d[detritus.conc,t] = $-0.005 \cdot$ r

Table 11.4 Pseudocode for the RPM system for inducing rate-based process models. Rather than generating complete model structures, it carries out heuristic search by inducing one equation at a time, using process knowledge to ensure consistency across equations

Generate all process instances consistent with type constraints.
For each process P, calculate the rate for P on each time step.
For each target variable X,
Estimate $d[X, t]$ on each time step with center differencing.
For each subset of processes with up to k elements,
Find a regression equation for $d[X, t]$ in terms of process rates.
If the equation's r^2 is high enough, retain for consideration.
Add the equation with the highest r^2 to the process model.

right-hand side. This approach factors the model construction task into a number of tractable components, combining the efficiency and robustness of linear regression with the use of domain knowledge to ensure explanations are internally consistent.

As expected, experiments revealed that RPM was not only vastly more efficient than SC-IPM (Bridewell & Langley 2010), an earlier system for process model induction, running 83,000 times faster on even simple tasks, but that it found both the structure and parameters of target models much more reliably. Heuristic search through the structure space led to reasonable scaling with increases in the number of variables and generic processes, and simple smoothing over trajectories let it deal well with noise. However, some important drawbacks remained, including an assumption that all variables were observed and reliance on exhaustive search through the equation space.

More recently, Arvay and Langley (2016) have presented another system, SPM, that combines sampling of rate terms with backward elimination to induce equations in the presence of many irrelevant processes. The new program also replaces greedy search through the space of model structures with a two-stage strategy. First, the system finds multiple differential equations for each variable, after which it uses depth-first search to find sets of equations that incorporate consistent processes. Experiments with synthetic time series suggest that this approach scales better to equation complexity and identifies consistent process models better in domains like chemistry, where many different equations predict each variable's derivative accurately, but where only a few combinations of these equations are consistent.

11.4   Extension to the Social Sciences

In the introduction, we mentioned our concern with computational discovery in the social sciences, and we are finally ready to return to that topic. In this section, we discuss briefly the relevance of process models to this area, consider some examples of social processes, outline how automated construction of social models might occur, and discuss some challenges that we must overcome to support the general form of this vision.

11.4.1   Relevance to Social Science

The social sciences share a number of features with ecology that suggest quantitative process models, and computational methods for their discovery, will prove as useful in the former disciplines as they have for the latter. These similarities concern both the nature of data that arise in these fields and the form of models that researchers often develop to explain them.

First, most data sets in the social sciences are observational rather than experimental in character. Not only would social experiments that involve large groups of people be prohibitively expensive, but many societies would view them as ethically unacceptable. The majority of data sets for ecological systems are also observational, for the same reasons, so the two fields must work with similar forms of nonexperimental evidence. They must also deal with dynamic behavior that requires explanation of changes over time.

Second, although social phenomena are composed of interactions among individuals, they are typically measured at the aggregate level. This produces values for a set of quantitative variables that describe summary features of the entire group, rather than those of their constituents. Most data about ecological phenomena also have this characteristic. As a result, many models in both fields postulate relations among aggregate, quantitative variables, as do the process models we have discussed in earlier sections.

Finally, many dynamic social phenomena appear to involve interactions among many variables. Endogenous terms both influence other variables and are influenced by them, often through feedback loops, although exogenous variables that only influence others also play a role. Thus, human behavior at the aggregate level is a complex system in the same sense as ecological networks. In other words, both are instances of system sciences that study interactions among entities.

Taken together, these similarities indicate that inductive process modeling offers a promising approach to discovery in the social sciences. At first glance, an important difference is that rate-based processes in ecology are described naturally in terms of inputs and outputs, often with an assumption that they involve variables that are conserved over time. This seems a less likely premise in social settings, but it is not a strict requirement on process models, so it does not prevent their application in this new arena.

11.4.2   Social Process Models

We can clarify the notion of social process models with some examples. First, consider some types of entities that might appear in a model. These might include social groups (e.g., different ethnicities, professions, or political parties) and physical resources (e.g., food, water, or power). Each entity will have one or more attributes that specify quantities on some dimension. For instance, a particular social group might have a membership count, an average annual income, a status score, and numbers who live in different neighborhoods. Consider two urban gangs, the *Jets* and the *Sharks*, with *Jets.count* and *Sharks.count* denoting their respective numbers, and with *Jets.status* and *Sharks.status* specifying their status scores.

Social processes produce changes in one or more such attributes. For example, a *migration* process might lead to an increase in the number of a group's members that live in one neighborhood and decrease those in another. Similarly, a *consumption* process might describe reduction in food or water when a group uses these resources. Or consider a *conversion* process that transfers some members of one group to another group:

conversion[Jets, Sharks]
    rate: $r = $ Jets.count $\cdot$ (Sharks.status $-$ Jets.status)
    equations: d[Jets.count,t] $= -1.0 \cdot$ rate
                  d[Sharks.count,t] $= 1.0 \cdot$ rate

The coefficient for *Jets* is -1.0, indicating that the process causes *Jets* membership to decrease, while *Sharks* is 1.0, stating that it leads *Sharks* membership to grow. The two constants have the same absolute value because every person who leaves the first group must joint the second. The rate of transfer depends on three factors:

the status of *Jets*, the status of *Sharks*, and the number of people in *Jets*. The rate increases with larger differences in status and with more people in the low-status group. Of course, different rate expressions are possible that depend on other attributes, but this example should clarify the notion of a social process.

A social process model would include a number of such elements, each of which describes change in one or more attributes and the rate at which they jointly occur. As we saw earlier, one can automatically compile these processes into a set of linked differential equations and then simulate the compiled model to generate multivariate time series. To the extent that the resulting trajectories match the observed social behavior, they provide an explanation of that behavior in terms of unobserved but still plausible processes.

11.4.3   Discovering Social Process Models

As in ecology, we can automate discovery of social process models using heuristic search through a space of candidate accounts. This requires that we provide a set of generic processes, instances of which might plausibly occur in the target setting. Each of these templates will specify the types of entities involved (e.g., a group or location) and associated attributes (e.g., count or status), whether the process causes the latter to increase or decrease, and the algebraic form of the expression that determines its rate. This set of generic processes may include different versions of the same process type. For instance, there may be variants of the conversion process with the same input and output relations but that differ in their rate expressions or even in the variables that influence them. These provide the building blocks for generation of candidate process models.

Given observations about dynamic social behavior and a set of target variables, a computational system like SPM (Arvay & Langley 2016) can search the space of social process models defined by these generic elements. The program would induce one or more differential equations, stated as linear combinations of process rates, for each target variable. The system would then find combinations of equations that make consistent assumptions about which processes actually determine social dynamics. As before, search would occur for individual equations (which rate terms to include in the right-hand side) and model structure (which equations and associated processes to incorporate). Heuristics at both levels would limit the effective branching factor, making tractable the discovery of complex social process models that explain observed behavior.

11.4.4   Challenges in Social Process Modeling

The approach we have just described should apply, in principle, to any dynamic social setting for which multivariate time series are available. However, in practice, modeling tasks are likely to introduce challenges that require additional research on computational methods for discovering process accounts. The most basic is current techniques' reliance on a library of generic processes that specify not only attributes that interact but the functional forms that determine their changes over time. These may not be as obvious for social systems as for biological, chemical, or physical ones, in that they are typically less well understood. Automating the discovery of candidate generic processes is one response. Langley and Arvay (2017) have reported progress on this front, describing a system that introduces new generic processes by combining conceptual relations with algebraic rate templates, but we need more work on this problem.

Another challenge is that social science observations are more difficult to obtain than data in many other disciplines. This means that time series may have relatively sparse sampling rates; for instance, US census data is only collected every ten years. This is not an issue for social systems that change at rates slower than samples are taken, or even if signs of derivatives remain the same during unsampled periods. Moreover, for similar reasons, some social variables may not be measured on any time steps. Jia (personal communication, 2016) has identified certain conditions under which one can induce rate-based process models when some terms are unmeasured, but they must each participate in the same processes as observed variables. We need more research on this topic before our discovery methods can contribute fully to the social sciences.

A more basic limitation of process model induction is that it assumes the entities remain fixed over time. An organism's population or a group's count can decrease to zero, which can mimic the disappearance of an entity, but a model has no means for creating new entities during a simulation run. This would make it difficult to explain events such as the fissioning of a group into two splinters or the merging of two groups into a new composite. We might expand the process formalism to allow discrete events of this sort that occur under certain conditions (e.g., a group splitting when it grows too large), and extend simulation methods to predict their behavior over time, but inducing models that include both continuous and discrete processes would take us into new territory for computational scientific discovery.

11.5 Related Work on Social Model Construction

We are not the first to propose using computational methods to construct accounts of social phenomena. In fact, this idea has a long history, and in this section we examine its various threads. In each case, we describe the formalism for representing models and the extent to which their construction has been automated.

Structural equation models have been widely used in the social sciences (Goldberger 1972). Such a model relates a set of quantitative variables, $X_1, \ldots X_n$, using a set of linear equations. The first variable, X_1, is a function of X_2 through X_n, the next one, X_2, is a function of X_3 through X_n, and so forth, with the final variable, X_n, being exogenous. This means one can display the model as a directed acyclic graph or as a coefficient matrix in which half of the nondiagonal entries are zero. Traditionally, a human would specify the graphical structure of such a linear causal model and invoke computational methods to estimate coefficients for each equation. Social scientists have applied this approach to observational data in many different settings, but standard approaches are limited nondynamical models with no feedback loops.

More recently, automated methods have emerged for inducing the structure of such causal models. The earliest example was TETRAD (Glymour, Scheines, Spirtes, and Kelly 1987, Spirtes, Glymour and Scheines 1993), which used relations among partial correlations (e.g., the product of two partials equals the product of two others) to identify constraints on causal links. The system carried out search through a space of model structures, eliminating links that were inconsistent with these inferred constraints. TETRAD's developers applied it to a variety of observational data sets from the social sciences, but their approach did not support the discovery of dynamical models that explained change over time. More recent efforts, including related work in inducing the structure of Bayesian networks, have typically adopted greedy search through the space of model structures, based on degree of fit. However, Maier, Taylor, Oktay, and Jensen (2010) report an extension of the constraint-based approach that handles discrete relations among entities, rather than linear influences among continuous variables.

An alternative paradigm for explaining social behavior involves *agent-based* models (Epstein & Axtell 1996). These are stated as collections of individual entities that interact over time in simulated environments. Members of an agent category follow the same decision-making rules, but they may differ in their parameters. As with differential equation models, simulation occurs in discrete time steps, but each agent responds separately to its situation. Activities are aggregated into summary statistics for groups or the entire population, which in turn are compared to measurements made at the aggregate level. Simulations that involve millions of agents are not uncommon. Researchers in this tradition develop their agent-based models by hand, but one can imagine automating their discovery by providing elements of agent programs and using computational methods similar to inductive process modeling to search the space of candidates.

11.6 Concluding Remarks

In the preceding pages, we reviewed computational advances in our understanding of scientific discovery. We recounted early research in this area, which treated the induction of numeric equations as heuristic search through a space of candidate laws. We then examined more recent work on inductive process modeling, which finds sets of processes and their associated differential equations that reproduce and explain multivariate time series. Contemporary efforts on this problem partition each process into a rate that is an algebraic function of known variables and a set of derivatives that are proportional to this rate. This assumption allows the use of multiple linear regression to find constituent differential equations, with process knowledge constraining their combination into models. This provides reliable, efficient, and scalable methods for discovering explanatory process models of dynamical observations, as repeated experiments have demonstrated.

We also discussed applications of process model induction to the social sciences. We argued that these disciplines have much in common with ecology, which has served as the main testbed for work on process modeling. These included a focus on nonexperimental data, quantitative measurements at the aggregate level, and dynamic interactions among variables. We provided examples of processes that might appear in explanations of social phenomena and how computational discovery might construct them using heuristic search. We also noted challenges that the social sciences pose to process model induction, such as fewer insights into candidate processes, difficulty in obtaining time-series data, and discrete events that remove entities or introduce new ones. Despite these challenges, inductive process modeling offers a promising approach to automating the discovery of explanatory models in the social sciences.

Acknowledgements The research reported in this chapter was supported by Grant No. N00014-11-1-0107 from the US Office of Naval Research, which is not responsible for its contents. We thank Will Bridewell, Sašo Džeroski, Ruolin Jia, and Ljupčo Todorovski for useful discussions that led to the results reported.

References

Asgharbeygi, N., Bay, S., Langley, P., & Arrigo, K. (2006). Inductive revision of quantitative process models. *Ecological Modelling, 194*, 70–79.

Arvay, A., & Langley, P. (2016). Selective induction of rate-based process models. In *Proceedings of the Fourth Annual Conference on Cognitive Systems*. Evanston, IL.

Bradley, E., Easley, M., & Stolle, R. (2001). Reasoning about nonlinear system identification. *Artificial Intelligence, 133*, 139–188.

Bridewell, W., Bani Asadi, N., Langley, P., & Todorovski, L. (2005). Reducing overfitting in process model induction. In *Proceedings of the Twenty-Second International Conference on Machine Learning* (pp. 81–88). Bonn, Germany.

Bridewell, W., Langley P., Racunas, S., & Borrett, S. R. (2006). Learning process models with missing data. In *Proceedings of the Seventeenth European Conference on Machine Learning* (pp. 557–565). Berlin: Springer.

Bridewell, W., Langley, P., Todorovski, L., & Džeroski, S. (2008). Inductive process modeling. *Machine Learning, 71*, 1–32.

Bridewell, W., & Langley, P. (2010). Two kinds of knowledge in scientific discovery. *Topics in Cognitive Science, 2*, 36–52.

Bruk, L. G., Gorodskii, S. N., Zeigarnik, A. V., Valdés-Pérez, R. E., & Temkin, O. N. (1998). Oxidative carbonylation of phenylacetylene catalyzed by Pd(II) and Cu(I): Experimental tests of forty-one computer-generated mechanistic hypotheses. *Journal of Molecular Catalysis A: Chemical, 130*, 29–40.

Colton, S., Bundy, A., & Walsh, T. (2000). Automatic identification of mathematical concepts. In *Proceedings of the Seventeenth International Conference on Machine Learning* (pp. 183–190). Stanford, CA: Morgan Kaufmann.

Džeroski, S., & Todorovski, L. (1995). Discovering dynamics: From inductive logic programming to machine discovery. *Journal of Intelligent Information Systems, 4*, 89–108.

Džeroski, S., & Todorovski, L. (Eds.). (2007). *Computational discovery of communicable scientific knowledge*. Berlin: Springer.

Džeroski, S., & Todorovski, L. (2008). Equation discovery for systems biology: Finding the structure and dynamics of biological networks from time course data. *Current Opinion in Biotechnology, 19*, 360–368.

Epstein, J. M., & R Axtell, R. (1996). *Growing artificial societies: Social science from the bottom up*. Cambridge, MA: MIT Press.

Fajtlowicz, S. (1988). On conjectures of GRAFFITI. *Discrete Mathematics, 72*, 113–118.

Falkenhainer, B. C., & Michalski, R. S. (1986). Integrating quantitative and qualitative discovery: The ABACUS system. *Machine Learning, 1*, 367–401.

Fayyad, U., Haussler, D., & Stolorz, P. (1996). KDD for science data analysis: Issues and examples. In *Proceedings of the Second International Conference of Knowledge Discovery and Data Mining* (pp. 50–56). Portland, OR: AAAI Press.

Forbus, K. D. (1984). Qualitative process theory. *Artificial Intelligence, 24*, 85–168.

Glymour, C., Scheines, R., Spirtes, P., & Kelly, K. (1987). *Discovering causal structure: Artificial intelligence, philosophy of science, and statistical modeling*. San Diego: Academic.

Goldberger, A. S. (1972). Structural equation models in the social sciences. *Econometrica, 40*, 979–1001.

Gordon, A., Edwards, P., Sleeman, D., & Kodratoff, Y. (1994). Scientific discovery in a space of structural models: An example from the history of solution chemistry. In *Proceedings of the Sixteenth Annual Conference of the Cognitive Science Society* (pp. 381–386). Atlanta: Lawrence Erlbaum.

Hempel, C. G. (1965). *Aspects of scientific explanation and other essays*. New York: Free Press.

Hempel, C. G. (1966). *Philosophy of natural science*. Englewood Cliffs, NJ: Prentice-Hall.

King, R. D., & Srinivasan, A. (1996). Prediction of rodent carcinogenicity bioassays from molecular structure using inductive logic programming. *Environmental Health Perspectives, 104*(Supplement 5), 1031–1040.

King, R. D., Whelan, K. E., Jones, F. M., Reiser, P. G. K., Bryant, C. H., Muggleton, S. H., Kell, D. B., Oliver, S. G. (2004). Functional genomic hypothesis generation and experimentation by a robot scientist, *Nature, 427*, 247–252.

Kokar, M. M. (1986). Determining arguments of invariant functional descriptions. *Machine Learning, 1*, 403–422.

Koza, J. R., Mydlowec, W., Lanza, G., Yu, J., & Keane, M. A. (2001). Reverse engineering of metabolic pathways from observed data using genetic programming. *Pacific Symposium on Biocomputing, 6*, 434–445.

Langley, P. (1981). Data-driven discovery of physical laws. *Cognitive Science, 5*, 31–54.

Langley, P. (2000). The computational support of scientific discovery. *International Journal of Human-Computer Studies, 53*, 393–410.

Langley, P., & Arvay, A. (2015). Heuristic induction of rate-based process models. In *Proceedings of the Twenty-Ninth AAAI Conference on Artificial Intelligence* (pp. 537–543). Austin, TX: AAAI Press.

Langley, P., & Arvay, A. (2017). Flexible model induction through heuristic process discovery. In *Proceedings of the Thirty-First AAAI Conference on Artificial Intelligence* (pp. 4415–4421). San Francisco: AAAI Press.

Langley, P., Simon, H. A., Bradshaw, G. L., & Żytkow, J. M. (1987). *Scientific discovery: Computational explorations of the creative processes*. Cambridge, MA: MIT Press.

Langley, P., Sanchez, J., Todorovski, L., & Džeroski, S. (2002). Inducing process models from continuous data. In *Proceedings of the Nineteenth International Conference on Machine Learning* (pp. 347–354). Sydney: Morgan Kaufmann.

Langley, P., Shiran, O., Shrager, J., Todorovski, L., & Pohorille, A. (2006). Constructing explanatory process models from biological data and knowledge. *Artificial Intelligence in Medicine, 37*, 191–201.

Maier, M., Taylor, B., Oktay, H., & Jensen, D. (2010). Learning causal models of relational domains. In *Proceedings of the Twenty-Fourth AAAI Conference on Artificial Intelligence* (pp. 531–538). Atlanta: AAAI Press.

Mitchell, F., Sleeman, D., Duffy, J. A., Ingram, M. D., & Young, R. W. (1997). Optical basicity of metallurgical slags: A new computer-based system for data visualisation and analysis. *Ironmaking and Steelmaking, 24*, 306–320.

Moulet, M. (1992). ARC.2: Linear regression in ABACUS. In *Proceedings of the ML 92 Workshop on Machine Discovery* (pp. 137–146), Aberdeen, Scotland.

Murata, T., Mizutani, M., & Shimura, M. (1994). A discovery system for trigonometric functions. In *Proceedings of the Twelfth National Conference on Artificial Intelligence* (pp. 645–650). Seattle: AAAI Press.

Nordhausen, B., & Langley, P. (1990). A robust approach to numeric discovery. In *Proceedings of the Seventh International Conference on Machine Learning* (pp. 411–418). Austin, TX: Morgan Kaufmann.

Park, C., Bridewell, W., & Langley, P. (2010). Integrated systems for inducing spatio-temporal process models. In *Proceedings of the Twenty-Fourth AAAI Conference on Artificial Intelligence* (pp. 1555–1560). Atlanta: AAAI Press.

Popper, K. R. (1961). *The logic of scientific discovery*. New York: Science Editions.

Saito, K., & Nakano, R. (1997). Law discovery using neural networks. In *Proceedings of the Fifteenth International Joint Conference on Artificial Intelligence* (pp. 1078–1083). Yokohama: Morgan Kaufmann.

Schaffer, C. (1990). Bivariate scientific function finding in a sampled, real-data testbed. *Machine Learning, 12*, 167–183.

Schmidt, M., & Lipson, H. (2009). Distilling free-form natural laws from experimental data. *Science, 324*, 81–85.

Shrager, J., & Langley, P. (Eds.) (1990). *Computational models of scientific discovery and theory formation*. San Francisco: Morgan Kaufmann.

Simon, H. A. (1966). *Scientific discovery and the psychology of problem solving*. In R. Colodny (Ed.), *Mind and cosmos*. Pittsburgh, PA: University of Pittsburgh Press.

Spirtes, P., Glymour, C., & Scheines, R. (1993). *Causation, prediction, and search*. New York: Springer.

Todorovski, L., Bridewell, W., Shiran, O., & Langley, P. (2005). Inducing hierarchical process models in dynamic domains. In *Proceedings of the Twentieth National Conference on Artificial Intelligence* (pp. 892–897). Pittsburgh, PA: AAAI Press.

Todorovski, L., Džeroski, S., & Kompare, B. (1998). Modeling and prediction of phytoplankton growth with equation discovery. *Ecological Modelling, 113*, 71–81.

Valdés-Pérez, R. E. (1994). Human/computer interactive elucidation of reaction mechanisms: Application to catalyzed hydrogenolysis of ethane. *Catalysis Letters, 28*, 79–87.

Washio, T., & Motoda, H. (1997). Discovering admissable models of complex systems based on scale types and identity constraints. In *Proceedings of the Fifteenth International Joint Conference on Artificial Intelligence* (pp. 810–817). Yokohama: Morgan Kaufmann.

Żytkow, J. M. Zhu, J., & Hussam, A. (1990). Automated discovery in a chemistry laboratory. In *Proceedings of the Eighth National Conference on Artificial Intelligence* (pp. 889–894). Boston: AAAI Press.

Index

© Springer Nature Switzerland AG 2019
M. Addis et al. (eds.), *Scientific Discovery in the Social Sciences*,
Synthese Library 413, https://doi.org/10.1007/978-3-030-23769-1

Printed by Printforce, the Netherlands